The University of Chicago
FOUNDED BY JOHN D. ROCKEFELLER

A LEXICOGRAPHICAL STUDY OF THE GREEK INSCRIPTIONS

A DISSERTATION SUBMITTED TO THE FACULTIES OF THE GRADUATE
SCHOOLS OF ARTS, LITERATURE, AND SCIENCE, IN CANDIDACY
FOR THE DEGREE OF DOCTOR OF PHILOSOPHY

DEPARTMENT OF
SANSKRIT AND INDO-EUROPEAN COMPARATIVE PHILOLOGY

BY

HELEN M. SEARLES

WIPF & STOCK · Eugene, Oregon

Wipf and Stock Publishers
199 W 8th Ave, Suite 3
Eugene, OR 97401

A Lexicographical Study of the Greek Inscription
A Dissertation Submitted to the Faculties of the Graduate Schools of Arts,
Literature, and Science, in Candidacy for the Degree of Doctor of Philosophy
By Searles, Helen M.
ISBN 13: 978-1-60608-757-2
Publication date 5/26/2009
Previously published by University of Chicago Press, 1898

A LEXICOGRAPHICAL STUDY OF THE GREEK INSCRIPTIONS.

By Helen M. Searles.

THE words discussed in this paper have been for the most part taken from material collected for a Lexicon of the Greek Dialect Inscriptions. When Professor Buck, in the spring of 1896, suggested the latter work, it seemed possible to accomplish the task within two or three years. But, as the work developed, the necessity of more time became evident. It was then decided to discuss the new and rare words in a preliminary paper, which should at the same time serve as a study for the lexicon. The original plan for a full treatise has not been abandoned, but on the contrary somewhat extended. It was not the intention at first to include words from the Attic inscriptions, but according to the present plan this dialect will have its place with the others. For this paper, however, the Attic material has not been collated with the same fullness as that of the other dialects. In fact, its treatment here is mainly restricted to the citation in the list of "New Words" of such hapaxlegomena as are noted in the indices of the Attic Corpus, or have been met with in desultory reading. Under "New Words" are included not only words which are strictly unknown outside of inscriptions, but also those known elsewhere only in glosses.

There has been some difficulty in deciding what formal differences should be taken as constituting a new word; of course mere dialectic variation has not been so regarded, not even such as represents a different ablaut grade. So, forms like δείλομαι, βέλλομαι for Attic βούλομαι are not given. But words showing different suffixes from the corresponding Attic forms are included, though not if the difference is merely a variation between verbs in -άω and -έω.

1

The work is based upon a collection of the material accessible to the author and published before the end of 1897. It can hardly be expected that the list will prove absolutely complete, but it is hoped that not many of the important new words have been omitted. Under "Rare Words and Rare Meanings" are cited words which are so infrequent in literature that an additional citation is of interest, and also words which are used in a sense different from the usual meaning in literature. As no rigid rule as to the degree of infrequency or divergence in meaning can be applied, the choice of words for this second list is necessarily somewhat arbitrary. A brief list of "Poetic Words" found in prose inscriptions is added; further, a discussion of a few groups of synonyms drawn from the various dialects.[1]

There are few existing works of this character. The Συναγωγὴ Λέξεων Ἀθησαυρίστων of Kumanudis (1883) treats, as its title indicates, only of words which are not to be found in the Thesaurus; while the aim of the present work has been rather to show as a whole the important contribution to the lexicography of the Greek language furnished by the inscriptions. No word has been rejected because it is already in the Thesaurus, or even in Liddell and Scott. This is the more justifiable since, owing to recent discovery and study, it is possible in nearly every case to add something to the lexicographical work already done. Again, the work of Kumanudis includes a large proportion of late Roman and Byzantine words. In this paper such words have been omitted. So far as the dates are known, no words have been taken from inscriptions belonging to the Christian era, with a few exceptions. The scope of this work is also different from that of the Συναγωγή, in that it includes a brief discussion of the form whenever it has seemed desirable, either for interpretation or on account of some phonetic peculiarity.

In the Commentationes Woelflinianae, pp. 350–362, Dr. Ludwig Bürchner has some "Addenda lexicis linguae Graecae," chiefly late Roman and Byzantine words. Also, in the Zeitschrift

[1] It has been found necessary to postpone the publication of this section on synonyms, to which some references are made in the other parts.

f. d. österr. Gym., 42 (1891), pp. 481–486, J. Simon gives a "Probesammlung" from a new collection which, so far as I am able to learn, has not yet appeared. His plan is very similar to that followed by Kumanudis, and the examples given are words which do not occur in the Συναγωγή. For the poetical words there are two important articles—"Poetic Words in Cyprian," H. W. Smyth, AJP. VIII, p. 467, and "Vocabula Homerica in Graecorum dialectis" (1876), Kleemann. This latter work deals largely with glosses. It is, of course, out of date, as so many valuable additions to the material have been made since its publication.

A partial list of abbreviations is given below. The Collitz Sammlung der griechischen Dialekt-Inschriften is made the basis of the work, and the inscriptions which have been published therein are always cited first by their number in this collection, even where a different reading is adopted. *All citations by numbers only, without designation of the work, refer to this collection.* Other sources are given in the list of abbreviations. Inscriptions not included in any of the larger collections are cited by reference to the journal in which they were first published. A few exceptions are noted in the list below. The question of transcription has been a difficult one. For the word under discussion certainly the exact testimony of the stone must be given. Where this differs in any way from the transcription, it is shown by inscriptional capitals in parentheses. But since the citations of context are made for the purpose of interpretation, it has seemed best to give these only in transcription. If words occurring on the stone have been omitted as unnecessary for the purpose of the citation, their absence is indicated by dashes. Words missing from the stone are either supplied in brackets as edited or replaced by dots.

Quantities are marked only in the headings. In "New Words" the headings are given in the form cited. Under "Rare Words" the Attic form is used.

Dates are given approximately, according to the best authority available, for the earliest occurrence of the word. If other dates are of significance, these, too, are given; otherwise not. The Gortynian Law-code has been assigned to the fifth century with Kirchhoff and the French editors of Insc. Juridiques, though with some hesitation. The new Delphian Labydean inscription seems in character to belong rather to the fifth century than to the fourth, notwithstanding its representation of the long vowels. This, too, is the decision of Homolle. The Elean inscriptions are dated according to Dittenberger in "Olympia." The Cyprian inscriptions are left for the most part undated; cf. Meister, GD. II, pp. 192 ff.; Hoffmann, GD. I, pp. 38 ff. The dates are too much a matter of conjecture to make anything more than tentative dating possible. The dates given are inclosed in square brackets immediately after the definition.

I am unwilling to offer even this preliminary paper without expressing my indebtedness to my former instructors, Professor Walter Ray Bridgman, of Lake Forest University, and Professor Benjamin Ide Wheeler, of Cornell University. To my present instructors, Dr. Alfred William Stratton, who has made many valuable suggestions in the course of the proofreading, and Professor Carl Darling Buck, who not only suggested the work, but has also given it constant and invaluable criticism, I am especially indebted.

ABBREVIATIONS.

AJA. = American Journal of Archaeology.

AJP. = American Journal of Philology.

And. = Inscription concerning the Mysteries, found at Andania. Cauer[2] 47; Dittenberger, Sylloge 388; Sauppe, Ausgewählte Schriften, pp. 261 ff.

Arch. Zeit. = Archaeologische Zeitung.

BB. = Beiträge zur Kunde der indogermanischen Sprachen, herausgegeben von A. Bezzenberger.

BCH. = Bulletin de Correspondance Hellénique.

Ber. d. sächs G. d. W. = Sitzungsberichte der Königlichen sächsischen Gesellschaft der Wissenschaften.

Berl. Woch. = Wochenschrift für klassische Philologie. Berlin.

Boisacq, DD. = Les Dialectes Doriens. 1891.

Br. Mus. = The Collection of Ancient Greek Inscriptions in the British Museum. Part I, Hicks, 1874. II, Newton, 1883. III, Hicks, 1886. IV, Hirschfeld, 1893.

Brugmann = Grundriss der vergleichenden Grammatik. Vol. I (second edition), 1897. Vol. II (first edition).

Cauer = Delectus Inscriptionum Graecarum. P. Cauer. Second edition, 1883.
CIA. = Corpus Inscriptionum Atticarum.
CIG. = Corpus Inscriptionum Graecarum.
CIGS. I. = Corpus Inscriptionum Graecarum Septentrionalis. I. Ed. W. Dittenberger. (Megara, Oropus, Boeotia.) 1892.
CIGS. III. = Same. Vol. III. (Phocis, Locris, Aetolia, Acarnania, Islands of Ion. Sea.) 1897.
Crete (or Gort.) Comp. = Le Leggi di Gortyna e le altre Iscrizioni Arcaiche Cretesi. Domenico Comparetti. 1893.
Curt. Stud. = Studien zur griechischen und lateinischen Grammatik. 1868–78.
Danielsson. Epigr. = Epigraphica, O. H. Danielsson. Upsala, 1890.
Ditt. Syll. = Sylloge Inscriptionum Graecarum. 1883.
Epid. K. = Fouilles d'Epidaure par P. Kavvadias. 1893.
'Εφ. 'Αρχ. = Εφημερὶς ἀρχαιολογική. Athens.
Gilbert = Handbuch der griechischen Staatsaltertümer.
Hoffmann GD. = Die griechischen Dialekte. I, 1891 ; II, 1893.
IF. = Indogermanische Forschungen, Zeitschrift für indogermanische Sprach- und Altertumskunde.
IG. Ins. = Inscriptiones Graecae Insularum. De Gaertringen. 1895.
IG. Sic. et It. = Inscriptiones Graecae Siciliae et Italiae. Kaibel. 1890.
Ins. Jurid. Gr. = Recueil des Inscriptions Juridiques Grecques. 1895.
Ion. Bechtel = Inschriften der ionischen Dialekte. 1887.
Jbb. f. Philol. = Jahrbücher für classische Philologie. Fleckeisen.
Kaibel = Epigrammata Graeca ex lapidibus conlecta. 1878.
Kühner-Blass = Ausführliche Grammatik der griechischen Sprache. Third edition, 1890.
Kum. = Συναγωγή Λέξεων 'Αθησαυρίστων. A. Kumanudis. 1883.
KZ. = Zeitschrift für vergleichende Sprachforschung, begründet von A. Kuhn.
Lac. M = De titulorum Laconicorum dialecto. P. Müllensiefen. 1882.
Latyschew = Inscriptiones antiquae orae septentrionalis Ponti Euxini. 1885.
LeB.-F. = LeBas, Voyage archéologique, ed. Foucart.
Meister GD. = Die griechischen Dialekte. Vol. I, 1882 ; Vol. II, 1889.
Meyer = Griechische Grammatik. G. Meyer. Third edition, 1896.
Mitth. = Mittheilungen des deutschen archäologischen Instituts in Athen.
Mus. Ital. = Museo Italiano di Antichità classiche. Florence, 1885 ff.
Ol. = Die Inschriften von Olympia. W. Dittenberger and K. Purgold. 1896.
PBB. = Beiträge zur Geschichte der deutschen Sprache und Literatur. H. Paul and W. Braune.
PH. = Inscriptions of Cos. Paton and Hicks. 1891.
Philol. = Philologus. Zeitschrift für das klassische Altertum.
Rev. Arch. = Revue Archéologique. Paris, 1844 ff.
Rev. d. Ét. Gr. = Revue des Études Grecques.
Rh. M. = Rheinisches Museum für Philologie.

Roberts = Introduction to Greek Epigraphy. E. S. Roberts. 1887.
Schmidt, Plur. = Die Pluralbildungen der indogermanischen Neutra. 1889.
Schulze, Quaest. Ep. = Quaestiones Epicae. W. Schulze. 1892.
SGDI. = Sammlung der griechischen Dialekt-Inschriften. Collitz and Bechtel.
Skias, Kr. D. = περὶ τῆς κρητικῆς διαλεκτοῦ. Athens, 1891.
Swoboda = Die griechischen Volksbeschlüsse. H. Swoboda. 1890.
Tab. Heracl. = Tables of Heracleia. Cauer 40, 41; Meister, Curt. Stud. IV, p. 355.
Wien. Stud. = Wiener Studien: Zeitschrift für classische Philologie.
Z. f. öst. G. = Zeitschrift für die österreichischen Gymnasien. Wien.

NEW WORDS.

ἀγαῖος, *admirable, desirable.* [V] Delph. BCH. 1895, 1 ff. D_{38} ἐπέδωκε — — καὶ τὰν ἀγαίαν μόσχομ. Cf. Hesych. ἀγαῖον· ἐπίφθονον; Etym. M. 8, 50, ἀγαῖον· ἐπίφθονον ἢ θαυμαστόν. As Homolle, l. c., p. 60, says, this adjective is vague, but it is hardly to be rejected with Dragumis, BCH. 1895, 297, who reads ἀγατάν.

ἀγέρτᾱς, *collector.* [I] Taur. IG. Sic. et It. 424 I_{35}, II_{35}, III_{35} παρὰ δὲ ἀγέρταις τοῖς . . . . This word is defined in L. & S. as a "collection of dues," but σιταγέρτης is given correctly.

ἀγνέω = ἄγω. [II] Aetol. 1413_5 ἀγνηκώς, 1411_{145} ἀχνηκότας; Lac. (Amyclae) Cauer 32_9 διεξαγνηκέναι; Berl. Pap. I, 17–20 (Meyer, p. 587) ἀγνέουσι. Cf. Hesych. ἀγνεῖν· ἄγειν. Κρῆτες; ἀγνεῖ· λαμβάνει; also ἄγνηκε· (for ἀγνησόει of the text; cf. Ahrens II, p. 337) ἀγήοχε. Λάκωνες. Both ἀγν- and ἀγ- are used in the same inscription 1411_{12} εἰ δέ τις ἄγηι — — —τοὺς ἀχνηκότας, and $1413_{5·20}$ ἀγνηκὼς—εἰ δέ τίς κα ἄγη — —. The Laconian inscription shows traces of Aetolian influence, nevertheless it is quite possible that διεξαγνηκέναι, in view of the gloss, is to be taken with Cauer as Laconian. Then, this inscription, too, shows both roots. In no inscription from Crete is ἀγνέω found, although Hesychius cites it from this dialect. The reduplicated perfect of ἄγω does not occur in Aetolian and seems to have been replaced by the perfect of ἀγνέω. The χ in ἀχνηκότας is to be taken with Meyer, § 279, as purely graphic. The development, however, of γ to a spirant is hardly to be assumed in the absence of other evidence.

ἀγωνάριον, *"a kind of college examination or competition among the members."* [138] Cos PH. $43a_7$, b_8 καὶ ἀγωνάριον ἀνήβων.

ἀδηνέως, *without fraud, plainly.* [V] Ion. (Chios) Bechtel $174b_{10}$ κηρυσσόντων καὶ διὰ τῆς πόλεως ἀδηνέως γεγωνέοντες — —. Cf. Hesych. ἀδηνέως· ἀδόλως, ἁπλῶς, χωρὶς βουλῆς; Bekk. Anecd. I,

p. 341 ἀδηνέως : ἁπλῶς καὶ ἀταλαιπώρως, κατὰ στέρησιν τῶν δηνέων καὶ μεριμνῶν. See Smyth, § 716, who prefers this explanation, which is given by Haussoullier, BCH. 1879, 23, to that of Röhl, who explains as = ἄδην (*quantum opus erit*). ἀδηνής is suggested by Valckenaer in Sim. Amorg. 7, 53, where Bergk reads ἀληνής.

ἀζετόω, *convict*. [186] Delph. 2034₁₆ εἰ δέ τί κα ἀζετωθέωντι περὶ Νεοπάτραν πεπονηρευμέναι ἢ τῶν Νεοπάτρας ὑπαρχόντων τι, κύριοι ἐόντων οἱ ἐπίνομοι κολάζοντες αὐτάς, etc. Cf. Hesych. ἄζετον· ἄπιστον. Σικελοί, cited by Hartmann, de dial. Delph., p. 5. The complete explanation is given by Baunack, Stud. I, 248, who compares 1819₉ εἰ δέ τι νοσφίξαιντο Κωμικὸς ἢ Ἰωνὶς τῶμ Μαρα[ί]ου καὶ ἐξελεγχθείη <ι>σαν, etc. ἀζετόω is the equivalent of Attic ἀναζητέω, while in the gloss of course the *a* is the negative prefix. For ἀ- = ἀνα- see also Kretschmer, KZ. 33, 566. ζετόω is formed from a participle ζε-τός seen in the gloss, as ζητέω from *ζη-τός, the relation of ζετός to ζη-, δί-ζη-μαι being the same as that of θε-τός to θη- in τίθημι.

ἀϝλανέως, *openly, without concealment* (?). [V] Elis 1156₄ = Roberts 296 = Ol. 7, ἐξαγρέων καὶ ἐνποιῶν σὺν βωλαῖ [π]εντακατίων ἀϝλανέως (ΑΥΛΑΝΕΟΣ) καὶ δάμοι πληθύοντι δινάκοι. Cf. Hesych. ἀλανές· ἀληθές ; ἀλανέως· ὁλοσχερῶς. Ταραντῖνοι ; ἀλλανής· ἀσφαλής. Λάκωνες. It can hardly be doubted that the word must be explained by the glosses cited. Its exact meaning, however, is not clear. The order of the words would indicate that it modifies what precedes, and it was so interpreted by Röhl, IGA. Add. N. 113c, and by Bücheler, RhM. XXXVI, 621 f. The latter translated by "ungefähr," and made the word a modifier of πεντακατίων ; the former, laying stress on the gloss ὁλοσχερῶς and bringing into connection ἀολλής and ἀλής, interpreted it as a modifier of the phrase βωλᾶι πεντακατίων and translated "senatu pleno." Meister, GD. II, p. 72, criticises fully both these interpretations. He thinks that a quorum in a matter of religious observance would not be defined as *about* five hundred. His objection to Röhl's explanation: that, if a modifier of βουλή, the word should be an adjective, not an adverb, is convincing. Dittenberger, Ol. 7, sustains this objection. He thinks irregularity in the order of words in an Elean inscription of this character is not important. He inclines to interpret the word as = ἀσφαλῶς, used in the sense of ἀνατεί (sine fraude sua). Meister, GD. II, p. 24, translates "sicher (i. e., ungefährdet) ändern." It seems, however, that the gloss ἀσφαλής should be regarded as secondary, and the real meaning be sought in ἀληθές. Professor Buck has suggested that an adverbial meaning, *certainly, without fail*, which would suit this connection and at the same time indicate the line of development which led to the gloss ὁλοσχερῶς, might be assumed for the passage in question, and be taken in close connection with the preceding words. It would then be translated: "Amendment may be made with the consent of the council without fail and with the full assembly." But I am inclined to think that, while some such general meaning may be inferred from ὁλοσχερῶς, the word has a more specific meaning here. I would translate: "Amendment[1] may be made with the Boulé of five hundred *openly* and with a majority[1] of the assembly." The -ϝλ- suits admirably the gloss ἀλλανής; cf. also ἀλλαθεάδας.

ἀί, ἀίν = ἀεί. [319–317] Aeol. 304 A$_{34-36}$ ἄι; Thess. 361 B$_{12}$ ἀίν and in the compounds ἀίσιται, CIA. II, 329$_{41}$, ἀίδασμος, Bechtel 183a$_{30}$, b$_{30}$. These words are to be taken with J. Schmidt, KZ. XXVII, 298 ff., as forms of an old *i*-stem, as Goth. *aiwins*. See Meyer, p. 401, n. 1. (Otherwise Meister, GD. I, p. 72; Hoffmann, I, p. 387.) Schmidt argues rightly that -ν must denote a case-form, since ν-movable is unknown to Thessalian, and that ει is not represented by ι in Thessalian.

ἀίδασμος, *subject to perpetual payment*, as land *on perpetual lease*. [IV] Ion. Bechtel 183a$_{30}$, b$_{30}$ = BCH. 1879, 244. (Here the inscription is given entire. For citation see below.) The larger part of this inscription is in the κοινή, but a few words belong to the local dialect. This word has been generally confused with ἄδασμος. Haussoullier, l. c., p. 250, says "pour ἄδασμον;" Smyth, Ion. Dialects, § 210, "ἀίδασμος is an unexplained form for ἄδασμος." Bechtel, l. c., says "neu und nicht zu rechtfertigen ist zweimaliges ἀίδασμος = ἄδασμος, von der Abgabe befreit." As for

[1] See πληθύοντι and δινάκω.

the meaning, Hausoullier understands as "not subject to taxation," contrasted with ἑκατοστηρία, which was land subject to a special tax both before and after the lease. But this would separate the word from the δασμός of l. 19. For, comparing A, ll. 5ff. τετρακόσιαι εἴκο[σι δρα]χμαί. Ἀναξίδημος Ἡραγόρου Κλυτ[ίδαις κ]αὶ Κλυτιδέων τῶι ἄρχοντι Ἀργέ[αι Ἀρισ]τομήδους· ἡ γῆ ἡ ἐν Δελφινίωι ἡ τ[είως Κ]αυκασίωνος τοῦ Βασιλεΐδου, καὶ [τὰ ἐπό]μενα τῆι γῆι πάντα ἐστὶν ἐμὰ καὶ [ἡ οἰκίη] ἡ ἐν Ἀνδίνηι ἦν οἱ ὁρισταὶ ὤρι[σαν Κλυ]τιδῶν εἶναι καὶ ἦν Λεώφρων ὁ Δε[.... ἐδ]ίκασεν ἑκατοστηρίην εἶναι· ἔσ[τιν δὲ ἡ] ἀξίη πεντακισχιλίων στατήρω[ν, ἀποδί]δοντος ἐμοῦ Κλυτίδαις ἔτεος ἑ[κάστου] τριάκοντα τάλαντα ξύλων ἐν [τῶι ....]τωι ἄλσει κείμενα, ὅταν ἡ ἀγὴ ᾖ[ι καὶ τετ]ρακοσίας εἴκοσι δραχμὰς ἐμ μ[ηνὶ Ἀρτε]μισιῶνι, τὸμ πρῶτον δασμὸν ἅμα [πρώτωι] ἔτει μετὰ "Αλσωνα πρύτανιν καὶ [τοὺς ἄλ]λους ἅμα ἐνιαυτῶι ἕκαστον with B$_{37}$ ὁ ἀνε]λόμενος τὴγ γῆν τὸ ἐνηλά[σιον ἀποδώσε]ι ἐμ μηνὶ Ἀρτεμισιῶνι τῶ[ι μετὰ ....]ην πρύτανιν καὶ τῶν ἄλλω[ν ἕκαστον ἀμ' ἐ]νιαυτῶι, it is clear that τὸμ πρῶτον δασμὸν refers to the first yearly payment of the lessee to the owners, the first installment of the ἐνηλάσιον.

By taking this word as a possessive adjective formed from a compound of αἰ and δασμός we account for the form and at the same time secure a meaning which brings the word into connection with the δασμός of l. 19. It simply states what according to Haussoullier, p. 250, was tacitly understood, namely, "La durée du bail, n'étant pas indiquée, est illimitée;" cf. the phrase κατὰ βίω of the Heraclean Tables, εἰς τὸν ἅπαντα χρόνον, Munychia, and other similar expressions. See BCH. 1879, 250, n. 1. The word δασμός may indicate a recognition of the proprietary rights of the Klytidae and a feeling that the annual payments were really of the nature of tribute.

ἀκαταβολέω, *fail in making payment.* [171] Delph. 1804$_3$ κατενεγκάτω δὲ Ἀφροδισία τὸν [ἔ]ρανον τὸν βρομίου οὗ ἐγγυενει Ἰατάδας μὴ ἀκαταβολέουσα μηδὲ καταβλάπτουσα Ἰατάδαν· εἰ δὲ μὴ κατενέγκαι Ἀφροδισία τὸν ἔρανον ἢ καταβλάψ<α>αι τι - -.

ἀκεύω, *guard, watch.* [V] Gort. Law-code II$_{17 \cdot 18}$ αἴ κα τὰν ἐλευθέραν ἐπιπρήται οἴφεν ἀκεύοντος καδεστᾶ. Cf. Hesych. ἀκεύει·

τηρεῖ. Κύπριοι. This gloss gives the satisfactory explanation. The word must be separated from ἀκούω. See Comparetti, p. 164; Kretschmer, KZ. 33, 565.[1] The latter suggests that ἀκ-, *sharp*, is probably to be seen in ἀκεύω as well as in ἀκούω. The original meaning would then be general, *be keen*, which might easily be specialized to *guard*, *heed*. There is a proper name Ἀκευσώ Anaphe 3451, which seems to contain the same verbal stem.

ἀκροσκιρία, *wooded height*. [IV] Tab. Heracl. I$_{65.71}$ δύο (ὅροι) δὲ ἐν ταῖς ἀκροσκιρίαις, also δύο δὲ ἐπὶ τᾶν ἀκροσκιριᾶν - -. Cf. σκῖρος I$_{19}$ (common) and the glosses of Hesych. σκεῖρος· ἄλσος καὶ δρυμός, Φιλητᾶς δὲ τὴν ῥυπώδη γῆν; σκῖρα· χωρία ὕλην ἔχοντα εὐθετοῦσαν εἰς φρύγανα.

ἀλεκχώ(?) = ἄλοχος. [V] Delph. BCH. 1895, 1 ff. D$_{12}$. Homolle transcribes and translates as follows: καίκ' αὐτὸς θύηι ἱαρήιαν καίκα λεκχ' οἳ παρῆι καίκα ξένοι ϝοῖ παρέωντι ἱαρήια θύοντες καίκα πενταμαριτεύων τύχηι. "Soit que le Labyade sacrifie lui-même la victime, ou que sa femme avec son assistance, ou que des étrangers avec son assistance sacrifient des victimes, ou qu'il se trouve en fonctions de cinq jours." This passage follows the enumeration of the obligatory feasts to be observed by every member of the clan in one of the ways here described: 1) He may perform the sacrifice personally; 2) his wife may perform it in his stead (?); 3) the strangers present in his home may make the sacred offerings, or, 4) he may be engaged in the duties of a πενταμαρίτης. The clause containing this word is extremely difficult. Homolle, l. c., p. 57, gives six possible transcriptions. None is entirely satisfactory. Dragumis, p. 298, choosing the same reading as Homolle, cites Hesych. λέχος· γάμος and translates "ou qu'on célèbre des noces chez lui," which is even more incomprehensible than Homolle's explanation. Keil, Hermes XXXI, p. 508, objects to Homolle's transcription on the ground that in the dialect of this inscription ϝοῖ not οἷ is to be expected, as indeed it is written immediately below; λεκχοι

---

[1] For the various attempts to connect with ἀκούω see Baunack, Ins. v. G., p. 54; Skias, Kr.D. 131; Bechtel, SGDI. 3451; Meister, Gr.D. II, 232.

therefore forms one word, presumably in the dative case. On this assumption Keil takes παρῇ from παρίημι and translates "or if he has given it over to his wife," thinking that in Doric conditions of society the wife might possibly perform priestly duty. I have, however, been unable to find any Greek parallel for such an arrangement. The other difficulty which Keil sees in the use of a different word for γυνά does not seem serious. In the Delphian manumission decrees there is a single occurrence of ἑρπούσας instead of the usual ἀποτρέχουσας, and δείληται occurs three times in the place of θέλῃ. Keil seems to prefer λεκχώ,[1] though he takes up the discarded ἀλεκχοῖ of Homolle as not wholly impossible. It has seemed to me more probable that the compound was used. The omission of the article on this assumption may be due to the apparent identity of the recurring καῖκα. ἄλοχος is a poetical word, but is cited as Cyprian in Bekk. Anecd. III, p. 1095, Κυπρίων· ἄλοχος· γυνή. The spelling -κχ- is purely graphic. See Blass, Ausspr., p. 101.

ἀλίασμα, 1) *assembly* (not technical), 2) *decree*. [211] Agrig., Cauer 199 = IG. Sic. et It. 952 ἀλίασμα[2] ἔκτας διμήνου,[3] Gela, Cauer 198 = IG. Sic. et It. 256 βουλᾶς ἀλίασμα τᾶ(ς) δευτέρας ἑξαμήνου, Rhegium, Ditt. Syll. 251 = IG. Sic. et It. 612 τὰν δὲ βουλὰν τὸ ἀλίασμα κολαψαμέναν εἰς χαλκώματα δισσά. The word is a derivative of *ἀλιάζω = ἐκκλησιάζω. There is evidently a double development in meaning. In the inscriptions from Gela and Agrigentum the word can hardly mean other than *coming together*. But in the inscription from Rhegium it is as plainly used for *decree of the assembly*. Cf. Ditt. Syll., l. c., n. 4, "I. e., τὸ δόγμα τᾶς ἀλίας·" wrongly adding "Vocabulum praeterea nusquam exstat."

ἄλινσις, *rubbing* (*painting* or *polishing*?). [IV] Epid. 3325A$_{39}$ = K. 241. Σαμίων ἔλετο ἄλινσιν τοῦ ἐργαστηρίου καὶ κονίασιν.

[1] Λεχοῖ occurs on an ancient Spartan inscription. Roberts cites also from a later inscription, Mitth. 1877, 440, ΑΓΙΓΓΙΑΛΕΧΟΙ.

[2] For smooth breathing cf. ἀλία and ἀλίασις (under "Rare Words").

[3] See Swoboda, p. 308, for the different systems of dating assemblies. It must be assumed that βουλᾶς is omitted here, hardly that ἀλίασμα stands for the council itself.

Verbal substantive from ἀλίνω. Cf. Hesych. ἀλίναι· ἐπαλεῖψαι and ἀλίνειν· ἀλείφειν; also Bekk. Anecd. 383,11 ἀλίνουσιν : ἀντὶ τοῦ λεπτύνουσι. Σοφοκλῆς (Fr. 826). In the building inscription, CIA. II, 167 ἀλοιφή, ἀλοιμός, and περιαλείψει occur. Hesych. glosses ἄλοιμα by χρίσμα τείχων. and in Etym. M. 69, 41, we find ἀλοιμός· τὰς χρίσεις καὶ τὰς ἐπαλείψεις ἀλοιμοὺς ἔλεγον. The general meaning of these words is clear, but the special use cannot be asserted with any certainty.

ἀλλαθεάδες, *rites in memory of the dead.* [174–157] Delph. 1796,5 ποιήσας τὰ νομιζόμενα τὰ ἐν τὰν ταφὰν καὶ ἀλλαθεάδας; 1731,10 θαψάτω Κίντος καὶ τὰς ἀλλαθεάδας ποησάτω καθὼς νομίζεται; 1775,29 ποιησάτω δὲ καὶ τὰς ἀλλαθεάδας καὶ τὰ λοιπὰ τὰ νομιζόμενα πάντα. The above are the only occurrences of this word, so far as I am able to ascertain. Baunack in a note to 1731 defines as "Erinnerungsfeierlichkeiten," which is undoubtedly correct, though why he should divide the word ἀλ-λαθ-εάδες rather than ἀ-λλαθ-εάδες is not clear. The -λλ- is probably due to the presence of two original consonants. Cf. ἀλλανής : ἀϝλανέως.

The suffix -ας -αδος is not common. It is used chiefly in nouns of agency and in feminine abstracts from numerals. It may be that the form of this word was influenced by τριακάδες. The general term τὰ ὥρια is used in two inscriptions of Phocis outside of Delphi, 1545 and 1546. But it is likely that ἀλλαθεάδες may have denoted a definite observance not always kept.[1]

ἄλϝον, *garden* or *orchard.* [IV] Cypr. (Edal.) 60,9·18·21 τὸ(ν) χρανόμενον "Ο(γ)κα(ν)τος ἄλϝω (9), τὸ(ν) χῶρον τὸ(ν) χραυζόμενον 'Αμηνίδα ἄλϝω (18), τὸ(ν) Διϝείθεμις ὁ 'Αρμανεὺς ἦχε ἄλϝο(ν), τὸ(ν) ποεχόμενον πὸς Πασαγόραν τὸν 'Ονασαγόραν (21). The neuter τὸ ἄλϝον is to be assumed here with Deecke, SGDI. I, p. 30, and Meister II, p. 243. The Hesychian ἄλουα· κῆποι. Κύπριοι is the equivalent of the Hom. ἀλωή and agrees with our word in

---

[1] For the ordinary funeral customs see Becker, Charicles III,155, and Hermann-Blümner, p. 372, n. 2.

In the manumission decrees directions for the freed person after the death of his master occur in only about a dozen of the seven or eight hundred inscriptions of this character which we have. They are very elaborate in 1801, 1807.

stem only. ἄλως, which Hoffmann would see here, is rare in inscriptions. It occurs on a late Delph. inscription, BCH. 1881, 157. Hoffmann would translate, GD. I, p. 71, *threshing-floor*, which hardly suits the context as well as *garden* or *orchard*. His objection to the form ἄλϝο(ν), 21, that -ν would not be lost before τὸν ποεχόμενον, since the latter is not a modifier of ἄλϝον, but of κᾶπον, is to be met by the fact that -ν is lost in τὸ(ν) Διϝείθεμις of the same line and also that τὸν ποεχόμενον is logically closely connected with ἄλϝον.

ἀλλοπολία = ἀλλοδημία. [V] Gort. Law-code VI₄₇ ἔκς ἀλλοπολίας ὑπ' ἀνάνκας ἐχόμενος κελο[μ]ένω τις λύσηται. Comparetti in note to place explains this word as an abstract to *ἀλλόπολις, while Baunack cites the πολία which occurs in πολιανόμος, πολιατεύω, etc.

ἄλωμα = ἀνάλωμα. [III] Boeot. 488₁₃₉ κὴ τὸ ἄλωμα ἀπολογίτταστη ποτὶ κατόπ[τ]α[ς]. CIGS. I, 2426₁₄, 4131₃₄, 4263₂₉ (similar expressions); Ceos, Ἐφ. Ἀρχ. II, 3267 quoted by Keil, Mitth. 1895, 51, in criticising Pridik, De Cei ins. rebus, p. 164, for correcting to (ἀν)άλωμα.

ἀμάτη, *single part*. [III] Cos PH. 367₄₆ ποταπογραφέσθων δὲ καὶ τὰν πατρίδα καὶ τινος (ἐ)[νά]της καὶ ἀμάτη[ς ἔλαχ?]ε. See Keil, Mitth. 1895, 32. He derives from the same stem as εἷς, μία, citing the Hesych. glosses, ἀμάκις· ἅπαξ. Κρῆτες and ἀμάτις· ἅπαξ. Ταραντῖνοι.

ἀμεῖ, *together*. [V] Delph. BCH. 1895, 1 ff. D₄₈ συμπρηίσκεν haμεῖ. Cf. μηδαμεῖ of the same inscription.

ἀμμόνιον, *deposit*. [V] Delph. BCH. 1895, 1 ff. A₄₈·₅₄, hόστις δέ κα μὴ ἄγηι τ'ἀπελλαῖα ἢ τὰν δαράταν μὴ φέρηι ἀμμόνιον κατθέτω στατῆρα ἐπὶ ϝεκατέρω, τῶι δὲ hυστέρωι ϝέτει ἀγέτω τ'ἀπελλαῖα καὶ τὰν δαράταν φερέτω. αἰ δέ κα μὴ ἀγηι, μηκέτι δεκέσθων ἀμμόνια. The word is defined at length by Homolle, l. c., as "un dépôt, une consignation faite en attendant pour donner patience, un gage, ou une compensation." Apocope is constant in this inscription. There is but one apparent exception, ἀναποτθέθηι, as read by Homolle, but this is to be otherwise explained. See θιγάνα.

ἀμοιϝά, *change*. [VI] Corinth 3119 = IGA. 20, 108ₐ τὺ δὲ δὸ[ς χα]ρίεσ(σ)αν ἀμοιϝάν. This word occurs in the same expression as ἀφορμάν, ἀμοιβάν in other inscriptions of this group. It is to be connected with ἀμεύσασθαι. See Schmidt, KZ. 32, 374, who sets up *ἀμοϝια, which becomes by epenthesis ἀμοιϝά. Cf. Meyer, p. 173; Brugmann I, p. 271; Kretschmer, Vas. Insc., p. 48.

ἀμπέτιξ(?) = περιαμπέτιξ = πέριξ. [Late.] Crete, CIG. 2554₁₁₈. Cf. Helbig, de dial. Cret., p. 5; Böckh, CIG., p. 405.

ἀμπώλημα, *price paid for readjudication on account of broken agreement*, technical term. [IV] Tab. Heracl. I₁₁₀·₁₅₅ τό τε μίσθωμα διπλεῖ ἀποτεισεῖ τὸ ἐπὶ τῶ ϝέτεος καὶ τὸ ἀμπώλημα τοῖς τε πολιανόμοις καὶ τοῖς σιταγέρταις - - (110) and (155) τὼς δὲ πρωγγύως τὼς ἀεὶ γενομένως πεπρωγγυευκῆμεν τῶν τε μισθωμάτων καὶ τῶν ἐπιζαμιωμάτων καὶ τῶν ἀμπωλημάτων. The ἀμπώλημα is further explained in l. 111 ὅσσῳ κα μείονος ἀμμισθωθῇ πὰρ πέντε ϝέτη τὰ πρᾶτα. It is, therefore, a payment made as guarantee to the state against loss which might be incurred through a new lease at a lower rental. This is the explanation given by Kaibel, IG. Sic. et It. 645. Cf. Ins. Jurid. Gr., p. 233.

ἀμυωτός (?) = ἀμύητος. [VII, VI] Cret. Comp. 44 AMVOTON. The word is written retrograde and is without context. Comparetti's suggestion that it is a possible variant for ἀμύητος as ὀφήλωμα : ὀφήλημα 152 VI₁₅ is as probable a disposal of the word as can be made in the absence of evidence.

ἀμφαντύς, *state of adoption*. [V] Gort. Law-code XI₂₁ τῶν δὲ πρόθθα, ὄπαι τις ἔχει ἢ ἀμφαντύι (ΑΜΠΑΝΤVΙ) ἢ παρ' ἀμφάντω, μὴ ἔτ' ἔνδικον ἦμεν. See Dittenberger, Hermes 20, 573, whose explanation of the word as the dative of an abstract noun with meaning given above is undoubtedly correct. Comparetti explains as an adverb in -ῦι, but the abstract is quite as satisfactory in form and suits the context better. Cf. Blass, Jahrb. f. Philol. 131, 485; Meyer, p. 202.

ἀμφεικάς, *one and twentieth*. [II] Cos 3720 Πανάμου, ἀμφεικάδι· [ἔδ]οξε τοῖς φυλέταις - -. Thera, Cauer, 47 C₁ τᾷ δὲ ἀμφεικάδι. Hesych. ἀμφεικάς· ἡ περὶ εἰκάδα. This gloss, formerly read ἀμφ'εἰκάς, is confirmed by the inscriptions.

ἀμφιθύσανος, *fringed.* [346/45] Ion. Bechtel 220₂₂ πρόσλημμα τῆς θεοῦ παραλοργὲς ἀμφιθύσανον.

ἀμφίμωλος, *defendant in a law suit.* [V] Gort. Law-code X₂₇ ἄνθρω[π]ον μὴ ὠνήθα[ι] κατακείμενον πρίν κ' ἀ[λλ]υ(σ)ήται ὁ καταθένς, μηδ' ἀμφίμωλον (ΑΜΓΙΜΟΛΟΝ).

ἀμωλεί, *without contest.* [V] Gort. Comp. 156 II₄ κ' ὅττον ἐγράττai ἀμωλεὶ (ΑΜΟΛΕΙ) πραδέθαι. The inscription is badly mutilated, but this seems to be the context. This conjecture, made by Comparetti, is possible, but necessarily uncertain.

ἀνασάξιμος, *reopened after having once been worked,* as a mine. [III] CIA. II, 780₂₀ πα(λ)αιὸν ἀνασά[ξιμον—., 781₁₀ ἀνασάξιμον στήλην ἔχον, 782 and IV, 1078b Κ]ρωπίδης κατέλαβε [ἀ]νασάξιμον μέταλλον. See Hicks Br. Mus. I, XXXVl. He repeats Böckh's explanation as above. The word is apparently a miner's term and might be from σάττειν, used first of loading ore, then of working the mine generally. These are all mine inscriptions. II, 781₁₀ would apparently show application of the word to the slag which is worked for the second time.

ἀνάτως, *with impunity.* [V] CIGS. III, 333 τὸν δὲ συλῶντα ἀνάτω(ς) συλῆν τὰ ξενικὰ ἐθαλάσ(σ)ας hάγειν ἄσυλον, πλὰν ἐλιμένος τῶ κατὰ πόλιν. This reading is preferred by Dittenberger, l. c. Bechtel in SGDI. 1479 reads ἀνὰ τὸ συλῆν. Cf. ἀνατεί.

ἀνδιχάζω, *disagree.* [V] Locris 1479₁₀ = CIGS. III, 333₁₀ αἴ κ'ἀν διχάζωντι (ΑΝΔΙΧΑΖΟΝΤΙ) τοὶ ξενοδίκαι, ἐπωμότας hελέστω – –. Denominative from ἄνδιχα.

ἄνερμα, *necklace*(?) [330] CIA. IV, 767b₂₄ δακτύλιος ἀργυ[ροῦς . . . .] IC· ἄνερμα τοῦ . . . ου ἀργύρου. The exact meaning of this word is uncertain, since the following letters cannot be read. Köhler's note, l. c., suggests *necklace* or *earrings.* From ἀνείρω. Cf. ἕρματα, ὅρμος.

ἀνκριτήρ, *official of Megara.* [Late.] Meg. 3055 ἀνκριτῆρες τοὶ ἐπὶ βασιλείος. These officers are mentioned only in this inscription. Three names follow. Foucart, BCH. 1887, 296, thinks their duty is "de faire l'*ἀνάκρισις* ou instruction préparatoire des procès."

ἀνπαιστήρ, *knocker*(?). [IV] Epid. 3325 B₇₉ = K 241₇₉ Εὐκράτης εἵλετο ἀσπίδα κ[αὶ] ἀνπαιστῆρα τῶι μεγάλωι θυρώματι. Cf.

Hesych. ἀναπαιστρίδες· σφῦραι, παρὰ τοῖς χαλκεῦσιν. See Baunack, Aus. Epid., p. 80, who thinks the ῥόπτον, 3340₄₁, is here called ἀναπαιστήρ because on the temple it is used only for closing the door. He compares ἐπισπαστήρ, which also replaces ῥόπτρον.

ἀντίθεμα, *final addition to structure* (?). [Ionic characters "d'une bonne époque" (Foucart.)] Troiz. BCH. 1893, 117 ἀντιθέματα ταῖ περιφανεῖ καὶ ταῖ πράτα[ι]. Le Grand, 1. c., thinks this word designates the stones which form the finish of the wall on the two faces.

ἀντίθημα, probably same as preceding. [400] CIA. I, 321₇ (without context). The word is used in the plural. The interchange of -ημα, -εμα is common, the variation one of periods. Cf. Lob. Phryn., p. 249.

ἀντίμορος, *opposite, corresponding to.* [400] CIA. I, 322₂₆ γογγύλος λίθος ἄθετος, ἀντίμορος ταῖς ἐπικρανίτισιν.

ἄντομος, *road.* [IV] Tab. Heracl. I₁₅ (com.) ἐπὶ τὸν ἄντομον τὸν ὁρίζοντα.

ἄντορος, *opposite boundary-stone.* [IV] Tab. Heracl. I₆₀·₆₂·₇₅·₇₈ ἄλλως δὲ ἀντόρως τούτοις ἐστάσαμες ἐπὶ τᾶς ἀμαξιτῶ.

ἀνυπόζωστος, *without benches for rowers.* ⌊375/3⌋ Attic, Mitth. 1883, 173. The inscription is an inventory of triremes. The others had each four ὑποζώματα, the last two were apparently ἀνυπόζ[ωστοι].

ἄνφανσις, *act of adoption.* [V] Gort. Law-code X, 33 ἄνφανσιν (ΑΝΠΑΝϟΙΝ) ἦμεν ὦ ποκά τιλ λῆι. For technical use cf. ἀμφαίνομαι, ἀμφαντύς.

ἀνφιδήμᾱ, *jewelry, ornament.* [V] Gort. Law-code V₄₀ θνατῶν δὲ καὶ καρπῶ καὶ ϝήμας κ'ἀνφιδήμας (ΑΝΠΙΔΕΜΑϟ) κ'ἐπιπολαίων χρημάτων αἴ κα μὴ λείωντι δατήθαι, etc., also Comp. 154 I₂₀₋₂₁ τὰ δὲ τρίτρα τᾶς ϝήμας καὶ τᾶς ἀνφιδήμας (ΑΝΠΙΔΗΜΑϟ). Cf. Hesych. ἀμφιδέαι· ψέλλια. κρίκοι. δακτύλιοι. The genitive proves conclusively that the word belongs to the *ā*-nouns. A similar transfer is found in ἡ χάρμη: τὸ χάρμα, et al. Cf. also Cret. ϝήμᾱ : ϝῆμα.

ἀνφιμωλέω, *contest at law, bring suit.* [V] Gort. Law-code X, 27. See μωλέω for related words and discussion.

ἀξιόσυλος, owning property which can be taken for debt. [VI] Elis 1151₆ = Ol. 16 = Roberts 298 αἰ δ'ἀξιόσυλος γένο[ιτο].

ἀπαμπαίω, beat back. [V] Gort. Comp. 152 II₁₇ κύναυς ἀπαμπαιομένο[υς].

ἀπάρβολος, without deposit. [II?] Corcyra 3206₁₁₅ κρίσιν ἀπάρβολον. ἀπαραβόλως occurs in Schol. to Il. N. 141.

ἄπατος, free from liability. [V] Gort. Law-code, II₁, IV₁₇. Comp. 152 V₆, 153 II₁₄, 154 II₁₃₋₁₄, 194₆ (Eleuthera) ἄπατον ἦμεν. For discussion of this and similar expressions see section on synonyms.

ἀπεκδίδωμι, 1) give to another, 2) let out on contract. [III] Delos, CIG. 2266₄ ἐξέστω τοῖς ἐπιστάταις καὶ ἀπεκδοῦναι τὰ κατα[λειφθέντα?]; Priene, Brit. Mus. 415₃₁ τὸν νεωποίην Λεωμέδοντα ἀπεγδοῦναι, ὅπως στήλη τε κατασκευασθῇ καὶ ἀναγραφῇ εἰς αὐτήν—., 420₇₂ (same use). Keil, Mitth. 1895, 34, note, cites in addition ἀπέγδοσις found on Egypt. papyrus. In the inscriptions from Priene ἀπεγδοῦναι = ἐκδοῦναι. Fabricius, Hermes 17, 4, compares the verb of the Delos inscription with ἀπομισθοῦν in an inscription from Amorgus. See also Fabricius, de Architectura, p. 32.

ἀπέλλα, assembly. [I] Lac. M. 50₂₁ = LeB.-F. 243a₂₁, M. 51₄ = LeB.-F. 242a₄₁ ἔδοξε τῶι δάμοι ἐν ταῖς μεγάλαις ἀπέλλαις. Cf. Hesych. ἀπέλλαι· σηκοί. ἐκκλησίαι. ἀρχαιρεσίαι and ἀπελάζειν· ἐκκλησιάζειν. Λάκωνες; Plut. Lyc. VI, quotation from the oracle at Delphi, ὥρας ἐξ ὥρας ἀπελλάζειν. Cf. also ἀπελλαῖα (below).

The inscriptions in which ἀπέλλα occurs are from Gytheum, one of the cities of the league of coast towns formed in 146 B. C. The constitutions of these towns were modeled after that of Sparta. See Gilbert I (trans.), p. 29. Swoboda, p. 105, says, in substance, that there was at that time no council in Gytheum, and decisions were made in the μεγάλαι ἀπέλλαι by the citizens upon proposal of the ephors, perhaps also after action in a smaller[1] assembly. Both inscriptions in which ἀπέλλα occurs are late. Swoboda, p. 270, places the second in the time of Sulla,

---

[1] In Syll., p. 381, note 19, Dittenberger compares the relation of ἁλία to ἔσκλητος in 251 as probably similar to that of the ἀπέλλα to a smaller assembly.

the first somewhat earlier. The word is not, however, a late formation. Cf. ἀπελλαῖα, Ἀπέλλαι. The derivation has been much discussed.[1] It is probably ἀ-πελ- from $\sqrt{quel}$ seen in Gr. τέλος, O.B. čeljati, Lith. kiltis, Sans. kula-, Lat. concilium.

Ἀπέλλαι, *feast at which the ἀπελλαῖα offerings were made by the members of the clan of the Labyadae.* [V] Delph. BCH. 1895, 1 ff., A_{31} τὰ δὲ ἀπελλαῖα ἄγεν Ἀπέλλαις καὶ μὴ ἄλλαι ἀμέραι. A_{36} αἰ δέ κα [δέ]ξ[ω]ν[τ]αι ἄλλαι ἀμέραι ἢ Ἀπέλλαις, D_3 θοῖναι δὲ [h]αίδ[ε νόμιμ]οι· Ἀπέλλαι καὶ - -.

ἀπελλαῖα, *offerings made at the Ἀπέλλαι festival.* [V] Delph. BCH. 1895, 1 ff., A_4 ταγευσέω δικαίως κατὰ τοὺν νόμους τᾶς πόλιος καὶ τοὺς τῶν Λαβυαδᾶν πὲρ τῶν ἀπελλαίων καὶ τᾶν δαρατᾶν. A_{23} τοὺς τάγους μὴ δέκεσθαι μήτε δαράταν γάμελα μήτε παιδήϊα μήτ' ἀπελλαῖα, αἰ μὴ τᾶς πατρίας ἐπαινεούσας καὶ πληθυόσας ἇς κα ἦι. A_{31} τὰ δὲ ἀπελλαῖα ἄγεν Ἀπέλλαις καὶ μὴ ἄλλαι ἀμέραι. A_{44} ἄγεν δὲ τἀπελλαῖα ἀντὶ ϝέτεος καὶ τὰς δαράτας φέρεν. Cf. $A_{47\cdot51\cdot54}$ and B_4 πάντες δὲ τοὶ Λαβυάδαι Εὐκλείοις περὶ τᾶν δαρατᾶν ἐπικρινόντων καὶ Ἀπέλλαις περὶ τῶν ἀπελλαίων παρεόντες μὴ μείος hενὸς καὶ hεκατόν. B_{45} καὶ hὸ κα δέξωνται ἢ δαράταν ἢ ἀπελλαῖα πὰρ τὰ γράμματα μὴ ἔστω Λαβυάδας μηδὲ κοινανείτω τῶν κοινῶν χρημάτων μηδὲ τῶν θεμάτων. The feast at which these offerings are made is mentioned among those which are obligatory on the members of the clan, D_3. ἀπελλαῖα is coördinate with δαράτα. The verb φέρεν is always used with the latter, ἄγεν with the former. It may, therefore, be fairly assumed that the ἀπελλαῖα were animal offerings. There is nothing to indicate what animal was used. It may have varied under different circumstances. The importance of this festival and the offerings is clearly shown by the citations. But just what event in the life of a member of the clan of the Labyadae was so celebrated we can only infer. It seems probable that it has to do with membership in the clan; very possibly the admission of the youth to full rights.

[1] See Bezzenberger, BB. XVI, 245; Fick, BB. XVIII, 134, 135; Fröhde, BB. XIX, 317; Müllensiefen, De tit. Lac. dial., p. 49 (179); Brugmann, Curt. Stud. IV, 122.

The month Ἀπελλαῖος is the first of the Delphian civil year, corresponding to the Attic Hecatombaeon. It is a widely used name for a month, though not always with the same value. Cf. Reinach, Traité d'Épigraphie Grecque, p. 481.

ἀποθρίγκωσις, *the capping of a wall*, building term. [Late.] Troiz. BCH. 1893, 117 f. Cf. SGDI. 3362₃₉ τοίχων λιθίνων ἀποθριγκώσιος. ἀποθριγκόω is a late verb which means *to wall off*. Le Grand, l. c., translates "l'opération qui consiste à couronner un mur."

ἀποινίζω, *take vengeance*. [V] Mant. BCH. 1892, 577 ἀποινίξασθαι. This is not from *ἀποινίγω, as Fougères thinks, but it is a regular formation in -ίζω. The -ξ- in the aorist is simply an extension of the so-called Doric future; cf. Kühner-Blass II, 159₈.

ἀπολαγάζω, *release, let go* (?). [Late.] Crete, Mus. Ital. III, p. 693, n. 133₃ ἀπολ]αγαθένσα, n. 134₆ ἀπολγάσα[ντα. Cf. Hesych. λαγάσσαι· ἀφεῖναι; Bekk. Anecd., p. 106, 5, λαγγάζει· ἀντὶ τοῦ ἐνδίδωσιν. Ἀντιφάνης Ἀντερώσῃ. There is no context, so that it is not certain what effect on the meaning the preposition may have. See λαγάζω, λαγαίω (below).

ἀπολάγαξις, *release* (?). [Late.] Crete, Mus. Ital. III, p. 693, n. 134 ἀπ]ολαγάξιος κα[ὶ τ]ᾶς χρηματίξιος. Cf. preceding. The inscription is so badly mutilated that a certain interpretation is impossible.

ἀπομωλέω, *contest in a suit*. [V] Gort. Law-code VI₂₆ αἰ δέ κ' ὁ ἀντίμωλος ἀπομωλ(ῇ)ι (ΑΠΟΜΟΛΕΙ) ἀνφὶ τὸ χρέος - -. IX₁₈ αἰ δ' ὁ ἀντίμωλος ἀπομ[ωλ]ίοι - -. See μωλέω.

ἀπονάϝω, *consecrate*. [V] Lac. IGA. 61a Εὐμυδι[ς] ἀπόναϝ[ε] (ΑΠΟΝΑϜϜ). This was interpreted by Röhl as from πονάω. He compared ἀπόεσεν, IGA. 557, to which may now be added ἀϝρήτευε Arg. AJA. 1896, 43. But even so it is hardly possible to take ἀ- as the augment. There is also another interpretation for each of these forms, which seems preferable. ἀπόναϝε may well be, as Stolz, Wien. Stud. VIII, p. 159, points out, for ἀπό-ναϝε, "*dedicavit*." He compares the Hesychian gloss ναύειν· ἱκετεύειν. Cf. also ναύω of the Gort. Law-code I₃₉.₄₂. For ἀϝρήτευε see below. ἀπόεσεν also can be read differently. It is quite possible that another form may be discovered which would reverse this opinion, but so far as present evidence goes, this seems the safest. Cf. Meyer § 474.

ἀπόπαξ, *altogether.* [V] CIA. I, 288, 286 [καθ' ἡμέ]ραν μισθοὶ κατὰ [τὰ εἰρημέν]α ἀπόπαξ (ΑΠΟΠΑΧϟ). Cf. Hesych. ἀπόπαξ· ξύμπαν, ἢ σύμπαν.

ἀποπολιτεύω, *change citizenship.* [III] Aetol. 1415₁₆ εἰ δέ κα ἀποπολιτεύωντι Πηρεῖς ἀπὸ Με[λι]ταέων—; Phocis 1539a₅₅ μὴ ἐξέστω δὲ ἀποπολιτεύσασται τοὺ[ς] Μεδεωνίους ἀπὸ τῶν Στιρί[ων].

ἀποσκουτλόω, *deface.* [Late.] CIA. III, 1423, 1424 εἴ τις ἀποκοσμήσει τοῦτο τὸ ἡρῷον ἢ ἀποσκουτλώσει.

ἀποστέγασις = ἀποστέγασμα. [Late.] Troiz. 3362₂₆ ἀ[π]οστεγάσσιος τῶν τοίχων τῶν λιθίνων.

ἀρέσμιον, *fee for sacrifices to be performed.* [181] Phocis 1539a₂₅ λανβανέτω [δ]ὲ ὁ ἱεροταμίας ἀρέσμιον ὃ τ[οὶ ἄ]ρχοντες ἐλάμβανον, ἡμι[μ]ναῖον καὶ τῶν χοῶν τὸ ἐπ[ιβ]αλὸν τῶ ἱεροταμίαι. The meaning given is suggested by Dittenberger, Syll. 294. ἀρεστήρ is another derivative from the same root which also has specialization of meaning. Cf. Kum., who says wrongly πιθανῶς ταὐτο τῷ ἀρεστήρ. Cf. ἀρεστηρίαν, CIA. IV, 834b, Col. II, 90.

ἀρήν, ϝαρήν, nominative to ἀρνός. [VII/VI] Gort. Comp. 12–13 καὶ ϝαρήν (FAPEN) τυτυῖ ἔτι δὲ φοῖρος; CIA. I₄,₂₂ Ἑρμ]ῆ ἀρὴν (APEN) κριτός; Cos. 3638 Ἡρακλεῖ ἐς Κο[νίσαλο]ν ἀρὴν καυτός. Cf. PH. 39, note, which says the word is used to denote a lamb less than a year old; Poll. 7, 184, whose apparent identification as a poetical form corresponding to ἀρνειός is explained by Paton as probably referring to ῥήν which is used only by Alexandrian poets.

ἀρήτευε, ἀϝρήτευε, *was the speaker*(?). [500] Argive, AJA. 1896, 43 (AFPETEVE), SGDI. 3277 ἀρήτενε Λέων [β]ωλᾶς σευτέρας, 3315 ἀρήτευε[1] δαμιοργῶν Δελφίων Τ[ι]μοκρίτου Δαιφοντεύς, 3316 ἀρήτ[ενε]. LeBas III, 1 gives the inscription cited here as 3277. He translates "était prêtre du second sénat," and derives from ἀρητήρ. Tszuntas, Ἐφ. Ἀρχ. 1887, 157, commenting on

[1] For this reading see Richardson, l. c., 46 f.

3315, in which he read ἀρίστευε, says the phrase may mean either that Delphion was the first of the δημιουργοί or be equivalent to εἶπε τὴν γνώμην. He prefers the former and compares ἀριστῆρες.[1] Swoboda, p. 171, after defining ἀρίστευε as "praesidierte," adds that the use of ἀρήτευε in 3316 is another reason for coming to this conclusion. This was, however, before the form with ϝ had appeared. It seems impossible to connect this form with ἀρητήρ or with ἀρετή, ἄριστος which Blass suggests as related, Jahrb. f. Philol. 143, 560. The root must be, as Richardson thinks, ϝρē-. The ἀ- is then either for ἀνα-, as in ἀζετόω, or prothetic, as in ἀμέλγω. See Brugmann, Grundriss I, p. 824.

ἀριστήρ (ἀρ[τ]ιστήρ?), a magistrate. [III] CIGS. III, 97. 105 τὰν δὲ [σ]τάλαν τοὺς ἀριστῆρας θέσθαι. In 97 Lolling's copy apparently shows ἀ[ρτ]ιστῆρας. Dittenberger adds that it is doubtful which is an error, but, as he says, ἀρτιστήρ would have a satisfactory derivation with suitable meaning, while ἀριστήρ has not. This new reading is of special interest in view of the change in the reading ἀρίστευε of 3277. See preceding word.

ἄρκαλον, porcupine(?). [V] Lac. M. 11 [ἐ]δήδοϝας ἄρκαλον. Cf. Hesych. ἄρκηλα· ᾠόν. Κρῆτες τὴν ὕστριχα. The inscription is incomplete and of somewhat doubtful reading (Fourmont).

ἄρνηας, ewe. [IV] Aeol. (Aegea) Hoffmann II, 155a=Reinach, Rev. d. Ét. Gr. IV, 268 ff. ἔπεροι καὶ ἀρνήαδες ἐρίων ἀτέλεες. See Meister, IF. I Anz. 203, who explains as feminine to ἀρνειός, comparing χιμαίραδες of the same inscription.

ἀρρέντερος, male. [V] Mant. BCH. 1892, 570 KATOPPENTE- PON. This was first read correctly by Dittenberger, Hermes 28, 473, as κατώρρέντερον = κατὰ τὸ ἀρρέντερον, in male succession. This reading is generally accepted.[2]

ἀρτιλιθία, close joining of stone. [IV] Oropus, CIGS. I, 4255_{25} = 'Εφ. 'Αρχ. 1891, 71 ἐπικόψας δὲ [κ]ατὰ κεφαλὴν εὐτενῆ συνστ[ρώ]σει λίθοις συντιθεὶς πρὸς ἀλλήλους ἁρμόττοντας καὶ εἰς ἕδραν ἀσκάστους τιθείς, ἀρτιλιθίαν μηδαμοῦ ποιῶν. Cf. ἀρτίκολλος,

---
[1] See below.
[2] Cf. Keil, Gött. Nachr. 1895, 349; Solmsen, KZ. 34, 452; Larfeld, Ber. ü. gr. Epigr. 1888–1894, 143; Danielsson, Eranos II, 26.

Hesych. ἀρτίτονον; Hippocr. 809g οἱ σπόνδυλοι (τῆς ῥάχιος) ἐντὸς ἄρτιοί εἰσιν ἀλλήλοισι, καὶ δέδενται πρὸς ἀλλήλους. See Tszuntas, 1. c., who says that he has been informed by Homolle of a late occurrence of the word in the phrase φεύγων ἀρτιλιθίαν τὸ ἐλάχιστον ἡμιποδι....

ἀρτοπωλικός, *having bake-shops*, name of a street. [III] CIA. II, 860 εἰς τὸ ἀρτοπωλικόν.

ἀρτυτήρ, official of Thera. [II] Thera, Cauer 148 E_1 ὑπὸ τοῦ κατατυγχάνοντος ἀρτυτῆρος, E_5 ἀρτυτήρ—ἀποδιδότω ἐπὶ σύλλογον καὶ δανειζέσθω. E_{26} ὁ δὲ ἀρτυτήρ, εἴ κα μὴ ἐξοδιάξει τοῖς ἐπιμηνίοις κατὰ τὰ γεγραμμένα, ὁ μὲν ἐπιμήνιος πάντως δεχέσθω - - ; also $E_{16 \cdot 20 \cdot 23 \cdot 30 \cdot 31}$. Cf. ἀρτύνας, Argive magistrate.

ἀρχιδαυχναφορέω = *ἀρχιδαφνηφορέω. [Late.] Thess. 372. Cf. Hesych. δαυχμόν· εὔκαστον ξύλον δάφνης and Schol. to Nicander, Ἀντίγονος δὲ λέγει δαύχμου· ἔστι δὲ δάφνη πικρά. The word probably contains a local name for δάφνη.[1] Its etymology is quite uncertain, though Meister, GD. I, p. 301, tries to connect with Sans. √dah.

ἄσσιστα = ἔγγιστα. [V] Lac. M. 21b = Cauer 10 εἰ δέ κα μὴ νόθοι ζῶντι, τοὶ ἄσσιστα ποθίκες ἀνελόσθω. Cf. Hesych. ἄσσιστα· ἔγγιστα. Müllensiefen, de tit. Lac. dial., p. 65, explains rightly as a superlative which has been influenced by a comparative with ι-suffix.

ἀστεροβλῆτα, *smiting with sun-stroke*. [IV?] Sybaris 1654 = IG. Sic. et It. 641 ἀλ(λ)ά με μο(ῖ)ρα ἐδάμασ(σ)ε<καὶ ἀθάνατοι θεοὶ ἄλλοι> καὶ ἀστεροβλῆτα κεραυνόν. Kaibel makes the comment that the nominative ἀστεροβλῆτα was taken as an accusative, hence the writing κεραυνόν. Hoffmann, l. c., writes κεραυν(ῶ)ν, part. to κεραυνόω; cf. note.

ἄσχαστος, *not split, without a flaw*. [IV] Boeot. CIGS. I, 4255_{26} ἄσκαστοι λίθοι, 3073_{164} ἄσχαστοι λίθοι. From σχάζω.

ἀτιτάλτᾱς, *nurseling*(?). [VII] Gort. Comp. 40 (ΤΙΤΑΛΤΑϚ). There is no context. Comparetti conjectures that we have here a substantive from ἀτιτάλλω. Cf. Hesych. ἀτίταλ(λ)ον· ἔτρεφον; ἀτίτηλα· ἀνέθρεψα, and other similar glosses. The verb is used

[1] See Hehn, Culturpfl.⁶, p. 572; Meyer, p. 276, note 2.

in Homer referring to the young of animals, but more especially to children.

ἀφεδριατεύω, *acting as* *ἀφεδριατεύς (?). [III] Boeot. 494₅, 570₂, 571₄, 865₄, N. 807ª₃.₄. Since the names of *seven* officials are given, they have been generally identified with the Boeotarchs, but as Gilbert II, 56, says, it is hardly probable that the Boeotarchs had another title, and, if so, it would not be so uniformly used in these similar inscriptions. The number seven is not to be considered significant, since it is a sacred number among the Boeotians. Gilbert thinks that these officials are named as a special commission in charge of the dedication of a tripod. Lolling, Mitth. 1878, 91, has thought that they had religious functions.

ἀφέργνυμι, *keep off, prevent*. [IV] Tab. Heracl. I₁₃₁ οὐδὲ ἐφέρξοντι τὸ ὕδωρ οὐδ' ἀφέρξοντι.

ἀφηρωίζω, *canonize as a hero*. [I?] Anaphe 3437 ὁ δᾶμος Εὐάνασσαν Κρινοτέλους - - διὰ τὰς εἰς αὐτὸν εὐεργασίας ἀφηρώιξε.; Thera, CIG. 2467–73, 2480, etc., Att., Mitth. 1884, 291, l. 46.

ἀχύριος, *place for chaff*. [IV] Tab. Heracl. I₁₃₉ οἰκοδομήσηται δὲ καὶ οἰκίαν - - ἀχύριον - - τὸν δὲ ἀχύριον μὴ μεῖον τὸ μὲν μᾶκος ὀκτὼ καὶ δέκα ποδῶν, τὸ δὲ εὖρος ὀκτὼ καὶ δέκα ποδῶν. Cf. Hesych. ἄχυρος (I. ἀχύριος)· ὁ ἀχυρών. ἀχυροδόκη, ἀποθήκη τῶν ἀχύρων. Kaibel, IG. Sic. et It., in the commentary to 645, after giving the glosses as above, adds, "Aristoph. Vesp. 1310 (coll. schol.) non ἀχυρμόν cum Meinekio sed ἀχύριον videtur corrigendum."

ἀχυρών, *barn for chaff*. [279] Delos, BCH. 1890, 426 ἀχυρῶνα ἄθυρον.

βενέω, *hold sexual intercourse*. [VI] Elis 1156₂ = Ol. 7 = Roberts 296 αἰ δὲ βενέοι (BENEOI) ἐν τἰαροῖ, βοί καὶ θωάδ(δοι) καὶ κοθάρσι τελείαι, καὶ τὸν θεαρὸν ἐν τα[ὐ]ταῖ. Blass, l. c., compares ENEBEOI of 1158₃ and questions whether the words are not identical and to be connected with ἐνηβητήριον, "Vergnügungsort." He would then assume that it implied remissness in performing the required service to the god. Meister, GD. II, p. 22, derives from El. *βενά : Boeot. βανά. But such an Elian form is very doubtful, as with this vocalism a dental would be expected.

Brand, Hermes 21, 312 compares βινέω, citing the passage from Herod. II, 64 καὶ τὸ μὴ μίσγεσθαι γυναιξὶ ἐν ἱροῖσι - - οὗτοί (Αἰγύπτιοι) εἰσιν οἱ πρῶτοι θρησκεύσαντες. Dittenberger, l. c., comments on this as an obscene word not used in good Attic prose, but frequent in comedy. Its use here would be similar to that of οἴφην in Gortynian.

βίδεος = ϝίδεος, Laconian official. [II] CIG. 1241 II$_{18}$, 1242$_{23}$, 1268, 1269, 1364a, b, LeB.-F. 180$_7$, BCH. 1877, 369, Bull. dell' inst. 1873, 213.

βίδυος = ϝίδυος, same as preceding. [II] CIG. 1270, LeB.-F. 281b$_4$. Cf. Suid. βείδιος· ὁ ἔνδοξος; Hesych. ἰδυῖοι· μάρτυρες. No distinction in usage can be found in the Laconian inscriptions which would correspond to the difference in suffixes. For the latter see Brugmann II, 412, -εια : -υια. In meaning both words are rather to be explained by the gloss of Suidas. Other words from this root are given by Müllensiefen, de tit. Lac. dial., p. 47. βιδιαῖοι, Paus. III, 11$_2$, 12$_4$; βιδάταν, βιδατάω, Crete, Helbig, p. 9; ϝίστορες, Boeot. 429$_7$ et al. The technical use of this word seems to have been limited to Laconian. For discussion of the duties of these officials see Böckh, CIG. I, pp. 88, 609.

βόλιμος = μόλυβδος. [IV] Delph. BCH. 1896, 199 ff. $_{43·91·93·112}$ βολίμου εἰσφορᾶς δρ. τρεῖς; Epid. 3325, B$_{275·284·302}$ Πυρομάχωι βολίμου (275). Cf. Etym. M. μόλιβος παρὰ Συρακουσίοις, κατὰ ἐναλλαγήν. Prellwitz, l. c., compares Rhod. περιβολιβῶσαι, Cauer 176$_{10}$, which presupposes a form *βόλιβος, probably due to confusion between μόλιβος and βόλιμος. See J. Schmidt, Sonanten-Theorie, p. 28; Brugmann, § 972 and § 1000; Keil, Mitth. 1895, 435.

βουλογράφος, *clerk of βουλή*. [III] El. 1172$_{37}$ = Ol. 39 περὶ δὲ τῶ ἀποσταλᾶμεν τοῖρ Τενεδίοιρ τὸ γεγονὸρ ψάφισμα ἐπιμέλειαν ποιήαται Νικόδρομορ ὁ βωλογράφορ.

βοών, *cattle-shed*. [IV] Tab. Heracl. I$_{139·143}$ οἰκοδομήσηται - - βοῶνα - - τὸν μὲν βοῶνα τὸ μὲν μᾶκος ϝίκατι καὶ δυῶν ποδῶν, τὸ δὲ εὖρος ὀκτὼ καὶ δέκα ποδῶν. Kaibel, CIG. Sic. et It. 645, further compares the gloss of Hesych. βοωνία· αὔλειος θύρα. Κρῆτες, which suits much better than βοῶνα· ὁδόν. The latter is secondary. Cf. also Etym. M., p. 203₉ ἔρριψεν εἰς βοῶνα; Bekk Anecd. 29, 32 βοών · ἡ τῶν βοῶν στᾶσις. The word occurs also in a Carian inscription, CIG. 2694b₁₂, a sale of land and buildings, καὶ τῷ ὀρνιθῶνι καὶ τοῖς βοῶσι καὶ τῷ φρέατι. Similar forms are γαιών and τοφιών.

γαιών, *heap of earth.* [IV] Tab. Heracl. I₁₃₆ οὐδὲ γαιῶνας θησεῖ πὰρ τὼς ὑπάρχοντας —. γαεών occurs in a Sicilian inscription, CIGS. I, 352, II₈₃·₈₅ ἀνὰ μέσον τῶν γαεώνων. Cf. Hesych. χόρτος – – – καὶ τὸν ὅρον τὸν ἐκ γαιών (for γαιώνων). See Meister, Curt. Stud. IV, p. 437, who cites a number of similar collectives in -ών ἀχυρών, δενδρων, etc. Cf. also τοφιων, I₁₃₈, βοών, I₁₃₉·₁₄₃·

γάμελα = γαμήλια. [V] Delph. BCH. 1895, 1 ff., A₂₃, B₃₆ μήτε δαράταν γάμελα μήτε παιδήια μήτ' ἀπελλαῖα. Cf. ἀπελλαῖα, δαράτα, παιδήια.

γεροντεύω, *act as γερων.* [II] LeB.-F. 162h, CIG. 1261.

γράσσμα, *theft, despoliation.* [V] Argive, Fröhner, Rev.-Arch. 1891; Robert, Monumenti Ant. I, 593 ff.; Reinach, Rev. d. Ét. Grec. IV, 171, V, 357; Peppmüller, Wochenschrift. f. kl. Phil. 1891, N. 31; Meister, IF. Anz. I, 200 (review of previous translations); Blass, Jbb. f. Phil. 143, 559. ἡ δικάσζοιτο τῶν γρασσμάτων (ΓΡΑΣΣΜΑΤΟΝ) ἕνεκα τᾶς καταθέσιος ἐ[τ]τᾶς ἀλιάσσιος τρήτω καὶ δαμενέσθω ἐνς Ἀθαναίαν. This difficult passage is variously interpreted. Reinach reads γδασσμάτων = δασμάτων and thinks it is dependent upon κατάθεσις, translating "versement des impôts." Blass, with the same reading, connects with the Hesychian gloss δάσματα · διαμερίσματα. Robert thinks the word intended is γραμμάτων. But the original reading may be retained and the word be taken from γράω with Fröhner. Meister's interpretation, however, is to be preferred to that given by F.: "le caissier infidèle limait les pièces d'or qu'il avait en depôt." M. would translate by "aufgezehrtes" and defends its harshness by the citation of δωροφάγοι, οἶκος ἐσθίεται and ἔσθιε. ἀνάλισκε, Hesych.; to which may be added the Locrian παματοφαγείσται. The definite date of the inscription ἀνφ' Ἀρίσστωνα accords with the use of the article before γρασσμάτων.[1]

[1] For another untenable view of ἀνφ' Ἀρίσστωνα see Meister, l. c.

δαῖσις, *division*. [V] Gort. Law-code IV₂₅, V₄₇ αἰ δέ κα χρήματα δατιομένοι μὴ συνγιγνώσκωντι ἀνφὶ τὰν δαῖσιν. In Crete, Comp., 147y, is found δαῖσ[ιν.

δαμέτᾱς = δημότης. [III] Rhodes IG. Ins. 1032₉ = Cauer 171 οὐ μόνον τῶν δαμετᾶν ἀλλὰ καὶ τῶν παροικεύντων, l. 13 πολλοὺς τῶν δαμετᾶν. Here the word seems to replace πολιτᾶν. The form shows rather a different suffix than an unusual representation of -o-. See Meyer, p. 64.

δαράτα, *cake of unleavened bread*. [IV] BCH. 1895, 1 ff., A₅·₄₅·₄₇·₅₁·₅₈· B₆·₄₆ A₄₅ ff. καὶ τὰς δαράτας φέρεν. hόστις δέ κα μὴ ἄγηι τἀπελλαῖα ἢ τὰν δαράταν μὴ φέρηι, ἀμμόνιον κατθέτω στατῆρα ἐπὶ ϝεκατέρωι, B₄ [πάντες δὲ το]ὶ Λαβυάδα[ι Εὐκλείοι]ς περὶ τὰν δα[ρατᾶν ἐπι]κρινόντων, B₄₅ καὶ hὸ κα δέξωντι ἢ δαράταν ἢ ἀπελλαῖα πὰρ τὰ γράμματα μὴ ἔστω Λαβυάδας μηδὲ κοινανείτω τῶν κοινῶν χρημάτων μηδὲ τῶν θεμάτων. Cf. Hesych. δαράτῳ· ἀζύμῳ; Ath. who defines δάρατον as ἄζυμον ἄρτον and, under δαρόν - - καὶ ἑορτήν, καὶ ἄρτον τινές, τὸν ἄζυμον, also, 114 B, δάρατον δ'ὑπὸ Θεσσαλῶν. From these glosses it is to be inferred that the δαράτα was made of unleavened bread. It seems probable also that the word was Thessalian and that a feast had been named from the δάρατον-offering.[1] δαρίτα in this inscription refers to the offerings used at the Εὐκλεῖοι feast and includes the γάμελα and παιδήια offerings. It is probable that with the transfer of declension the word took on a specialized meaning.

δασέα, *fur, skin of furry animal*. [V] Ion. 100₂·₃₆ ἦν ἐν θ[ύη]ται, λά[ψεται γλῶσ]σαν, ὀσφύν, δασέαν, ὥρην. Dittenberger, Syll. 376, n. 3, says with Rayet, Rev. arch. XXVIII, 106, that this is plainly a noun and denotes the furry skin. That the skin was a perquisite of the priest is seen from Cos 3636₅₁ γέρη τοῦ βοὸς τῶι ἱερῆι δέρμα; Halicarnassus Ditt. Syll. 371₁₂; Arist. Thesm. 758, and also in this inscription, l. 1, λαμβάνειν δὲ τὰ δέρματα [καὶ] τὰ ἄλλα [γ]έρεα, ll. 7, 8 (of a stranger) διδόναι δὲ τῶι ἱερεῖ τὰ γέρεα ἄπερ ἡ πόλις διδοῖ χωρὶ[ς] δέρματο[ς].

---
[1] Homolle thinks the feast also was probably Thessalian. Cf. Solmsen, KZ. 34, 555, who discusses briefly the points of contact between Thessalian and Phocian, adding from this inscription δαράτα, τάγος, and ταγευσέω.

δεκάω, *accept*. [VII] Attic, Mitth. 1893, 225. In Roberts 34, the "oldest Attic inscription," is found ὃς νῦν ὀρχηστῶν πάντων ἀταλώτατα παίζει τοῦ τόδε . . . . . This has been completely read by Studniczka, l. c., τοῦτο δεκᾶν μιν. For the vocalism of δεκάω, Wackernagel compares πεδᾶν, περᾶν.

δεμελεῖς, *leeches*. [IV] Epid. $3339_{98 \cdot 99}$ = K. 1 Ἀνὴρ Τορωναῖος δεμελέας. τὰ στέρνα μαχαίραι ἀνσχίσσαντα τὰς δεμελέας ἐξελεῖν – –. Cf. Hesych. δεμβλεῖς· βδέλλαι. See Prellwitz, l. c., who says rightly that there is no necessity for changing the Hesych. δεμβλεῖς to δεμελεῖς, and Baunack, Stud. I, p. 128. Prellwitz connects with Lat. *lumbricus* for *lumblicus, *dumblicus. See also Brugmann, Ber. k. sächs. G. d. W., 1897, p. 24, who affirms this connection. βδέλλα is probably not a related form.

δενδρύω, *sink*. [IV] Epid. 3340_{20} = K. 2 οὗτος ἀποκολυμ-[βάσ]ας εἰς τὰν θ[άλασσ]αν ἔπειτα δενδρύων εἰς τόπον ἀφίκετο ξηρόν, κύκ[λωι] πέτραις περ[ιεχό]μενον, καὶ οὐκ ἐδύνατο ἔξοδον οὐδεμίαν εὑρεῖν. Cf. Etym. M. δενδρυάζειν· εἰς δρῦς καταδύεσθαι κυρίως. καὶ τὸ καθ' ὕδατος δύεσθαι καὶ ἀποκρύπτειν ἑαυτόν. This word is not to be connected with δρῦς, but, as Prellwitz suggests, it may belong to Sanskr. *dravati*. The general meaning seems to be *to go unseen*. It is correctly explained by Wilamowitz, Isyllus v. Epid., as an intensive to δρύεται· κρύπτεται, Hesych. Cf. Danielsson, Gram. u. Etym. Stud. I, p. 54.

δερτά = δέρματα. [Late.] Mycon. Ditt. Syll. 373_{26} = BCH. 1888, 461 δερτὰ μέλανα ἐτήσια. This is the reading given by Latyschew. Dittenberger reads δ' ἐ[π]τὰ, but this is wrong, as Latyschew proves, since the marks on the stone indicate that this is the beginning of a passage; moreover, according to Dittenberger's reading δέ would be too far removed from the beginning of the phrase. Kumanudis gives as equivalents δαρτά, θύματα. From δέρω, as Coan ἔνδορα, ἐνδέρεται, used in a similar inscription.

διακαλίζω = διακόπτω(?). [IV] CIA. IV, 834b, col. II_{22} μισθωτοῖς τοῖς διακαλίσασιν τὰ ξύλα. This apparently refers to the σάνιδες spoken of in ll. 20, 21. See Kavv. Epid. 242_{47} (note). Cf. διακάλισις (below).

διακάλισις, *removal of wooden crating in which valuable stones have been shipped.* [Late.] Hermione 3385$_{12}$ διακαλίσιος. It is necessary to consider with this word παρκάλισις Epid. K. 242$_{47\cdot63}$ παρκαλίσιος τῶν λίθων ἐπὶ λιμένι and ἐσκάλισις 242$_{85}$ ἐσκαλίσιος ἐμ Πιραι[ε]ῖ ἐπὶ τὰν ἄνθεσιν. Hesychius cites καλιοί· τὰ εὐτελῆ οἰκήματα; κάλιον· ξυλάριον. βακτηρίδιον; καλιός· τὶ δεσμωτήριον, καὶ ξύλον, ᾧ ἐδέοντο, καὶ οἱ μικροὶ οἶκοι καλιαὶ καὶ καλίδια and καλίς· σκέπαρνον. These glosses imply a double development in meaning: 1) inclosure of wood, 2) tool for working in wood. It is the latter which is seen in the verb διακαλίζω; the former in the nouns διακάλισις, ἐσκάλισις, παρκάλισις. The first satisfactory explanation of these words is given by Keil, Mitth. 1895, 425. After noting the glosses cited, he explains ἐσκάλισις as the crating of the stones for shipment, ἐπὶ τὰν ἄνθεσιν. παρκάλισις and διακάλισις then would denote the removal of this crating, which is done ἐπὶ λιμένι. Otherwise Kumanudis, who thinks διακάλισις a possible error for διασκάλισις, and Kavvadias, l. c., who would derive from καλίω = κυλίω. Cf. Bekk. Anecd. I, 5 ἔστι τι ῥῆμα κυλίω, ὃ ᾿Αττικοὶ διὰ τοῦ ᾱ καλίω. This word is very rare, though the root is seen in καλινδέω, κάλινσις. The inscription shows a considerable difference in the prices paid, that for the ἐσκάλισις being much larger than for διακάλισις or παρκάλισις. This fact also is accounted for by Keil's interpretation.

δίαλσις = βίβασις(?). [V] Crete, Comp. 183$_8$ ἰν ἀντρηίωι διάλσιος. This is an incomplete inscription from Oaxos. Comparetti makes this suggestion and connects with διάλλομαι, δίαλμα. The verb is rare, but is used in prose, meaning *leap across*. δίαλμα is used by the schol. to Pindar as equivalent to ἅλμα, so that the force of the preposition may be slight. Baunack, Phil. Woch. 1887, 156, suggests that the root is the same as in ἅλ-δαίνω ἄν-αλτις and thinks the expression may be synonymous with τροπὰν ἰν ἀντρηίωι, l. 15, of the same inscription. Roberts, p. 333, accepts the interpretation given above, though with some hesitation. Skias, Kr. D., p. 86, on the other hand, prefers Baunack's suggestion. Certainty is not possible, but ἅλσις, δίαλμα, διάλλομαι seem to favor Comparetti's explanation, while βίβασις proves the possibility of a "sacred dance."

διαλιαίνω, cancel. [III] Boeot. 488₁₅₇ κὴ τὰς ἐ[σ]πράξις τὰς ἰώσας Νικα[ρ]έτη [κ]ὰτ τᾶς πόλιος Ξεν[ο]κρίτω ἄρχοντος ἐν Θεισπιῆς πάσας διαλιάνασ[θη] τὼς πολεμάρχως. Cf. 488₇₃ ἐσλιανάτω Νικαρέτα τὰς οὐπεραμερ[ί]ας ἂς ἔχι κὰτ τᾶς πόλιος. Compounds of λεαίνω. ἐκλεαίνω is used in a new sense, and διαλεαίνω does not occur elsewhere.

διατειχισμός = διατείχισμα. [III] Troiz. 3364₂₁·₃₅·₄₂ ἐς τὸν διατειχισμόν καὶ τὰν σωτηρίαν τᾶς πόλιος.

διεξαγνέω = διεξάγω. [I] Lac. (Amycl.) Cauer, 32₉. See ἀγνέω.

δικαδία, double κάδος. [III] CIA. II, 856.

δικαστάγωγος, official who brings in the dicasts. [II] Aeol. 215₁₂·₄₂·₄₈·

δικαστήρ = δικαστής. [V] Locris 1478₃₃; Pam. 1267₁₁.

δίκρεας, double portion of flesh. [IV] Cos 3636₅₄ = PH. 37₅₄ [ν]ώτου δίκρεας. Cf. μερίδα δικρέων, Chios, Mitth. 1888, 166, which probably means διμορία κρέων. Paton, l. c., compares δεισίας κρέων CIA. II, 631₆, and thinks it may mean a portion of both cuts of the sirloin. Cf. Müllensiefen, l. c.

διλήμνιον, kind of woolen fillet. Rhodes, Cauer, 180₅₆ = IG. Ins. 155 καὶ πριάσθων στέφανον καὶ διλήμνιον - -. λημνίσκος is used by Polybius, Plutarch, etc.

διμάω, having two mothers (?). Cypr. 69. This is read by Deecke τιμῶ τὰ(ν) δίφατο(ν) δίμαο(ν) Παφίια(ν) γε διμώοις. Hoffmann, GD. I, p. 78, reads Τίμω τ' Ἀ(ν)τιφάτω· τιμάω Παφίια(ν) .... Meister, GD. II, p. 159, reads τιμωτὰ διφάτω διμάω Παφίια γε διμώοις and translates "zu ehren sind die beiden doppelnamigen von zwei Müttern geborenen paphischen Göttinnen mit Doppelliedern." He explains the two names as the Phoenician Astarte and the Grecian Aphrodite; the two mothers as the Ἔλ-α· Ἥρη ἐν Κύπρῳ, Hesych. and Διωνη; the two songs, Phoenician and Greek. The whole is very doubtful, but it hardly seems probable that the repetition of δι- is accidental, as Hoffmann's reading would imply. There is also a difficulty in Deecke's reading τιμῶ, which Meister avoids. The objection which Hoffmann makes to δίφατος, that it could not mean doubly *named*, but only *doubly said*, is not important. See Meister, Zum El. Ark. und Kypr., p. 32. Nor does διμάω to μαῖα seem unlikely.

δινάκω, *change, amend*. [V] Elis 1156₅ = Ol. 7 = Roberts 296. τῶν δέ κα γραφέων ὅτι δοκέοι καλ(λ)ιτέρως ἔχην πο(ῖ) τὸν θ[ε]όν, ἐξαγρέων καὶ ἐνποιῶν σὺν βωλαῖ [π]εντακατίων ἀϝλανέως καὶ δάμοι πληθύοντι δινάκοι· (δινά)κοι, etc. This interpretation was given by Meister, GD. II, p. 24, who connects this word with δίνω, δινεύω, etc. Dittenberger, 1. c., characterizes this explanation with the word "bedenklich." But it is to be preferred to any of the other readings and explanations which have been offered. Röhl reads δῖνα κῷ, Blass changes to δικάδδοι and Comparetti to διανικῶ. Johansson, Sprachkunde, p. 67, thinks the form obscure, as δινήκοι is to be expected if it is from δινέω, as the gloss δινήσας· στρέψας. κινήσας would imply. But there may easily have been a verb δινάζω beside δινέω from which δινάκω would be derived through the Doric aorist or future. Meister compares ὀλέκω, στενάχω, and δώκω.

The meaning of the verb is plainly *amend*, as is shown by the expression ἐξαγρέων καὶ ἐμποιῶν. δινάκω may imply a reversal of previous action, which would not seem a strange development of *whirl, turn around*.

διοικοδόμησις, *walling off, fortification*. [III] Troiz. 3364a₄₃. b₃₂ ἐς τὰν διοικοδόμη[σιν ἐπὶ σωτη]ρία[ν τ]ᾶς [πόλιος].

διορθωτήρ = διορθωτής. [Late.] Corc. 3206₁₃₈ εἰ δέ κα διόρθωσις τῶν νόμων γίνηται, ταξάντων οἱ διορθωτῆρες εἰς τοὺς νόμους καθώς κα δῆ τὸ ἀργύριον χειρίζεσθαι.

διπενθητήρ, *doubly bereaved*. Cypr., Berl. Phil. Wochenschrift 1890, 1355, 1381 'Ονασαγόραν τῶ Σιτασαγόραν τῶ διπε(ν)θητῆ[ρος] ἠμι. This is one of two stones found together, the other bearing the epitaph of a woman. Meister thinks this was erected by the father. One thinks of the use of δι- in Cypr. SGDI. 69. The word πενθητήρ is rare. It is cited by Meister from Aesch. Sept. 1054 and Pers. 949.

διπλεθρία, *area of two plethra*. Corc. 3198₂₁. Cf. τετραπλεθρίαν and τετραπελεθρίαν from the same inscription.

δυσαγέω, *be accursed.* Taur. IG. Sic. et It., 432₄ δυσαγείτω καὶ αὐτὸς καὶ γέ[νος το - -. From δυσαγής. For various forms of imprecation see section on synonyms.

δώκω = δίδωμι. [IV] Cypr. (Edal.) 60₁₆. This is a new formation from the κ-aorist.

ἐγγυεύω = ἐγγυάω. [171] Delph. 1804 τὸν [ἔ]ρανον τὸν Βρομίου οὗ ἐγγυεύει Ἰατάδας, etc. Argos, AJA. 1896, 55 ἐγ]γυεύσαντας εἰς αὐτοὺς followed by list of proper names.

ἔγγωνον, *rectangular piece of land.* [IV] Tab. Heracl. II₁₀₇ ϝέκτα μερὶς τὸ ἔγγωνον τὸ πὰρ τὰς ἀμπέλως τὸ ποτικλαίγον ποττὰν Ἡρακλείαν καὶ ποττὸν ποταμόν.

ἐγδοτήρ, *building commissioner.* [IV] Epid. K. 242₄ ἐγδοτῆρσι, l. 45 ἐγδοτέρσι. Arcad. (Tegea) 1222₆ ἐσδοτῆρες; cf. ἐξιδώκαμες 242₁₄₈; ἀτεκδίδωμι (above).

Keil, Mitth. 1895, 34, thinks the ἐγδοτῆρες are the same as the θυμελοποῖαι and explains, according to the suggestion of Dörpfeld, as follows: After other buildings in the hieron had been begun, the general name of the commissioners who had the oversight of the Tholos was changed for a more specific title. Kavvadias, l. c., regards them as two distinct bodies, but Keil's view is more in accordance with the whole. Cf. Fabricius, de Architectura, p. 32, n. 1. For the form in -ερσι cf. ἐγκαυτέρσι.

ἐγκαυτήρ = ἐγκαυστής. Nemea 3318 ἐγκ]αυτέρσι. The word is without context.

ἐγκόνῑμα, *place for preparing the body with dust for wrestling.* Aen. 1436₂ τὸ ἐγ]κόνιμα Ἑρμᾶι καὶ τᾶι πόλει, cf. ἐγκονίομαι, ἐν κονιστής (below). For -μα in noun denoting place cf. ἐνδιαίτημα, ἐνόρμισμα, etc.

ἐδδίομαι = *ἐκδίομαι. [V] Gort. Comp. 174 (without context) ἐδδίεται. Cf. ἐπιδίομαι.

ἔδραμα = ἔδρασμα. [IV] Epid. 3339₁₁₅, ἐπὶ ἐδράματός τινος καθῖζε. For variation between -μα and -σμα see Solmsen, KZ. 29, 117.

εἰλύτᾱς, *rolled cake.* [IV] Boeot. 413₄·₆ δέκα δραχμάων εἰλύτας δέκα. With this must be considered also—

ἐλλύτᾱς = εἰλύτας. [III] Thera, Cauer 148 E₃₇ ἐλλύτας ἐκ πυρῶν χοινίκων πέντε. Cf. Hesych. ἐλλύτης· πλακοῦς τις. The

Thesaurus gives ἐλύτης Theognost. Crameri Anecd. II, 44₂₂. See Meister, SGDI., p. 393, who takes these words as dialectic variations, with transfer between dialects, from a stem ϝελϝυ-, but this is impossible, since ϝελϝυ- would not give Boeot. ϝειλυ-, Dor. ϝηλυ-, but ϝελυ- in both, just as in Attic (cf. ξένος, ὄρος, etc.); and even for Aeolic there is no inscriptional evidence for λλ from λϝ (or ρρ, νν from ρϝ, νϝ). Attic has εἰλύω, and this ει is found also outside of the present beside ἐλ, e. g., εἰλυσθείς, εἴλυμα : ἐλυσθείς, ἔλυτρον. So it might well have εἰλύτης beside ἐλύτης if the latter is to be accepted. Boeot. ει = Attic ει, unless the latter is a genuine diphthong, and in εἰλύω it must be spurious. It is probably like εἰρύω, ἐρύω, but εἰρύω is not to be taken from ἐϝρύω with Blass and Meyer, p. 559, but rather from ἐ-ϝερύω with Schulze, Quaest. Ep., p. 317. Hence the Boeotian form makes no difficulty. The ἐλλύτας of Thera and the Hesychian gloss may owe their ἐλλ- to a possible *ἔλλω (from *ϝελιω) beside εἰλύω. The existence of such a form may perhaps be inferred from Att. εἴλλω beside εἰλύω. Cf. also Att. εἴλλω, *ward off*, apparently a compromise between εἴλω (from *ϝέλνω) and ἔλλω (from *ϝέλιω).

εἰσοδοιπορέω, *go into, enter.* [IV] Rhodes, Cauer 177₁₁ εἰσοδοιπορεῖν ἐς τὸ τέμενος.

ἑκαστάκις, *in each case.* [III?] Corc. 3196₁₁ τοῖς ἑ]καστάκις προβούλοις, 3206₈ ἐλέσθω δὲ ἁ βουλὰ ἑκαστάκις εἰς ἐνιαυτὸν --. 3206₂₂ οἱ ἑκαστάκις ἐόντες ἄρχοντες. This exactly corresponds to the use of ἀεί in similar expressions.

ἑκατοστηρίη, *land subject to a tax of one per cent.* [Late.] Ion. Bechtel 183a₁₃ = BCH. 1879, 244 ff. ἐδ]ίκασεν ἑκατοστηρίην εἶναι, 183₃₀ τῆς ἑκατοστηρίης τὰ δύο, 183₄₇ ἐκ τοῦ ἐνηλ]ασίου τὴν ἑκατοστηρίη[ν. See ἀίδασμος and ἐνηλάσιον. For the form cf. ἑκατοστός, ἑκατοστήρ. Locrian ἐνετήριον and Attic ἀφετήρια have a similar development of meaning.

ἐκπετέω, *fall down.* [IV] Tab. Heracl. I₁₂₀·₁₇₄ αἰ δέ τινά κα γήρᾳ ἢ ἀνέμῳ ἐκπέτωντι. (Of the trees on the land leased.)

ἐκτίμᾱτρον, *honorary gift*(?). [III] Cnid. 3517 Δάματρι καὶ Κούραι καὶ τοῖς θεοῖς τοῖς παρὰ Δάματρι καὶ Κούραι χαριστεῖα καὶ ἐκτίματρα ἀνέθηκε Πλαθαινὶς Πλάτωνος γυνά. Hirschfeld, Brit.

Mus. IV, 810, commenting on this word, is doubtful whether it can mean *atonement* or *sin-offerings*, as usually understood (so Kum. and L. & S.), since for this an expression like ἔκνιντρον would be expected. After rejecting various other possibilities as inconsistent with the meaning of ἐκτιμᾶν, he concludes that the word has some special meaning, unknown to us. Keil, Mitth. 1895, 51, cites this form together with Gort. τρίτρα and κόμιστρα as examples of an abnormal use of the suffix -τρον, without, however, suggesting any definite meaning. Can it have the force of *valued, valuable?* In this case χαριστεῖα would also have a general meaning, and the whole phrase be translated *acceptable (or pleasing) and valuable offerings*. On the other hand it is not clear why the suffix may not have its usual meaning, since ἐκτιμᾶν means *honor highly* as well as *estimate*.

ἔμπᾱσις = ἔγκτησις. [III] Boeot. 493$_6$ ἔππασις, 806$_6$, etc. ἔπασις 492$_{10}$, 719$_8$; Arcad. 1234 ἔμπασιν, 1233$_2$ ἴνπασιν; Corcyra 3199 = CIGS. III, 682$_{10}$ ἔμπασιν;[1] Megara 3005 ἔμπασιν, 3009, 3014. The word is of course related to πᾶμα, πᾶσασθαι, etc. Boeot. ἔππασις must be from ἔμ-ππασις, the ππ showing itself also in Θιό-ππαστος, etc., and in τὰ ππάματα Boeot. 488$_{164 \cdot 168 \cdot 174}$, as is probably to be read with Cauer and others. Cf. especially J. Schmidt, Plur., p. 415; Schulze, KZ. 318 ff. The root, however, is not to be taken with J. Schmidt, Plur., pp. 411 ff., as identical with that of κτήσασθαι, but as wholly distinct, probably k̑u̯ā, with Brugmann, Totatität, p. 62, note, where the extensive literature is cited. See also Meyer, p. 343.

ἔναγος, *offering to the dead* (?). [V] Delph. BCH. 1895, 1 ff. C$_{38}$ τὸν δὲ νεκρὸν κεκαλυμμένον φερέτω σιγᾶι, κἤν ταῖς στροφαῖς μὴ καττιθέντων μη[δ]αμεῖ, μηδ' ὀτοτυζόντων ἔ[χ]θος τᾶς ϝοικίας πρίγ κ'ἐπὶ τὸ σᾶμα hίκωντι, τηνεῖ δ'ἔναγος ἔστω hέντε κα ha[σ]ιγ' ἀναποτθέθηι. The above is the reading of Homolle, who translates as follows: "et en ce lieu, la soillure persistera jusqu'à ce que le silence ait été rétabli." This involves 1) the elision of -ā before ἀναποτθέθηι; 2) the assumption of a solitary occurrence of ἀνα- without apocope; 3) an interpretation which is hard to

---
[1] ἔγκτασιν is used in 3200, 3201, 3203 = CIGS. III, 688, 687, 685.

reconcile with the context. Dragumis, p. 298, offers a solution which is too fanciful to commend itself. Bechtel, BB. XXII, 281, would read τηνεῖ δὲ (μηδὲ)ν ἄγος· ἔστω, which would be a very possible slip on the part of the stonecutter, and also remove the difficulty of the interpretation which seems to demand permission for a renewal of the lamentation, if we accept hέντε κα ha[σ]ιγ' ἀναποτθέθηι. Then the clause would be translated, "silence must be observed until they arrive at the grave, there there shall be no attaint until silence is again resumed." But this interpretation does not in any way satisfy the first two objections to Homolle's reading. It also involves a mistake, which one is loth to assume if another explanation is to be found. It is also difficult to understand why the question of attaint should occur at this point. A word denoting lamentation or some ceremony at the grave, in contrast to the strict silence hitherto maintained, is rather to be expected. There is a verb ἐναγίζω, *offer sacrifice to the dead*. Cf. Hesych. ἐναγίζειν· τὸ χοὰς ἐπιφέρειν, ἢ θύειν τοῖς κατοιχομένοις. This may be from a substantive ἔναγος = ἐνάγισμα, which is a later formation. I would also change Homolle's transcription to hέντε κα hà [θ]ιγάνα[1] ποτθέθηι and translate, "there there shall be offering until the covering is put on."

ἐναιέτιον, *pediment statue*. [IV] Epid. 3325_{112} = Epid. K. 241_{112} Ἑκτοριδα[ι] ἐναιετίων τᾶς ἀτέρας κερκίδος. Cf. αἰετιαῖος, ἀέτωμα.[2]

ἐναιλέω = *ἐναιρέω. [V] Gort. Law-code II_{30} προφειπάτω δὲ ἀντὶ μαιτύρων τριῶν τοῖς καδεσταῖς τῶ ἐναιλεθέντος ἀλλύε(θ)θαι ἐν ταῖς πέντ' ἀμέραις. ἐναιρέω does not occur, and the preposition apparently does not alter the force of the verb here. Cf. αἰλεθῆι II_{20}. αἱρέω is found in the earlier Cretan inscriptions, Comp. 28, 29, 31. αἱλέω is a new formation peculiar to Cretan and probably due to confusion between the aorist and present stems. See Meyer, § 160.

ἐναράτιον, *collection of booty* (?). [III] Rhodes 924_{20} [τοίδε ἐμ]ι[σ]θώσαν[το καὶ ἀνε]θήκατι ἄρχοντ ..... (proper names).

[1] See this word below.
[2] Ἐφ. Ἀρχ. 1884, Pls. 3–4, show the fragments of the ἐναιέτια which the excavators found.

[τ]ὸ δὲ ἐναράτιον [καὶ τὰν] πράταν καταβολ[ὰν ἐπὶ νου]μηνίας ἐπ' ἱερέω[ς τοῦ δεῖνος·] from ἔναρα, ἐναίρω.

ἐνατεύομαι, *perform a ceremony on the ninth day.* [III] Myconus, Ditt. Syll. 373₂₄ ἐνδεκάτηι ἐπι.... θος Σεμέλη ἐτήσιον· τοῦτο ἐνατεύεται. See Dittenberger, who interprets as above.

ἐνγᾱρέω = ἐπιδημέω. [Late.] Elis SGDI., Anhang II, p. 336 = Ol. 335. This inscription is in the κοινή, but this word is to be taken with Dittenberger as a survival of the local dialect. See Arch. Ztg. XXXV, 38, where he explains it as a denominative from *ἐγ-γᾱ-ρος, *belonging to the land.* Cf. note in Ol., l. c., where ἔγγειος is given as an equivalent in meaning of *ἔγ-γα-ρος.

ἐνδέρω = δέρω. [IV] Cos 3636₄₈, 3637₈ = PH. 37, 38. See ἔνδορα.

ἐνδοθίδιος, *belonging to the house.* [V] Gort. Law-code II₁₁ ἐνδοθιδίαν δώλαν. This word is to be taken with Comparetti as derivative from ἔνδοθεν = ἔνδον rather than with Baunack, Ins. v. Gort., p. 75, who compares with ἀίδιος.

ἔνδορα, *entrails* (?). [IV] Cos 3636₄₈, 3637₈ = PH. 37, 38. Ικάδι βοῦς ὁ κριθεὶς θύεται Ζηνὶ [Πολιῆ]ι καὶ ἔνδορα ἐνδέρεται· ἐφ' ἑστίαν θύεται ἀλφίτων ἡμίεκτον, ἄρτο[ι δύ]ο ἐξ ἡμιέκτου,—ὁ ἅτερος τυ[ρ]ώδης—καὶ τὰ ἔνδορα, and in 3637 γέρ[η] λαμβά[νει] δέρμα καὶ σκέλος· ταύτας ἀποφορά· ἔνδορα ἐνδέρεται, καὶ θύ[εται] ἐπὶ τᾶι ἱστίαι ἐν τῶι ναῶι τὰ ἔνδορα καὶ ἐλατὴρ ἐξ ἡμιέκτου [σπ]υρῶν· τούτων οὐκ ἐκφορὰ ἐκ τοῦ ναοῦ. Paton compares Hesych. ἔνδρατα· τὰ ἐνδερόμενα σὺν τῇ κεφαλῇ καὶ τοῖς ποσί. Cf. also δερτά (above). Just what parts of the animal are intended it is difficult to say. Paton at first suggested the parts usually sacrificed, i. e., head, feet, stomach, and entrails. But l. 51 ἥπατος ἥμισυ καὶ κοιλίας ἥμ[ισυ] and l. 55 τὸ κεφάλαιο[ν] seem to dispose of part of these otherwise. For the prepositional prefix ἐν- Paton compares ἔντομα and ἐντέμνειν, words which are especially used with reference to sacrifices to the Chthonian deities.

ἐνδόσε, *within.* [V] Ion. 43₁₃ (Funeral law of Iulis.) κ]αὶ τ[ὰ] σ[τρωμ]ατα ἐσφέρειν ἐνδόσε. Cf. ἐκεῖσε, παντόσε, etc. Blass-Kühner II, 310 A₅.

ἔνδω, *within*. [V] Delph. BCH. 1895, 1 ff. D$_{30}$ ἐν τᾶι πέτραι ἔνδω;[1] SGDI. 1767$_{10}$ ἔνδω μένουσα[ι] (used of the freed slave). Cf. ἔχθω and ϝοίκω of the Labyadae inscription, and in general for adverbs in -ω see Ahrens, DD., p. 374; Kühner-Blass II, 304d, e.

ἐνετήρια, τά, *entrance-tax*. [V] Locris 1478$_8$ = Cauer 229 = Roberts 231 ἄνευ ἐνετηρίων.[2] Cf. Vischer, Rh.M. 26, 50, who assumes, with Oikonomidas, that it is a derivative of ἐνίημι and means "Einlass-Geld." This explanation is practically undisputed by the various editors except Meister, Ber. d. königl. sächs. G. d. Wissenschaft., 1895, 295 ff., who holds the same interpretation as to form, but thinks the word means a *sacrifice* upon return rather than a *tax*. If so binding that admission without this sacrifice is specified in only two cases, it is practically a tax, even on this assumption, and it is not plain why the objections to the interpretation as tax would not also apply here. These objections are: 1) a general tax for citizenship did not hold anywhere during the period of Greek independence; the cases cited are rather exceptional; 2) this must, if a tax, have been a general one required of all returning citizens, or it would have been defined in this decree; 3) is an answer to the translation in Insc. Jurid. Gr., "sans payer de droit d'établissement,"[3] that this is not a question of change of residence within the same state or confederation, but of emigration from Naupactus to Hypocnemidian Locris, hence practically from one state into another. The first objection would not be final, since there may very possibly have been a law at this time in Naupactus which did impose a tax for entrance into citizenship which would be binding on the returning colonists unless specifically excluded.

---

[1] This word certainly seems superfluous in the phrase, but the letters are plain and there seems no possibility of another reading. Homolle thinks that this inscription of the cult of Bouzyga may have been cut on the *inside* face of the stone. The whole passage is somewhat obscure. See Homolle, l. c., pp. 58, 59.

[2] In addition to those already given cf. Hicks, Hist. Insc. 63; Insc. Jurid. Gr., p. 180; Ed. Meyer, Forsch. z. alt. Gesch. I, 291, and the latest, SGDI. III, 333.

[3] Cf. also Gilbert, Griech. Staatsalt. II, 41.

The decisive point, however, is the position of ἄνευ ἐνετηρίων. It occurs in a section which discusses taxes and nothing else. It is, moreover, separated from the only discussion of sacrifice and religious duty in the inscription by a law regarding taxes. The words which Meister cites as parallels are different formations, with the exception of εἰσιτήρια, which means, originally, simply *belonging to the entrance*. Both these words were specialized, but for different purposes. Cf. also ἀφετήρια.

ἐνηβέω = ἐνηβάω (?). [VI] Elis 1158_3 = Ol. 5 ἀποδὼς, ἐνηβέο[ι] (ENEBEOI) ὁ ξένος. See Blass, 1156_3, note, who explains BENEOI with this form. Though they do not probably belong together (see βενέω), the suggestion may very well stand for this word, which may mean *take pleasure in*, a usage similar to that of ἐνηβητήριον. The offense would then consist in neglecting the sacrifice first due to the god. Inscription 1158 is fragmentary, but line 9 δα]ρχμὰς ἀποτίνοι τοῖ Δὶ 'Ολυν[πίοι] implies guilt for which a penalty is enforced.

ἐνηλάσιον, rent. [Late.] Ion. 183_5 = BCH. 1879, 244f. ἐνηλάσιον, τετρακόσιαι εἴκο[σι δρα]χμαί, l. 37 ὁ ἀνε]λόμενος τὴγ γῆν τὸ ἐνηλά[σιον ἀποδώσε]ι, ἐμ μηνὶ 'Αρτιμισιῶνι., l. 48 ἐνηλ]ασίου. From ἐνελαύνω. For the lengthening of the vowel see Wackernagel, Dehnungsgesetz d. gr. Compos., p. 42.

ἐνηρόσιον, rent. [III] Delos, BCH. 1882, 6 ff., I, 145 καὶ τόδε ἄλλο ἀργύριον εἰσήκει τῶι θεῶι ἐνηροσίων., l. 152 ἐνηροσίων. Cf. προηρόσιον. From ἀρόω and applies only to rent of land.

ἔνθινος = ἔνθεος. [Late.] Crete, Cauer 116_{11}, 117_7 ἔνορκον τε ἔστω καὶ ἔνθινον. Cf. Gort. Law-code X_{42} τὰ θίνα καὶ τὰ ἀνθρώπινα. See Meyer, p. 110, n. 2; Solmsen, KZ. 32, 536. For discussion of -θινος see θείνος, θίνος.

ἔνθινος, *in that place*. [IV] Chers. BCH. 1881, 70 f., l. 30 εἴς τε τοὺς κατὰ βόσπορον τόπους χωρισ[θεὶ]ς κα[ὶ καταστασάμενος καὶ τὰ ἐν(θ)ινα καλῶς καὶ συμφερόντως βασιλεῖ Μιθραδάται Εὐπάτορι. This is the reading of Blass, Rh. M. 36, 612, taking ἔνθινος from ἔνθα as ἐκεῖνος from ἐκεῖ. Cf. Ditt. Syll. 252, note 18.

ἐνκοιωταί, *pledges*. [V] Gort. Law-code IX_{25} ἐνκ]οιωτὰνς (OIO-ΤΑΝΣ) ὀφήλων, IX_{35} ἀνδοκᾶ<δ> δὲ κ'ἐνκοιωτᾶν (ENKOIOTAN).

LEXICOGRAPHICAL STUDY OF GREEK INSCRIPTIONS 39

Cf. Hesych. κοῖον· ἐνέχυρον; κοιάζει· ἐνεχυράζει; κῶα· ἐνέχυρα; κωάζειν· ἐνεχυράζειν; κωαθείς· ἐνεχυριασθείς. These glosses surely give the explanation of the word. Cf. Baunack, Ins. v. Gort., p. 135, and Ins. Jurid. Gr., p. 383, n. 2, and κοιακτήρ (below). Comparetti, p. 220, objects that, since ἐνέχυρον, ἐνεχυράζω occur in Gortynian, Nos. 153, 154, 156, 159, it would probably be used here also to express the same idea. But, as Baunack had already assumed, a differentiation of meaning is very probable, and ἐνκοιωταί may indicate a more general kind of obligation than ἐνέχυρον. Comparetti's comparison of ἐγγύας, ἐγγνιωταί is incomprehensible, if it means anything more than similarity of use, for κοῖον is clearly connected with κεῖμαι.

ἐνκόλαψις, *carving.* [IV] Epid. 3325$_{265}$ = Epid. K. 241 Πασέαι γραμάτων ἐνκολάψιος κ'ἐνκαύσιος, Lebadaea, Ditt. Syll. 353$_{11}$ τῶν δὲ γραμμάτων τῆς ἐγκολάψεως καὶ [τῆς] ἐγκαύσεως. See Baunack, Aus. Epid., p. 43.

ἐνκόλλᾱσις, *inlaying.* [IV] Epid. K. 242$_{167}$ ἐνκολλάσιος εἰς τοὺς στυλοβάτας. Cf. ἐγκολλάω, *glue, join.* κολλάω is used of inlaid work. A word denoting ornament for the stylobates is more likely here than a word which means joining.

ἐνκονιστάς, *sprinkler, used to cover the body with dust before wrestling.* [III] Boeot. CIGS. I, 2420$_{38}$ ἐν οὗτο χροῦσιος ἐνκονιστάς, ὁλκὰ χροῦσιος, κὴ τριώβολον Ἀττικόν. Cf. Lucian, Amor., 45 πρὸς ἡλίου μεσημβρινὸν θάλπος ἐγκονίζεται τὸ σῶμα πυκνούμενον.

ἐνπεδέω, *remain steadfast.* [VI] El. 1150 = Ol. 10 = Roberts 297. κὠπότα[ρ]οι μῆνπεδέοιαν (ΜΕΝΠΕΔΕΟΙΑΝ). Kirchhoff, Arch. Zeit. XXXVIII, 119, thinks that the verb is used intransitively and is the equivalent of ἔμπεδον εἶναι rather than of ἐμπεδόω. This is confirmed by Dittenberger.

ἔνσιτος, Laconian title of honor. [III] Lac. LeB.-F. 168b.g, CI. 1240, et al. Cf. σύσσιτος, ἀείσιτος, and πρωτενσιτεύω.

ἐντιτός, *liable, responsible.* [Late.] Cret. Mus. It. III, 731 αἰ δὲ μ(ή), αὐτῶι ἐντιτὸν ἔστω ἐπὶ τᾶι δόσει. Cf. Hesych. ἐντιτόν· ἔνδικ(τ)ον. The idea of responsibility is seen also in the τίτανς of Comp. 148, who plainly correspond to the βεβαιωτῆρες of the Delphian inscriptions, the guardians of the freed slaves. The force of the preposition in ἐντιτόν is apparently the same as in ἔνδικον. See Insc. Jurid. Gr., p. 403. See also ἔνδικον (Rare Words).

ἐντοφήια, *burial rites.* [V] Delph. BCH. 1895, 1ff., C. 20 (compare p. 297) hόδ' ὁ τεθμὸς πὲρ τῶν ἐντοφηίων (ἐντοθηκῶν, as read by Homolle, is now generally given up). Bechtel, BB. 22, 280, compares Hesych. ταφήια· ἐντάφια, εἰς ταφὴν εὔθετα ἱμάτια. For the vocalism cf. τόφος : τάφος, κοθαρός : καθαρός, Meyer, p. 71.

ἐνωνά, *right of purchase.* Boeot. 380_7 κὴ ϝυκίας ἐνωνὰν κὴ ἀσφάλιαν. This is a proxenus inscription. The word ἔππασις is generally used in Boeotian in this phrase.

ἐξαίρημα = ἐξαίρετον. [Late.] Cos PH. $36c_6$ ἐξαιρεῖσθαι [δὲ] ἀ[ρ]γύριον ἀπὸ τῶν προσόδ[ων τῶν πιπτουσῶ]ν ἀπὸ τοῦ τεμέν[ους κ.τ.λ.] καὶ τὰ ἐξαιρήματα δ[ιελεῖν] κατὰ μέρη.

ἐξαιθραπεύω, *act as satrap.* [IV] Ion. (Mylasa) Bechtel 248_2 Μανσσώλλου ἐξαιθραπεύοντος. See Smyth, §§ 143, 211. Bechtel, l. c., approves Lagarde's connection with Av. *šōithra* rather than with Persian χšaθrapāvā, which is represented in Greek by ἐξατράπης and ξατράπης.

ἐξιεριστεύω = ἐξιερόω. [I] Rhodes, IG. Ins. 701_6. Cf. Brit. Mus., II, CCCLIII, to which Newton notes ἀρχιαρίστας in another Camirus inscription, BCH. 1881, 337_{15}. Kuster reads ἱερίστας in a gloss of Hesychius under ἀγνίτης, where Schmidt substitutes ἱερείτας. The development seems to have been -ίζω, -ιστής, -ιστεύω.

ἐξορύζω, *drive out from the boundaries.* [IV] Cypr. (Edal.) $60_{25\cdot 26}$ ἤ κέ σις Ὀνάσιλον ἤ τὼς παῖδας τὼς Ὀνασίλων ἐξ τᾶι ζᾶι τᾶιδε ἲ ἐξ τῶι κάπωι τῶιδε ἐξορύξη, ἰδὲ ὂ ἐξορύξη—. Hoffmann, GD. I, p. 72, derives from *ἐξορϝίζειν to ὄρϝος, *boundary-stone.* Cf. Schulze, Quaest. Ep., p. 113, n. 8.

ἐπᾱβολά, *share, portion.* [V] Gort. Law-code V_{50} δια[λ]ακόντων τ[ὰ]ν ἐπαβολὰν (ΕΠΑΒΟΛΑΝ) ϝέκαστος. Cf. Hesych. ἐπηβολή· μέρος.

ἐπᾱγάνωσις = γάνωσις. [I] Boeot. CIGS. I, 4149_{18} ἐπεσκεύασα δὲ καὶ τὸ προσκήνιον [καὶ εἰς] τὴν τῶν ἀγαλμάτων ἐπαγανώσιν. Holleaux, BCH. 1890, 184, thinks this is an error for ἐπα(να)γάνωσιν.

ἐπάναγκον = ἐπάναγκες. [V] Gort. Law-code IV_{28}, $XI_{1\cdot 2}$.

LEXICOGRAPHICAL STUDY OF GREEK INSCRIPTIONS   41

ἐπαρέομαι = ἐπαράομαι. [V] Gort. Law-code II$_{40}$ ΕΓΑRIOME-
NON. ἀρέομαι is found in Poll. III, 65 ; Cf. Smyth, § 688.
ἐπάνθεμα, *votive offering* (?). [III?] Arg. AJA. 1894, 357
ἀργύρεον ὀλκὰ μ[ναῖ?] | ἐπανθέματα λεῖο. | φιάλαν ὀλκὰν δρα[χμαι ?].
Cf. the use of ἐπάνθετα, Boeot. CIGS. I, 2420, 3498, where it is
simply a brief expression for the Attic formula ἐπέτεια ἐπεγέ-
νετο. The verb ἐπανατίθημι is used in the sense *lay upon* in
Aristoph. Wasps, and Plato uses it in the Laws with the meaning
intrust.
ἐπανιτάω, *return, go back*. [III] Elis 1172$_8$ = Ol. 39$_8$ ἐπα-
νιτακὼρ ἐν τὰν ἰδίαν. Hesych. εἰτακεῖν· ἐληλυθέναι. ἰτακώς is a
formation of the same kind as ἰτητέον, ἐξιτητέον, παριτητέα. See
Baunack, Rh. M. 37, 472; Dittenberger, l. c., note, which points out
the fact that citizenship is independent of residence, and if once
a citizen of Elis, one would so remain even after his return home.
ἐπάνχιστος, *nearest of kin*. [V] Locris 1478$_{18}$ = CIGS. III,
334 τὸν ἐπάνχιστον κρατεῖν. This is the provision for the estate
of a man who dies without leaving immediate family.
ἐπελάω = ἐπελαύνω. [IV] Tab. Heracl. I$_{127}$ καὶ ἐπελάσθω τὰ
ἐπιζάμια τὰ γεγραμμένα. Cf. Boisacq, p. 49; Meister (Curt.
Stud. IV), p. 377. For ἐπελαόσθω 3d pl. Cf. for the meaning
ἐπελασάσθων, Arcad. 1222$_{23}$.
ἐπενπάω, *fulfill, accomplish*. [VI] Elis 1152 = Ol. 2 = Roberts 292 αἰ ζὲ μήπιθεῖαν τὰ ζίκαια ὁρ μέγιστον τέλος ἔχοι καὶ
τοὶ βασιλᾶες, ζέκα μναῖς κα ἀποτίνοι ϝέκαστος τῶν μήπιποεόντων
κα(τ)θυταὶς τοῖ Ζὶ 'Ολυνπίοι, ἐπενπῶι (ΕΓΕΝΓΟΙ) ζέ κ'ἑλλανοδίκας
καὶ τἄλλα ζίκαια ἐπενπήτω (ΕΓΕΝΓΕΤΟ) ἀ ζαμιωργία, αἰ ζέ μὴ (πε)ν-
πῶι (ΕΝΓΟΙ), ζίφυιον ἀποτινέτω ἐν μαστράαι. See Roberts, p. 365,
who discusses the various readings. Bücheler, Rh. M. 35, 632,
and Bergk, Rh. M. 38, 534, compare ἔνπει with *inquit* and ἐπένπειν
with the phrase *multam indicere*. Dittenberger, l. c., approves
this explanation, but it would overthrow the generally accepted
derivation of *inquit*. Cf. Stolz, Lat. Gr. 157. Ahrens, Rh. M. 35,
578 ff., takes ἐπ-ένπω = ἐφέπω (*curare*), while Kirchhoff, Arch.
Zeit. XXXVIII, 68, reads ἐκπέμποι. Comparetti, Acad. dei Lincei,
Ser. III, Vol. VI, p. 70, also assumes omission of πε in l. 6, and

explains ἐπέντοι, etc., as due to the error of the stonecutter for ἐπενπ[οέ]οι; but, as Roberts says, the threefold error is very improbable. The explanation given by Curtius, Gr. Gr., § 201, more fully by Brugmann, Grundriss II, p. 348 (cf. also Meister, GD. II, p. 20), is on the whole the most satisfactory. He assumes *πᾶιω from *k̑u̯ā-i̯ō, the same root which is found in πᾶμα, παμῶχος; cf. Brugmann I, 312, 550, 557. It would seem most probable that the three verbs are from the same compound, and that the omission of -πε- is to be assumed in ΕΝΓΟΙ.

ἕπερος, ram. [IV] Aeol. (Aeg.) Ét. Gr. IV, p. 268 = Hoffmann, GD. II, 155a. ἕπεροι καὶ ἀρνηάδες ἐρίων ἀτέλεες. Cf. Meister, IF. I, Anz. 203, who questions whether ἕπερος is to be connected with Lat. *aper,* etc., and Hoffmann, GD. II, p. 305, who quotes ἕπεροι "eber," Lat. *aper,* etc. Schulze, KZ. 33, 132, connects with εὔερος (Ion. εὔιερος, Lob. Phryn., p. 146), and for the use of ἐπί compares such words as ἐπάργυρος, ἐπίχαλκος, etc., translating by *lanatus.* Its limitation to male or female is a secondary development; cf. Sans. *urabhra, ram,* Lat. *lānāta, sheep* (Juv. VIII$_{155}$). This explanation given by Schulze commends itself in that it offers a reasonable explanation of the form without going out of the domain of the Greek.

ἐπιβάω, *trespass* (on sacred lands). [IV] Tab. Heracl. I$_{128}$ αἰ δέ τίς κα ἐπιβῇ ἢ νέμει ἢ φέρει τι τῶν ἐν τᾷ ἱαρᾷ - - -. Cf. Meister, Curt. Stud. IV, p. 425, who compares ἔμβη, Lysistr. 1303, and ἐκβῶντας, Thuc. V, 77, See also Boisacq, DD., p. 62.

ἐπιδικᾱτός = ἐπίδικος, *subject to judicial decision.* [V] Lac. (Teg.) M. 21$_5$. (To Xouthias the son of Philachaeus thirty minas. If he live, he shall have it himself. If he die, it shall belong to his children) ἐπεί κα πέντε ϝέτεα ηηβῶντι. αἰ δέ κα μὴ γένηται πέ(ντε ϝ)ετῶν, ἐπιδικατόν ἤμεν.

ἐπιδίομαι, 1) *lead, drive,* 2) *go away of one's own accord, flee.* [V] Gort. Comp. 152 I$_7$ αἰ δέ κα μὴ ἐπιδίηται τὸ παρωθὲν (animal) ἢ μὴ ἐπελεύσει τὸ τεθνακὸς ἢ μὴ δείκσει ἀι ἔγρ<α>τται, μὴ ἔνδικον ἤ<μ>ην, II$_5$ τὸ μὲν νυνατὸν ἐπιδίεθαι ἀι ἔγραττται, II$_8$ ἐπιδίεθθαι, II$_{14}$ αἰ ἐπεδίετο ἢ ἐπήλευσε ἢ ἐκάλη δεικσίων, VII$_2$ τὰ χρήματα ἐπὶ [ϝ]αὸν ἐπιδιόμεν[ον ἤ] ἐπελεύσαντα, IV$_2$ τὸν δὲ ϝοικέα τὸν ἐπιδιόμενον μὴ ἀπόδοθθαι, IV$_{6\cdot11}$ ἐπιδιομενος. Cf. Hesych. δίεσθαι· διώκειν, τρέχειν. In col. IV this word seems to be used in the same sense as δίω in Attic, while in the other citations the meaning corresponds to that of Homeric δίομαι, Il. XV, 681. In these it is used of the animal which is still in condition to walk, while ἐπελεύσω is used of the dead animal. Cf. also ἐδδίεται, Comp. 174. See discussion of meaning, Comp., pp. 272 f.

ἐπιζᾱμιώματα, τά = ἐπιζήμια. [IV] Tab. Heracl. I$_{155}$ ἐπιζαμιωμάτων. Cf. ἐπιζάμια I$_{127}$.

ἐπιζύγιον = ὑποζύγιον [IV] Arcad., Hoffmann, GD. I, p. 23, no. 29$_4$ τοῖ δὲ ξένοι καταγομένοι ἐξῆναι ἄμέραν καὶ νύκτα νέμεν ἐπιζύγιον. Cf. Hesych. ἐπιζύγιον· μέρος τῆς νεώς. See Danielsson, Epigr., p. 49.

ἐπικᾱπίς, *belonging to a garden* (?). Troiz. 3362$_{29}$ ἐς τὰν ὁδὸν τὰν πὰρ τὰς ἐπικαπίδας. Cf. κηπίδες νύμφαι in Aristaen. 1, 3; also ἐπικήπιος. A noun which this adjective modifies has apparently been obliterated.

ἐπιμηνιεία, 1) *office of ἐπιμήνιος,* 2) *special session of the temple officials at Delphi.* [II] Thera, Cauer 148 D$_{31}$ τὰν πράταν ἐπιμηνιείαν δωρεάν, F$_{20}$ εἰ δέ κα ἦ ἐπιμηνιεία δωρεάν; Delph. BCH. 1896, 198 ff., II$_{14}$ πυλαιᾶν πέντε καὶ ἐπιμηνιειᾶν δυοῖν. The πυλαῖαι were the two regular sessions of the Amphyctionic council, held in the autumn and spring. If an unexpected payment of money occurred between the two sessions, a special session was held called ἐπιμηνιεία and dated by the month in which it took place. Cf. Bourguet, BCH. 1896, 225, who gives this explanation.

ἐπιμηνιεύω, *act as ἐπιμήνιος.* [II] Cos 3635 [τ]οὶ ἀεὶ ἐπιμηνιεύοντες; Thera, Cauer 148 D$_{15\cdot32\cdot35}$, E$_{22\cdot35}$, F$_{32}$; Olbia, Ditt. Syll. 248$_{180}$ = Latyschew 16 B$_{83}$ ἐπιμηνιεῦσαι καὶ προνοῆσαι χρησίμως [τοῖ]ς τε δανεισταῖς – –; Delph. BCH. 1896, 198 ff., I$_{6\cdot90\cdot92}$, II$_{14}$. Cf. ἐπιμηνιεία.

ἐπιμωλέω, *bring suit against.* [V] Gort. Law-code IX$_{28}$ ἐπιμωλὲν (ΕΓΙΜΟΛΕΝ) ἰῶ πρὸ τῶ ἐνιαυτῶ, IX$_{31}$ αἰ μέν κα νίκας ἐπιμωλῆι (ΕΓΙΜΟΛΕΙ). See μωλέω.

ἐπιξοά, *smoothing, polishing.* [IV] Epid. 3225 A$_{70}$ = Epid. K. 241$_{70}$. Κάλις εἵλετο ἐπιξοὰν [το]ῦ στρώματος τοῦ ἔνδοι καὶ τοῦ προδόμου, Β₈₄ Γοργίας εἵλετο ἐπιξοὰν τοῦ στ[ρώ]ματ[ος] τοῦ ἔχ[θ]ω καὶ τοῦ σακοῦ καταξοὰν τὰ ἔξω, 242₁₇ ἐπιξοᾶς κρηπῖδος. Cf. καταξοάν 241, Β₈₅, et al., also παραξοήν, Lebadaea, CIGS. I, 3073₁₄₁ = παρατομή. Kavvadias, l. c., p. 90, n. 235, makes the distinction that ἐπικοπά is used of work on wood, these derivatives of ξέω when the work is to be done on stone. See also Baunack, Aus Epid., p. 75.

ἐπιπόλαιος, *movable property.* [V] Gort. Law-code V₄₁ ἐπιπολαίων (ΕΠΙΠΟΛΑΙΟΝ) χρημάτων. Mon. Ant. I, pp. 41 f., l. 15 τὰ δ'ἐπιπόλαια πάντα κοινὰ ἦμεν Γορτυνίων καὶ Κνωσίων ϝεκατέρων τὰν ἡμίναν. Cf. Hesych. ἔπιπλα· ἱμάτια γυναικεῖα. ἢ χρήματα, ἢ σκεύη, τὰ μὴ ἔγγεια, ἀλλ' ἐπιπόλαια.

ἐπιπρείγιστος, *next to the oldest.* [V] Gort. Law-code VII₂₀ (ΕΠΙΠΡΕΙΓΙSΤΟΙ). See πρείγιστος.

ἐπίσσοφος, Theran official. [II] Thera, Cauer 148 F₂₁ πολείτω ὁ ἐπίσσοφος, F₂₄ αἱρείσθω δὲ τὸ κοινὸν καὶ ἐπίσσοφον, F₃₁ καὶ ἐνγραφέτω τός τε ἐπιμηνίος καὶ τὸν ἀρτυτῆρα ἀνὰ πρεσβύτατα καὶ ἐπίσσοφον, G₁₀·₂₀·₃₅. ἐπεσ]όφευε is probably to be read in a Corcyrean inscription 3195₁₆ = CIGS. III, 691₁₆. Cf. Keil, Mitth. 1895, 435 (note). Although the ἐπίσσοφος of the Theran inscription was a private man, it is probable that the title was taken from that of a public official. Cf. Keil and Dittenberger, ll. cc.

Osthoff, PBB. XIII, 418 ff., connects Gr. σοφός with Lat. *faber.* The Greek word is from *τϝοφός from *θϝοφος, while *faber* is from *ƀvaf-ro-s.* In this way the -σσ- is satisfactorily explained. Cf. Brugmann I, p. 311; Prellwitz, Et. W. d. gr. Spr., p. 294; Meyer, p. 297.

ἐπωμότᾱς, "*additional sworn member of the tribunal,* chosen by the plaintiff." [V] Locris 1479₁₀ = CIGS. III, 333 αἴ κ' ἀνδιχάζωντι τοὶ ξενοδίκαι, ἐπωμότας (ΕΠΟΜΟΤΑS) hελέστω ὁ ξένος ὠπάγων τὰν δίκαν ἐχθὸς προξένω, etc.

ἐπώνιον, *tax on sales.* [V] CIA. I, 274₁₂, 277₅·₁₂ σὺν ἐπωνί[οις]; Erythrae, Bechtel 206 (com.) ἐπώνιον. Cf. Poll. 7, 15 τὰ δὲ καταβαλλόμενα ὑπὲρ τῶν πιπρασκομένων τέλη ἐπώνια λέγουσι; Bekk. Anecd. I, p. 40 ἐπώνια, τὰ ἐπὶ τοῖς ὠνίοις προσδιδόμενα ἔξωθεν χάριτος ἕνεκα. See Gilbert I, p. 333, II, p. 369. Apparently in

Cos 3632₄ (com.), ὠνά is used in this sense. See Töpffer, Mitth. 1891, 420.

ἐργωνέω, *contract for public works.* [III] Arcad. 1222₁₂ εἰ δέ τι(ς) ἐργωνήσας μὴ ἰγκεχηρήκοι τοῖς ἔργοις, etc.

ἐσκίχρημι, *lend money on interest.* [II] Thess. (Mondaia) 1557 πὲρ το(ἰ) [ἀρ]γύρροι τᾶς Θέμιστο(ς), αἰ ἀ(ν)εκτ[ό]ν ἐστι τᾶ Θέμι(σ)τι καὶ βέλτιον ἐ(σ)κιχρέμεν. This is an oracle-inscription from Dodona. ἐσκίχρημι = ἐκδανείζω. Cf. Prellwitz, de dial. Thess., p. 38, note.

ἔσκλητος, *small assembly* (technical term). [I] Rheg. IG. Sic. et It. 612 = Ditt. Syll. 251 ἔδοξε τᾶι ἁλία[ι] καθάπερ τᾶι ἐσκλήτωι καὶ τᾶι βουλᾶι. See Dittenberger, l. c., who gives this explanation. Cf. also Gilbert II, p. 239.

ἔταλον, *yearling.* [IV] Aeol., Hoffmann, GD. II, p. x, no. 155a₁₈ ἀρνηάδων ἔταλα ἀτέλεα ; Cos. 3721₁₁ ἀποδόμεν τοῦ μὲν ἐτέλου ἡμιωβέλιον, etc. From ϝέτος. Reinach, Rev. d. Ét. Gr. IV, 268, suggests that this may be the Aeolic form of ἄταλος, but as Meister, IF. Anz. I, 204, points out, η for α would not be Aeolic but Ionic. There is no difficulty in the derivation as given. For -ελ- to -αλ- cf. πύελος : πύαλος, μύελος : μύαλος, and the common interchange of -ερ- and -αρ-. See Meyer, p. 159.

εὐθυτοκίᾱ, *simple interest.* [I] Lac. M. 51 = LeB.-F. 242a₃₇ τοῖς δὲ ἄλλοις δανείοις ἄνωθεν ἀπὸ τῶν συνγραφῶν δραχμαῖον τόκον ἐξ εὐθυτοκίας ὥρισεν.

εὐστόν, *victim burned whole* (?). [V] Ion. 100₅ = Ditt. Syll. 376 ἦν δὲ εὐστόν θύηι ἡ πόλις, λάψεται γλῶσσαν, etc. Cf. Hesych. εὐστόν· τὸ σειόμενον. From εὕειν. Cf. Dittenberger, l. c., note, who gives the above interpretation. The definition of Hesychius may refer to the turning back and forth of an animal roasted on the spit.

ἐφανγρέω, *choose in addition.* [III] Thess. 345₄₁ ἐφανγρένθειν = ἐφαιρῶνται. Cf. προανγρέ[σι (below) and ἀγρέω (Rare Words).

ἐφακέομαι, *repair.* [380] Delph., Cauer 204₃₇ ἐφακείσθων (δρόμον), l. 41 γεφύρας ἐφακεῖσθαι. Cf. ἄκεσις (Rare Words). For the aspirate see Meyer, § 206.

ἐφέργνυμι, *shut in.* [IV] Tab. Heracl. I₁₃₁ ἐφέρξοντι. See ἀφέργνυμι.

ἐχεπάμων, *having the right of inheritance*. [V] Locris 1478₁₆ = CIGS. III, 334₁₆ αἴ κα μὴ γένος ἐν τᾶι ἱστίᾳ ἦι ἐχέπαμον. See Meister, Ber. d. sächs. G. d. W. 1896, 306.

ἔχθοι = ἐκτός [IV] Epid. 3325₆₆ = Epid. K. 241₆₆ τὰν ἔχθοι καὶ τὰν ἔνδοι. Cf. Hesych. ἔχθοι· ἔξω.

ἔχθω = ἐκτός [V] Delph. BCH. 1895, 1 ff. C₄₃ ἔχθω ἡομεστίων. This inscription shows also ἐχθός C₃₆ ἐ[χ]θὸς τᾶς ϝοικίας. Cf. Locris 1479₁₁ = CIGS. III, 333₁₁ ἐχθὸς προξένω. For the relation of these forms with χθ to the Att. ἐκτός see Wackernagel, KZ. 33, 40; Brugmann I, pp. 627, 754, 756; otherwise Keil, Hermes 25, 601; Meyer, § 209.

ϝαρήν. See ἀρήν.

ϝάριχος (?), *ram*. [VI] Elis 1158 = Ol. 5 ϝαρ]ίχως καθ(θ)ύσας ἐπὶ τοῖ βωμοῖ. Cf. Hesych. βάριχοι· ἄρνες and ἄριχα· ἄρρεν πρόβατον.

ϝάστιος = ἀστικός. [VII/VI] Crete, Comp. 32₂, 149₄ ϝαστίαν δίκαν.

ϝῆμᾱ = εἷμα. [V] Gort. Law-code V₄₀ θνατῶν δὲ καὶ καρπῶ καὶ ϝήμας (FEMA⋝) κανφιδήμας κἠπιπολαίων χρημάτων, αἴ κα μὴ ληίοντι δατῆ[θαι τινές]—. Comp. 154 I₁₉ τὰ δὲ τρίτρα τᾶς ϝήμας (FHMA⋝) καὶ τᾶς ἀνφιδήμας. Cf. ϝῆμα, Law-code III₃₈ ἢ ϝῆμα ἢ δυώδεκα στατήρανς. For similar variation of declension see ἀνφιδήμᾱ.

ϝέχω, *bring, present*. [II] Pam. 1267₂₄ ἄγεθλα ϝεχέτω – –; Cypr., Hoffmann, GD. I, p. 46, n. 66 αὐ]τάρ με ἔϝεξε ['Ονασί]θεμις, ἰ(ν) τύχαι. Cf. Brugmann I, p. 293.

ϝικατίδειον, *twenty-foot road* (?). [IV] Tab. Heracl. II₂₃·₄₄ (com.) ἀπὸ δὲ τῶ ϝικατιδείω τὰν ἐς ποταμὸν τὸν Ἄκιριν γᾶν ποτιγενομέναν, etc. This word occurs in close connection with ϝικατίπεδον, which has apparently about the same meaning, though an attempt to differentiate is made in Insc. Jurid. Gr., p. 215, n. 1.

ϝισοδᾱμιωργός, *having same rights as* δημιουργός. [V] Elis 1153₄ = Ol. 11 ϝισοπρόξενον (empty space) ϝισοδαμιωργόν.

ϝοίκω, *from the house*. [V] Delph. BCH. 1895, 1 ff., C₂₃ μήτε πριάμενο[ν] μήτε ϝοίκω. See Ahrens, DD., p. 374, for adverbs in -ω. This is undoubtedly a genuine ablative. Cf. Solmsen, Rh. M. 51, 303; Meyer, p. 485.

ϝρητάω, *promise.* [IV] Cypr. (Edal.) 60_{14} ἐϝρητάσατυ βασιλεύς κὰς ἁ πτόλις δοϝέναι - -, l. 4 εὐϝρητάσατυ. Hoffmann, GD. I, p. 219, thinks this is a derivative from Cypr. ϝρήτα, 60_{28}. Cf. Meister, GD. II, p. 245. But ϝρήτα : ῥήτρα = ῥόπτον : ῥόπτρον, θρέπτα : θρέπτρα, etc. Cf. Schulze, Berl. Phil. Woch. 1890, 1503; Meyer, § 301. ῥητάω is rather to be taken as an independent formation in -τ-ά-ω. Cf. Arg. ἀϝρήτευε.

ζευγῶχος, *driver of a cart drawn by yoked animals.* Hermione $3385_{7\cdot 9}$ ζευγώχωι.

ἡμιολίζω, *pay original amount increased by one-half.* [VI] Elis 1151_8 = Ol. 16 = Roberts 298. αἰ δὲ μὴ συναλλύ[οιτο - -, τὸ χρέος κ' ἠ]μιολίζοι ἁ πόλις τοῖ Δὶ 'Ολυνπίοι, etc. The above reading is according to Blass and is accepted by Roberts and Dittenberger. Blass compares ἡμιολιασμός = τὸ ἡμιόλιον δοῦναι, Harpocration. Dittenberger, l. c., further compares ἐφ' ἐμολίοι, CIGS. I, 1739_{15}. He thinks it doubtful whether τοῖ Δὶ 'Ολυνπίοι, etc., belongs to ἡμιολίζοι or is independent.

ἡμιρηναία, ἡμιρρήνιον, *hybrid animal.* [V] Delph. BCH. 1895, 1 ff., $D_{33\cdot 35}$ [Τ]ὰ δὲ [Φ]ά[ν]ατος ἐπέδωκε τᾶι θυγατρὶ Βουζύγαι, τὰ ἡμιρρ[ή]νια (HEMIPP. NIA) κήκτᾶς δυωδεκαιδος χίμαιραν καὶ τήμιρ[η]ναιᾶν δάρματα. Homolle explains as a compound of ἤμι and ῥήν similar to ἡμίονος. Cf. ἀρήν, πολύρρην, also Hesych. ῥῆνες· ἄρνες. πρόβατα and ῥήνεα· πρόβατα, οἶα.

ἡμιτύεκτος = ἡμίεκτος. Crete (Eleuthera), Comp. 200_3 τριώδελοντῶ [ἡ](μ)ιτυέκτω. ἤμιτυ for ἤμισυ. L. & S. cite ἡμισύτριττον, Kum. ἡμισυάρχης, ἡμισυάρχιον. Cf. Baunack, Berl. Phil. Woch. 1887, $57.^1$ For ἡμιτύ-: ἡμισύ see Meyer, § 268, end.

ἠχοῖ, *where.* [IV] Oropus, Bechtel 18_{16} = CIGS. I, 235 ἠχοῖ ἑκάστοις αἱ δίκαι ἐν τοῖς νόμοις εἴρηται, ἐντοῦθα γινέσθων. Cf. Hom. ἦχι. See Smyth, p. 612; Meyer, p. 454; Kühner-Blass II, p. 311, n. 7 (end).

---

[1] Baunack thinks ϝ is to be expected in -ϝεκτος as in ϝέξ. He explains its omission as due either to the similarity of the letters Ϝ and E, or to a feeling that υ alone was sufficient. The latter supposition seems the more probable. Cf. Comp. 194, 195, where ϝ alone is written ὠϝτο, ἀϝτόνς, and in other Cretan inscriptions we find αὐϝτ- for αὐτ-.

θεᾱροδοκίᾱ, *office of θεαροδόκος*. [III] Elis 1172_9 = Ol. 39 τῷ πατρὸρ θεαροδοκίαν διαδέδεκται; Tenos, Brit. Mus. 373_9 = CIG. 2329 καὶ τὴν θεαροδοκίαν τῶν Δηλίων.

θεᾱροδόκος, *person who receives the θεωροί*. [IV] Epid. K. 273 καὶ θεαροδόκον τοῦ 'Ασκλαπιοῦ; Hermione 3386 καταστᾶσαι δὲ καὶ θεαροδόκον, 3387, 3388; Elis 1172_{27} τοὶ λοιποὶ θεαροδόκοι; Mylasa, CIG. 2670_{14} τῶν θεαροδόκων; Crete, Rev. arch. XII, 396 θεα[ρ]οδόκος; Aetol. $1413_{24,28}$ θεωροδόκους. θεωρ- occurs also in 1424, an inscription found at Ceos which contains an agreement between the Aetolians and the inhabitants of Ceos. Inscriptions 1425, '27, '28 show θεαρ-. Cf. Meyer, p. 86, n. 2.

Θεοδαίσια = Διονύσια. Aeol. 272_{13} Θεο]δαίσια; Crete, CIG. 2554 I_{31} ἐν Θεοδαισίοις παραγγέλλουντες. Cf. Hesych. Θεοδαίσιος. Διόνυσος. Θιοδαίσιος occurs as the name of a Cretan month.

Θεοδαισίᾱ, *distribution at the Θεοδαίσια*. Aeol. 272_9 τ]ὰν θεοδαισίαν διέδωκεν τοῖς μὲν βολ[λάοις].

θηγανείτᾱs, *suitable for a whetstone* (?). Hermione 3247 = IG. Sic. et It. 317 τοῦ λίθου τοῦ θηγανείτα. See note, l. c., which compares ἀμμίτης, πυρίτης, χαλκίτης; Kühner-Blass II, 284.

θιγάνᾱ, *covering*. [V] Delph. 1895, C_{39} ἔναγος ἔστω ἥντε κα hὰ [θ]ιγάνα ποτθέθηι. Homolle's reading is [σ]ιγ' ἀναποτθέθηι. The objections to this are discussed under ἔναγος. Homolle admits them plainly on page 50, but, after discussing other possibilities, thinks that the reading indicated is the least difficult. But a derivative θιγάνᾱ, *covering*, from θιγ- as στεφάνη from στεφ-, στεγάνη from στεγ-, would not seem an unreasonable assumption. There are glosses of Hesychius, too, which should be considered. θίγωνος· κιβωτοῦ; θίβωνος· κιβωτός; θίβη· πλεκτόν τι κιβωτοειδές; θίβην· θήκην, etc. Homolle cites these, l. c., p. 51, and thinks that a word θίγα, θιγάνα might be assumed from the glosses, though he finally rejects this assumption in favor of the reading given.

θῖνος = θεῖος. [V] Gort. Law-code X_{42} τὰ θίνα καὶ τὰ ἀνθρώπινα, Comp. 184_4, 188_6 τὰ θίνα; Cauer 132_{33} καὶ πεδέχεν θίνων καὶ ἀνθρωπίνων. See Meyer, p. 110, n. 2, who says that θῖνος, θύινος, is to be explained from θίος and is formed after the analogy of θέινος. But as Solmsen, KZ. 32, 536, shows, ἔνθινον occurs in inscriptions from Hierapytna, and in that dialect θέος is found, not θίος. He thinks that probably θίνος replaces θεῖος by analogy with ἀνθρώπινος on account of its frequent use in the formula καὶ θεῖα καὶ ἀνθρώπινα. The θέινος which occurs in an inscription from Allaria, Cauer[1] 39₁₆, he explains by the full proportion ἄνθρωπος : θεός = ἀνθρώπινος : θέινος.

θοιναρμόστρια, *president of a feast* (fem.). [I] And.₃₂ εἶπεν ἁ θοιναρμόστρια ἁ εἰς Δάματρος καὶ αἱ ὑποθοιναρμόστριαι αἱ ἐμβεβακυῖαι, etc.; Lac. CIG. 1439, 1446, 1451, θυναρμόστρια 1435, 1436 (late).

θυᾱφόρος, *participating in the sacrifice* (official). Cos 3636₅₂ θυαφόρωι δὲ τοῦ σκέλεος - - [δίδ]οται ἀκρίσχιον. Cf. θυηπόλος CIA. III, 1337 et al. This official is named next after the ἱερεύς.

θυγατροποιΐᾱ, *adoption of daughter*. [II] Rhodes, IG. Ins. 115, 818₅ κατὰ θυγατροποίαν; Halicarnassus, Quest. de l'histoire de l'art., p. 133; θυγατροποιία Rhodes 646; Rayet, Ann. de l'assoc. pour ét. Gr. 1875, 319; Ross, Tagebuch, cited by Keil, Rh. M. 20, 537; Selivanov, Mitth. 1891, 122 ff., who notes the above citations and also Thessalian ὑοποίαν from Lolling, Preuss. Akad. d. W. 1887, 570 Πτολεμαίου τοῦ Ὁπλόνου καθ' ὑοποίαν δὲ Νικάρχου.

θυηχοῦς, *sacrificer, priest*. [IV] CIA. 322 τῷ βωμῷ τῷ τοῦ θυηχοῦ, 324 παρὰ τὸ[ν θ]υηχοῦ βωμό[ν].

θυμελοποῖαι (-ποιοι), *building commissioners in charge of the tholos*. [IV] Epid. K. 242₁₁₉·₁₃₄·₁₃₇·₁₃₉. See Mitth. 1895, 33 ff. Cf. discussion under ἐγδοτήρ. Similar compounds are θεατροποῖαι, ναοποῖαι. There is considerable variation of declension in this inscription. See Keil, Mitth. 1895, 440.

θύρωσις, *preparation of the doors*. [IV] Epid. 3325, A₃₈ = K. 241₃₈ Ἀρχέστρατος ἔλ[ε]το θύρωσιν τοῦ ἐργαστηρίου. See Baunack, Aus Epid., p. 76, where θύρωσις is explained as the *Anbringung der Thüren;* in the index *Anfertigung* is used. It seems probable that both are included.

θύρωτον, *jamb of the door*. [IV] Epid. 3325₃₀₄ Κλεινίαι θυρότοιν λευκώσιος, l. 305 θυρώτοιν (ΘΥΡΘΤΟΙΝ) φορᾶς Ἀρισταίωι, where Baunack would supply λευκώσιος. See Aus Epid., p. 78.

θωάζω, *inflict penalty.* [VI] Elis 1156₁ = Ol. 7 = Roberts 296 βοί κα θωάδ(δ)οι (ΘΟΑΔΟΙ) καὶ κοθάρσι τελείαι. CIA. II, 841₁₄ ἂν δὲ ἐλεύθερος εἶ, θοάσει αὐτὸν ὁ ἱερεὺ[s] μετὰ τοῦ δημάρχου πεντήκοντα δραχμαῖς. For discussion see θώιον.
θωάω, *inflict penalty.* [V] CIA. IV, 1, p. 139, ll. 8–10 ἐ]ξ[εῖ]-ναι θωᾶν (ΘΟΑΝ) [μέ]χρι τριῶν ὀβελῶν τοῖσι ταμ[ίασι].
θωέω, *inflict penalty.* [V] Delph. BCH. 1895, 1 ff., D₁₈ αἰ δέ τι τούτων παρβάλλοιτο τῶν γεγραμμένων, θωεόντων τοί τε δαμιοργοὶ καὶ τοὶ ἄλλοι πάντες Λαβυάδαι, πρασσόντων δὲ τοί πεντεκαίδεκα.
θωίασις, *fine.* [V] Delph. BCH. 1895, 1 ff., D₂₄ αἰ δέ κα ἀμφιλλέγηι τᾶς θωιάσιος, ἐξομόσας τὸν νό[μιμ]ον ὅρκον λελύσθω.
θώιον, *fine.* [V] Locris 1479₉ = CIGS. III, 333₉ Τὸν πρόξενον, αἰ ψευδέα προξενέοι διπλεῖ οἰ θώι' ἔστω. Cf. Bechtel, l. c., for the various readings of these last words.

The meaning of all these words is clear in so far, that it has to do with a *fine* or *penalty*. In the Elean inscription, however, there is doubt whether the verb is factitive or not. Meister, GD. II, p. 22, translates by *büssen,* also Dittenberger, l. c.; Comparetti, JHS. II, 373, likewise considers the word intransitive and equivalent in meaning to *atone,* or, connecting a Cyrillian gloss θόη δὲ λέγεται ἡ θυσία, *sacrifice;* but, as Bücheler, Rh. M. 36, 621, clearly shows, τὸν θεαρὸν would indicate that this verb is transitive. Brand, Hermes 21, 312, boldly and wrongly changes to θυάζοι, i. e., *sacrum facere.* Keil, Hermes 31, 513 ff., defines by *bestrafen,* and thinks the subject "der Richter." This seems to be implied in what follows, αἰ δέ τις πὰρ τὸ γράφος δικά(δ)δοι, ἀτελής κ' εἴη ἀ δίκα ἀ δέ κα ϝράτρα ἀ δαμοσία τελεία εἴη δικά(δ)δωσα. The other verbs are so clearly transitive that one would more naturally assume the same for this, but the inscription is obscure, so that an absolute decision cannot be made.

I have transcribed θωάζω, although there is no direct evidence for the ω except the derivative θωίασις. The only form, however, which certainly shows O in the inscriptions is the Attic θοάσει, as the Elean inscription does not differentiate the vowels. Outside this verb Ω is consistently used in the inscriptions as it is in the literary tradition for the word ἀθώιον. The only apparent exceptions are the Attic ΘΑΟΝ and ΘΟΑ, but neither of these inscriptions has Ω. The ο in Attic θοάσει is probably due to secondary shortening. Cf. Blass-Kühner I, p. 172, and Nachträge, p. 641.

Baunack, SGDI. 1746$_4$, thinks that the forms which have -ι̯- arise from the adjective; θω-ι-άζειν from θώ-ι-ος as προτεράζω from πρότερος. Cf. also Keil, l. c. The noun θωά apparently lost -ι- early, as it is found without in an inscription dating 411 B. C. Cf. Meisterhans, p. 52. θωάω, θωέω would seem to be from the noun. The θωίασις of the carefully written Delphian inscription would indicate that the verb θωάζω originally had -ι̯-. Dittenberger, CIGS. III, 333, reads θῳήστω, but his reasons for rejecting θώι(α) do not seem conclusive.

ιαρομάος, sacred official. [VII] Elis 1147$_2$ = Ol. 1 = Roberts 290 ἰ]αρομάοι αἰ μὰ πεν..., 1150 = Ol. 10 = R. 297 γνώμαν τῶ<ρ> ἰ[αρ]ομάω<ς> (I.. ΟΜΑΟ) τώλυνπίαι, 1154$_4$ = Ol. 4 = R. 295 γνώμα δέ κ'εἴη τιαρομάω. Cf. Hesych. ἱερόμας· τῶν ἱερῶν ἐπιμελούμενος.

ἱεραπόλος, *chief priest.* [II] Acarn. 1379 = CIGS. III, 513 ἐπὶ ἱεραπόλου τοῖ Ἀπόλλωνι τοῖ Ἀκτίοι Θευδότου, 1380$_{a,b}$ ἐπ' ἱεραπόλου.

ἱεροθυτεῖον, *place for sacrifice* (?). Rhodes (Lindus), IG. Ins. 846, 847, 848, 849, 853 σίτησις ἐν ἱεροθυτείῳ. Cf. ἱεροθυτέω, ἱεροθύτης.

ἱεροσαλπιστής = ἱεροσαλπικτής. Rheg., IG. Sic. et It. 617. The form σαλπιστής is found in CIA. 1285 and CIGS. I, 3197, also in late writers. It is evidently a later formation from σαλπίζω, due to confusion with dental stems in -ίζω.

ἱεροπαρέκτης, sacred official. Rheg., IG. Sic. et It. 617, 621. This word is probably to be connected with παρέχω, *furnish, provide.*

ἱεροφόρος, sacred officer of minor rank. [II] Acarn. 1389 = CIGS. III, 486. This title follows αὐλητάς and precedes μάγειρος. Plutarch uses ἱεραφόρος of the one who carries the sacred utensils.

ἰκμάω, *strike, wound.* [IV] Cypr. 60$_3$ τὼς ἀ(ν)θρώπως τὼς ἰ(ν) τᾶι μάχαι ἰκμαμένως. Denominative from *ἰκμή with the same root as Lat. *ico*, Gr. (Hesych.) ἰκτέα· ἀκόντιον. Cf. Ahrens, Philol. 35, 36 ff., who first suggested this derivation. See also Hoffmann, GD. I, p. 70; Meister, GD. II, p. 150.

ἱμάσκω = ἱμάσσω (?). [VI] Elis 1152$_{7\cdot8}$ = Ol. 2 = Roberts 292 αἰ ζ[έ] τις τὸν αἰτιαθέντα ζικαιῶν ἱμάσκοι, ἐν τᾶι ζεκαμναίαι κ' ἐνέχο[ιτ]ο, αἰ ϝειζὼς ἱμάσκοι. It would seem that this reading must be accepted[1] notwithstanding the difficulty of its interpretation, which makes it necessary to assume, as Dittenberger says, that αἰ ϝειζώς does not refer to ἱμάσκοι, but, as is very possible, implies knowledge of the fact that the person is under sentence. Another Elean verb which shows the suffix -σκω is πάσκω 1152$_8$.

ἰναλίνω, *write upon*. [IV] Cypr. (Edal.) 60$_{26}$ ἰδὲ τὰ(ν) δάλτον τά(ν)δε, τὰ ϝέπιϳα τάδε, ἰναλαλισμένα βασιλεὺς κὰς ἁ πτόλις κατέθιϳαν ἰ(ν) τὰ(ν) θιὸν τὰν Ἀθάναν τὰν περ' Ἠδάλιον. Cf. Hesych. ἀλειπ(τ)ήριον· γραφεῖον. Κύπριοι. See Hoffmann, GD. I, p. 72; Meister, GD. II, pp. 210, 278.

ἰνμενφής, *blameworthy, impious*. [V] Mant. BCH. 1892, 570$_{23\cdot28}$.

ἴνμονφος, *blameworthy, condemned*. [V] Mant. BCH. 1892, 570$_{34}$. These words occur in the same inscription and in similar phrases. I cite the occurrences together, using Danielsson's transcription, Eranos II, 8 ff., l. 22 ἴλαον ἦναι, εἰ δ'ἀλάξαι [δ]έατοι κατῶννυ, ἰνμενφές ἦν[αι.], l. 28 ἰνμενφὲ[ς ἦναι κα]τὸ χρηστήριον· εἰ δὲ μή, ἴλα[ον ἦναι], l. 33 κὰς μὴ προσσθαγενὲς τὸ ϝέ[ργον]τὸ τότΕΕ οὕτως ἴνμονφον ὀλ[έσθαι]. εἰ δὲ προσσθαγενὲς τὸ ϝέργ[ον] κὰς μὴ φονής, ἴλαον ἦναι. ἰνμενφές was first read by Homolle, BCH. 1892, 590, and explained as the opposite of ἀμεμφής. This is generally accepted. ἴνμονφον was read by Dareste, BCH. 1893, 202, and also by Bréal, Rev. d. Phil. 1893, 159. It is accepted by Danielsson, l. c., p. 37, and given as an alternative by Baunack, Ber. d. sächs. G. d. W. 1893, 104, though he prefers ἰν μόνφον, which Keil also reads, Gött. Nachr. 1895, 369. The context would seem to imply similar words in these phrases, both of which occur in direct contrast with ἴλαον ἦναι. It does not, however, seem

[1] Bergk, Rh. M. 38, 536 f., assumes ἱλλάσκοι, but this has not met with general acceptance.

necessary to take ἴνμονφος with Dareste and Bréal as identical in meaning with ἰνμενφής. It should rather be taken with Danielsson as slightly differentiated, in that it is personal and therefore stronger than the impersonal ἰνμενφές. Or even the adjective ἴνμονφον may be taken, as Baunack would take the phrase ἰν μόνφον, to denote the result of ἰνμενφὲς ἦναι, i. e., *condemnation to death*. ὀλ[έσθαι] is the most satisfactory completion which has been suggested, and the whole phrase would then be translated, *thus condemned he shall perish*.

ἰνφορβισμός, *act of seizing.* [IV] Arcad., Hoffmann, GD. I, p. 23, no. 29₂ εἰ δ'ἂν καταλλάσσῃ ἰνφορβισμὸν ἦναι. See following word.

ἰνφορβίω, *confine for unlawful grazing.* [IV]˙ Arcad., Hoffmann, GD. I, p. 23, no. 29 = BCH. 1889, 281 ff. l. 3 τὸν hιερομνάμονα ἰνφορβίεν· εἰ δ'ἂν λευτὸν μὴ ἰνφορβίη hεκοτὸν δαρχμὰς ὀφλὲν ἰν δᾶμον καὶ κάταρϝον ἦναι. l. 6 τὰ δ' ἀνασκηθέα ἰνφορβίεν, l. 10 εἰ δ' ἂν ἰν τοῖ περιχώροι, ἰνφορβίεν, l. 14 τὸ μὲν μέζον πρόβατον δαρχμὰν ὀφλὲν, τὸ δὲ μεῖον ἰνφορβίεν. Cf. l. 2 εἰ δ' ἂν καταλλάσσῃ ἰνφορβισμὸν ἦναι, and Hesych. ἐμφόρβιον·[1] τελώνημα.

Bérard, BCH. 1889, 289, translates by *saisir* and *saisie*, arguing that throughout the inscription the words are contrasted with νέμεν and should mean the opposite of free pasture. He derives from φορβεία, *bridle, halter*, defining ἰνφορβισμός as the action of attaching and "putting in pound." Meister, Ber. d. sächs. G. d. W. 1889, 71, derives from φερβ-, φορβ- translating *füttern, auffüttern*. Danielsson, Epigr., p. 35, thinks that Bérard's interpretation is very probable, and adds that the animal may have been prevented from further grazing either by confinement or by so fastening his head that he could not graze. Hoffmann, GD. I, p. 173, connects with Lith. *brizgi-las, halter*, and O. Bulg. *brŭzda* (for *brŭzgja) original stem *bhr̥sgi-*, which would become *φορσβι- *φορβι-. Solmsen, KZ. 34, 440, criticises this connection, with justice, on the ground that the analysis of the Slav. form is false, hence the vowel relationship of the Lith. word is not sufficiently

---
[1] A reasonably certain correction of ἐμφόρβων. See Solmsen, KZ. 34, 440, note.

clear to make it the basis of a derivation. Solmsen rests his own explanation on the Hesychian gloss given above, ἐμφόρβιον· τελώνημα, comparing for the form, ἐνοίκιον, ἐλλιμένιον, ἐννόμιον. Then to ἐλλιμένιον we have the verb ἐλλιμενίζω; cf. Hesych. ἐνλιμενίζειν· τελωνίζειν τὰ ἀπὸ λιμένων καὶ θαλάσσης. From such an analogy he thinks the assumption of a verb ἰνφορβίεν and a resulting ἰνφορβίζω, whence ἰνφορβισμός, is not difficult. The meaning would be then *tax for grazing*.

Whatever word is used as the starting point, there is no question that the root is φερβ- φορβ-, which makes derivatives meaning *pasturage, grazing*, and the like. Since the meaning of this verb is specialized in both φορβεία, *halter*, and ἐμφόρβιον, *tax*, the meaning of the word in this inscription is probably to be determined rather by its suitability to the context than by the meaning of a particular derivative. The fact that ἐμφόρβιον contains the same preposition as ἰνφορβίω, ἰνφορβισμός would not of itself be decisive. Meister's *auffüttern* does not seem reasonable. *To tax for grazing, a tax for grazing*, suits the context very well until we come to l. 14, where it would read, "the larger animal shall pay a drachma, the smaller, the hieromnemon shall tax." If ἰνφορβίεν means tax in this place, it presumably designates a fixed and known amount; but in the very next passage we find the same penalty for the larger animal, while the smaller animals are to pay an obol. There is only one difference in the two passages; the latter is the law concerning animals destined for the sacrifice. Of these animals ἰνφορβίεν or ἰνφορβισμόν ἦναι is never used. It would seem, then, that these words denote action which will prevent unlawful grazing, not applied to the sacred animals or to the larger animals of the traveler, though to both large and small which belong to the priest whose home is in Alea. Neglect to enforce this law would result in desecration of the sacred lands, hence the severe penalty, § 1. I am inclined to think the meaning here is some sort of confinement from which the animals of the priest could be released upon payment of money. If the smaller animals of the traveler should not be released, the hardship would not be very great.

ἱρών, *township, territory of the town.* [IV] Cypr. (Edal.) 60 A₈ τὰ (ζᾶι) ἰ(ν) τῶ ἱρῶνι. Cf. τὸ(ν) χῶρον τὸν ἰ(ν) τῶι ἔλει 1. 9. The above is the interpretation of Deecke, Curt. Stud. VII, p. 249. He connects with a Semitic loan-word '*īr, city,* which is Hebrew-Assyrian, but unfortunately not Phoenician. ἱρών is not a derivative of ἱερ-, as ἱερ- or ἱu̯ερ- occurs several times in Cyprian with no variant ἱρ-. Ahrens, Philol. 35, 42, assumes a noun ῥών, *Raum,* with no connection in Greek. Meister, GD. II, p. 151, accepts ἱρων, but Hoffmann, GD. I, p. 70, rejects it, though he offers no substitute.

ἰσχέγαον, *retaining earth* (?). [IV] Delph. BCH. 1896, 198 ff., I₇·₁₃ ἰσχεγάου—. Cf. p. 211. Homolle compares ἰσχέθυρον. Compounds with ἐχε- are very common.[1] Keil, Hermes 32, 419, note, says that it can hardly mean a support for embankment on account of its early mention in the account. One would think rather of a kind of mortar or a special kind of sealing earth.

κα(δ)δᾱλέομαι, *violate, make of no effect.* [VI] Elis 1149 = Ol. 9 = Roberts 291 τάλαντον κ' ἀργύρω ἀποτίνοιαν τοῖ Δὶ 'Ολυνπίοι τοὶ κα(δ)δαλήμενοι (ΚΑΔΑΛΕΜΕΝΟΙ) λατρειώμενον. αἰ δέ τιρ τὰ γράφεα ταὶ κα(δ)δαλέοιτο - - ἐνέχοιτο τοὶνταυτ' ἐγραμ(μ)ένοι. This is a new compound, though δηλέομαι is a Homeric word. For the form of the participle (-ημενος) see Meyer, § 523, note.

κάδδιχος, measure of quantity. [IV] Tab.Heracl. I₅₂·₁₈₁(com.). Cf. Hesych. κάδδιχον. ἡμίεκτον, ἢ μέτρον.

καθέσιμον, *payment of money.* [200/189] CIA. II, 444₁₄, 445₉, 446₁₂ ἔδωκεν δὲ καὶ τῇ βουλῇ καθέσιμον [δρ]αχμὰς ΧΗΗ, καὶ τοῖς πρυτάνεσιν εἰς θυσίαν H. From καθίημι. Kumanudis defines as *senatorial pay,* or payment for some other public expense (χορηγία), such as installation of the βουλή. Köhler also thinks it means *senatorial* pay.

καλλιέρησις, *auspicious sacrifice.* [V] CIA. I, 55, καὶ ἀργυρίου εἰς καλλιέρησιν (ΚΑΛΛΙΕΡΕΣΙΝ). The context is incomplete, but the word is probably to be defined as above. Cf. Hesych. καλλιέρημα· θυσία εὐπρόσδεκτος.

---

[1] Cf. also Aeolic Οἰσεξεία, Hoffmann, GD. II, p. 66, no. 90₁, beside the common compounds with φερε-.

καλλιτέρως = κάλλιον. [VI] Elis 1156₃ = Ol. 7 = Roberts 296 ὅτι δοκέοι καλλιτέρως (ΚΑΛΙΤΕΡΟΣ) ἔχην πο(τ)τὸν θ(ε)όν—. Cf. Homeric λωίτερος and modern Greek καλλίτερος. Meyer, p. 492, includes this among analogical formations. See Wackernagel, Vermischte Beiträge zur gr. Sprachkunde (1897), p. 11, on the extension of ι in place of the regular suffix, before the second member of bahuvrīhi compounds and also before suffixes in derivatives. -ίτερος, -ίτατος are not found in Attic.

κάμπτρᾱ, *small box, receptacle for the holy books.* [I] And.₁₂ τὰν δὲ κάμπτραν καὶ τὰ βιβλία. See Sauppe, Ausgewählte Schriften, p. 270. Cf. the use of Delphian ζύγαστρον.

καπναύγης, a minor official. Rheg. IG. Sic. et It. 617₉, 618. Dittenberger, l. c., thinks the meaning of this word is not clear, but refers to the words of Cyril (cf. Julian, p. 198) ἐκ τῶν θυσιῶν εἰς ἀέρα διᾴττοντας πολυπραγμονοῦντες καπνούς. It follows σπονδαύλης in the list of officials and precedes μάγιρος.

καρνεονίκᾱς, *victorious at the* Καρνεῖα (?). [I] Lac. M. 56₁₉. This word occurs in a list of petty officials for the feast. Δαμοκράτης χρυσωτάς, Φιλωνίδας Φιλωνίδα καρνεονείκας, Ἀριστόπολις Δαμοχάρισος κατὰ νόμον, etc.

καρπολογεύω = καρπολογέω. [II] Cos 3632₂₉ θυόντωι δὲ καὶ τοὶ καρπολογεῦντες τῶι Ποτειδᾶνι - -.

καρταῖπος, τό, used of *large cattle.* [V] Gort. Law-code IV₃₆ καὶ τὰ πρόβατα καὶ τὰ καρτα[ί]ποδα; Comp. 152, I₁₃₋₁₇ αἰ δέ κα σῦς καρταῖπος παρώσει ἢ κατασκένηι, τόν τε σῦν ἐπὶ τῶι πάσσται ἤμην ὦ κ'ἦι τὸ καρταῖπος, καὶ τὸ .. ; Mus. Ital. II, 678 II₃.₆.₉ = Ins. Jurid. Gr., p. 398. αἴ κα τὸ καρτα[ῖπος]. καρταῖπος αἱ πρίαιτο κ' ἀπόδομεν λέοι—. l. 9 [καρ]ταιπό[δος] - - τὸ καρταῖπος. Cf. κραταίπους, used by Pindar as a substantive, *bull.* The last inscription cited dates from the fourth century and shows Η = ē and Ω; hence it determines the form of this word. For similar compounds, cf. Meyer, § 77; Kühner-Blass I, p. 541. But this seems to be the first example of an accusative singular neuter in -πος.

κασσηρατόριν, *hunt, chase.* Lac. M. 57, 58 οἱ Νεικηφόρου νεικάαντερ κασσηρατόριν μῶαν καὶ λῶαν Ἀρτέμιδι βωρθέα ἀνέθηκαν.

The same expression probably is used in 58, though no part of it is legible except this word. It is explained by Baunack, Rh. M. 38, 293 ff., who discusses this word in connection with the θηρομαχία of the Greeks. κασσηρατόριν = *κατ-θηρατόριον from θηρατώρ, Il. IX, 544. This explanation was also given by Kouminos, 'Αθήναιον I, 390. See Meyer, p. 289. For nouns in -ιν from -ιον see Wagner, Quaest. Epig. Gr., p. 96.

καταβλαβής, *ruined, destroyed*. Taur., CIG. Sic. et It. 432$_{5.9}$ δυσαγείτω καὶ αὐτὸς καὶ γέ[νος - - - ἱερ]οῦ χρήματος καταβλαβέος. Cf. καταβλάπτω, ἀβλαβής.

καταδουλίζομαι = καταδουλόω. [II] Delph. 1713 (com.) εἰ δέ τις καταδουλίζοιτο 'Ηράκλειτον; Phocis 1523$_9$ (com.); Boeot. 500$_{5.6}$, 425$_{22}$, et al. There is also a late verb in -εύω.

καταδουλισμός = καταδούλωσις. [II] Delph. 1689 (com.) ἐπὶ καταδουλισμῶι, also καταδουλισσμῶι.

καταιϝεί, *forever*. [V] Locris 1478$_4$ = CIGS. III, 334 αἴ κα δείληται, θύειν καὶ λανχάνειν κῆδάμω κἠφοινάνων, αὐτὸν καὶ τὸ γένος καταιϝεί.

καταλοβεύς, *support*. [IV] Epid. K. 242$_{94}$ τῶγ καταγλυμμάτων ἐν τοῖν σταθμοῖν καὶ καταλοβεῦ[σι.], l. 96 τῶν ἐγγλυμάτων ἐργασία[ς ἐν] τοῖς καταλοβεῦσι καὶ ὑπερθύρωι τῶν δεδοκιμασμένων, l. 105 τῶν ἐν τῶι ὑπερθύρωι καὶ καταλοβεῖ ἐγγλυμάτων; Crete, Mitth. 1886, 181 = Mus. Ital. III, p. 617. ἐκ θεμηλίω ἄχρι ἐπὶ το[ν κ]αταλοβέ[α] τὸν ἐπὶ τῶι ὀρθοστά[ται]. Novosadsky, l. c., citing Hesych. λοβός· τὰ ἄκρα πάντα, connects with καταλείβειν and explains it as a *trough for carrying off rainwater*. Fabricius, Mus. It., l. c., discusses at length. He rejects Novosadsky's explanation, but offers no satisfactory derivation. He defines as a final covering placed on the ὀρθοστάται, cf. p. 621. As Kavvadias, l. c., says, this may apply to the Cretan inscription, but it does not satisfy the context of the Epidaurus inscription. Keil, Mitth. 1895, 420, gives a new and satisfactory derivation, καταλοβεύς = *καταλαβεύς, *der Träger*. For λο- : λα- he compares γροφ- : γραφ-. There are instances of this change in both dialects; cf. Epid. 3325$_{211}$ et al.; Cretan, Bergmann's 55. See also Skias, Kr. D., p. 87, and compare Hesych. ἀβλοπές· ἀβλαβές. Κρῆτες.

For the development of meaning Keil cites Hesych. καταλαβεῖς· πάσσαλοι. The covering of the ὀρθοστάται, which is indicated in the Cretan inscription, also sustains the upper wall (Hermes 17, 569), as in Epidaurus it will support the σάκος which is not yet in position. See Mitth. 1895, 88.

καταλυμακόω, *cover with stones.* [IV] Tab. Heracl. I₅₆ ὡς μὴ καταλυμακωθὴς ἀδηλωθείη καθὼς τοὶ ἔμπροσθα ὅροι. Cf. Hesych. λύμακες· πέτραι.

κατάμαστρος, *answerable to the μαστρός.* [II] Delph., Ditt. Syll. 233₂₁ εἰ δέ τις τούτων τι ποιῆσαι ἢ ἄρχων ἢ ἰδιώτας κατάμαστρος ἔστω. See ὑπόμαστρος, μαστρός (below).

κατανκτηρία, *fastening for doors.* [329/8] CIA. IV, 834 b, col. II₉₂ μοχλοὶ ταῖς κατανκτηρίαις παλαιοὶ κατεχρήσθησαν. Cf. ἀγκτήρ and ἀγκτηριάζω, which are, however, used chiefly as medical terms.

καταξύλωσις, *provision of wood* for use in building. [IV] Epid. Κ. 242₁₃₀ Δείνωνι καταξυλώσιος.

κάταρϝος, *accursed.* [IV] Arcad., Hoffmann, GD. I, p. 23, no. 29 εἰ δ'ἂν λευτὸν μὴ ἰνφορβίη - - - κάταρϝον ἦναι. See ἰνφορβίω for discussion of this passage.

κατασκευόω = κατασκευάζω. [II] Thera, Cauer 148 H₂₅; Delph. 1874₂₆·₂₈. With loss of -υ- 1928₈ κατασκεώσηται, 1938₂₁ κατεσκέωσται. Cf. note to the last citation.

κατεγγυεύω = κατεγγυάω. [I] And.₇₁ κατεγγυεύσας. Cf. ἐγγυεύω.

κατθυτά, *sacrifice.* [VI] Elis 1151₆·₁₂ = Ol. 16 = Roberts 298, 1152 = Ol. 2 = Roberts 292, 1157₄ = Ol. 3 ἀποτίνοι κα(τ)θυταῖς τοῖ Ζὶ 'Ολυνπίοι, and similar expressions.

κατοίκιος, *belonging to the house.* [II] Delph. 2141₂₃ με[ριξ]άντων τὰ κατοίκια πάντα. κατοικία, *village, dwelling,* is used by Polyb., Plut., etc.

κῆυα, *sacrifice, burnt offering.* [380] Delph. (Amphyctionic decree), Cauer 204₃₄ θύεν ἐν 'Ανεμαίαις τρικτεῦαν κῆυαν [τ]ῷ ('Απόλλωνι), τρικτεῦαν κηυ .... I also place here, with some hesitation, Lac. Μ. 59₄ = LeB.-F. 162 b₄ ἐπὶ πατρονόμω Γοργίππω (τῶ Γοργίππω) νεικάαρ κεαύαν 'Αρτέμιτι βωρσέα ἀνέσηκε. Böckh would explain the Delphian word as an adjective connected with the

LEXICOGRAPHICAL STUDY OF GREEK INSCRIPTIONS 59

Hesychian glosses κήια and κεῖα· καθάρματα, translating καθαρτηρίαν. Prellwitz, BB. XVII, 167, considers τρικτεῦαν for *τρικτεῖαν the adjective, and κῆυαν a substantive from *κηυιαν, root κέυ- : καίω. The strong form is seen in Hom. ἔκηα, κηώδης. There may be a middle form in Hesych. κεάσαι· σχίσαι, καῦσαι. In this form we find the connection with the Laconian word, which Baunack, Rh. M. 38, 297, separates into κε ΑΥΑΝ. He then assumes either a stonecutter's mistake or that Α is a ligature for ΛΑ, and reads λαῦαν, interpreting as an equivalent to Lac. λοαν, M. 57. But this is very doubtful. Unfortunately these inscriptions are from Fourmont's notes, and no great stress can be laid on their accuracy. The meaning *sacrifice, burnt offering*, would suit well in the Laconian inscription. It would be taken then as the object of ἀνέσηκε.

κλᾱίγω = κλείω. [I] And. $_{94}$ ὅπως κατασκευασ[θ]ῆντι θησαυροὶ λίθινοι δύο κλαικτοί. See Meyer, p. 294, note. Cf. ποτικλαίγω.

κλᾱικοφόρος = κλειδοῦχος. Epid. K. 245 Ἥρωος κλαικοφόρου. This is an inscription on an architrave. Though this word seems clear, the meaning of the whole is obscure.

κλισμάκιον, *small ladder*. [356/5] CIA. IV, 682c$_{28}$. This word occurs in a list of various articles for the temple.

κλώστᾱς, minor Laconian official. [I] Lac. M. 56$_{21}$ = LeB.-F. 163a. The word stands in the list after καρνεονείκας and before π[α]ιανίας. It is evidently a derivative of κλώθω. Cf. κλωστός, κλωστήρ, which, however, means *spindle*. Cf. also Etym. Mag. 1417 κατάκλωθες and κλώθειν γὰρ τὸ νήθειν· ὅθεν καὶ κλώστης, παρὰ τὸν κλώσω μέλλοντα καὶ κλωστήρ.

κοιακτήρ, minor Laconian official. [I] Lac. M. 55a$_{52}$ = LeB.-F. 163b.c, 163d (κοακτήρ). Cf. Hesych. κοιάζω· ἐνεχυράζω and κοῖον· ἐνέχυρον. The word occurs in the following series: κάρυκες, μάντις, αὐλητάς, γραμματεύς, τὸν σὺν φέρων, ἐπιγράφων, κοιάκτηρ, μάγειρος. It is too low in the list for us to think of κοίης, *priest* and the word should rather be explained by the Hesychian glosses Cf. Gortynian ἐν-κοιωτάνς. This κοιακτήρ is probably the official in charge of the amounts deposited, perhaps for the expenses of the feast itself.

κονδύλωτον (?), *small ornament.* [V] CIA. IV, 652b₁₀ χρυσίδες τρεῖς καὶ [κονδ]ύλωτον ἕν, στέφανος θάλλοῦ. From κόνδυλος.

κονιᾱτήρ = κονιατής (?). [IV] Epid. 3325₂₅₁ = Epid. K. 241 Ἀντιφίλωι κονιατῆρι παρδειχμάτων. Cf. Hesych. κονιαταί· ἀσβεστήριοι καὶ οἱ χρῖ(σ)ται and Suid. οἱ τοὺς τοίχους παραχρίοντες. See Kavv., l. c., who says that the παρδείχματα are the models of the ornaments for the decoration of the temple.

κόριλλα, *infant girl.* [Late.] Boeot. 635, 963–965. Cf. CIGS. I, 713–722, 2901, 3516. This word is taken by Meister as a proper name. Dittenberger, however, in a note to 690, l. c., suggests that it is rather a diminutive of κόρη. This seems very probable. Cf. πάλλος.

κοτυλέος, *containing a κοτύλη.* Cos 3637₂₅ = PH. 38 ἐλαί[ου] τέτορες κοτυλέαι, 3638₁₂ = PH. 39 μέλιτος τέτορες κοτυλέαι. κοτυλέα, an abbreviation for χύτρα κοτυλέα. Cf. Bechtel, note to 3637.

κραδευτά, article of temple property. [356/5] CIA. IV, 682c₂₀ κ[ρ]αδευταί π[έντε].

κτοίνᾱ, *a division of territory* in Rhodes. [III] Rhodes, IG. Ins. 694 τὰς κτοίνας τὰς Καμιρέων, 736 ἐν τᾶι κτοίναι, 978 (Roman period). ὁ δ[ᾶμος ὁ Καρπαθιοπο[λιτᾶν κα]ὶ ἁ κτοίνα ἁ Ποτιδαέ[ων], 1033 ἁ κτοίνα ἁ Ποτι[δαι]έων —. Cf. Hesych. κτύναι ἢ κτοῖναι· χωρήσεις προγονικῶν ἱερείων. ἡ δῆμος μεμερισμένος. For full discussion of the κτοίνα see Holleaux and Diehl, BCH. 1885, 115; Gilbert II, pp. 181, 307. κτοίνα among the Rhodians corresponds to κώμη in Corcyra, Leos, and Lampsacus, δῆμος in Aegina, Miletus Cos, and Calymna. Members of the same κτοίνα came together as a religious association. They held assemblies, τὸ κοινὸν τᾶς κτοίνας, and voted decrees in honor of certain men. This division existed throughout Rhodes and the Rhodian colonies on the continent. Cf. 694 τὰς ἐν τᾷ νάσῳ καὶ τὰς ἐν τᾷ ἀπείρῳ. They lasted until a late period, as is shown by πτοίνας in BCH. 1885, 261. Cf. Ditt. Syll. 305, n. 2. From κτίζω. Kretschmer, KZ. 33, 272, would connect πτοίνα. But cf. ὀπτίλλος and references.

κτοινάτᾱς, *member of the κτοίνα.* [III] Rhodes, IG. Ins. 694₁₄ ἐγ δὲ ταυτᾶν τᾶν κτοινᾶν ἀποδεικνύειν τοὺς κτοινάτας μάστρον ἐν τῷ ἱερῷ τῷ ἁγιωτάτῳ.

κυκλίστρια, *dancer* (?). CIA. II, 4112 Σαννὼ χρηστὴ | ἀγαθὴ κυκλίστρια. Kumanudis, Ἀττικῆς ἐπιγραφαὶ ἐπιτύμβιοι 3292, reports that the two lines are far apart, with a vacant space between, where probably there was formerly a picture of the woman, which would make this word clear. He also cites Mod. Gr. ἀνατσιουκλίζω, which is used of some part of the weaving process. κυκλίζω = κυκλέω, κυκλόω is quoted in the Thesaurus as a rare verb.

κυμερέω, *guide, direct*. Cypr. 68₄ θεοῖς κυμερῆναι πά(ν)τα, τὰ ἄ(ν)θρωποι φρονέωί· χαίρετε. Hoffmann reads Θεῶι, otherwise the same. See GD. I, p. 212, where κυμερνήτης, Etym. M. 543, 2, is cited as Aeolic. Hoffmann thinks the stem κυβερ- is from the strong form κυμερ- and the β due to κυβρ- (from κυμρ-) by analogy. Cf. Blass-Kühner, Gr. Gr. I, p. 155, Meyer, p. 252. J. Schmidt, Sonanten-Theorie, p. 27, n. 1, takes *κυμρνᾶν to be a word of the vulgar speech. From this resulted *κυβρνᾶν, though written κυβερνᾶν either from want of a sign ṛ or by comparison with κυμερ-. Otherwise Osthoff, IF. VI, 13 f., who, comparing Skr. *kūb-ara-*, Lith. *kumb-ra-s*, concludes with Curtius that κυβ- is the older form of the root, beside which there was also a *κυμβ-. He thinks the assumption of Curtius of a development to *κυμμ- and simplification to κυμ- not impossible.

κωποξύστᾱς, *polisher of oars*. [II] Cos 3632₁₇ θυόντωι δὲ [καὶ σ]κανοπαγείσθων τοὶ κωποξύσται τ[ῶ]ι (Π)οτ(ε)ιδᾶνι καὶ Κῶ - -. Bechtel, l. c., cites Theophrast, Hist. plant. 5.1.7, δι' ὃ καὶ τὰς κώπας ξύοντες ἀφαιρεῖν πειρῶνται καθ' ἕνα καὶ ὁμαλῶς.

λαγάζω, *release, let go*. [VII/VI] Crete, Comp. 46 λαγάσαι (no context), Gort. Law-code I₅ λαγάσαι (slave) ἐν ταῖς τρισὶ ἀμέραις, 1. 24 τὸμ μὲν ἐλεύθερον λαγάσαι, I₇·₉·₂₇·₃₁ λαγάσηι; cf. also late Gort. ἀπολαγ- (above). These words are undoubtedly to be explained by the Hesychian gloss λαγάσσαι· ἀφεῖναι.

λαγαίω = λαγάζω. [VI] Crete, Comp. 148₄ τὸν κσένιον κοσμὸν μὴ λαγαίεν.

λατρειόω, *consecrate*. [VII/VI] Elis 1149₇ = Ol. 9 = Roberts 291 τάλαντον κ' ἀργύρω ἀποτίνοιαν τοῖ Δὶ Ὀλυνπίοι τοὶ καδαλήμενοι λατρειώμενον (ΛΑΤΡΕΙΟΜΕΝΟΝ), Elis 1147₇ = Ol. 1 = Roberts

290 Ζὶ 'Ολυνπίοι λατρα[ιώμενον...]. From λατρεῖος as οἰκειόω from οἰκεῖος. Cf. Dittenberger and Roberts, ll. cc.

λειτορεύω, *act as priest*. [II] Thess. 1329₁ λειτορεύοντος τοῖ 'Ασκ[λ]απιοῖ 'Αντιμάχοι Φιλιουνεί[ο]ι, Hoffmann, GD. II, no. 4 λειτορεύσαντα, no. 19₃ λειτορ(εύο)ντος. Cf. Hesych. λείτεραι· ἱέρειαι, λείτορες· ἱέρειαι. Hesychius also has the glosses λητῆρες; λήτειραι; ἀλήτωρ, which indicate that the ει is simply the Thessalian development of η, not original ει. Cf. Hoffmann, GD. II, p. 328.

λειώλης, *accursed*. [VII] Rhodes, IG. Ins. 737, Ζεὺ(δ) δέ νιν ὅστις πημαίνοι λειώλη θείη. Cf. Hesych. λεώλης· τελείως ἐξώλης. λεώλεθρος· παντελῶς ἐξωλεθρευμένος. This was first read correctly by Wackernagel, Mitth. 1891, 243, who says: "Auf λειώλη führte mich eine Bemerkung F. Dümmler's, der die Trennung in ein Synonym von ἐξώλης u. θείη verlangte; (cf. Hesych., etc.—) sowie wegen des ει in der ersten Silbe, λείως bei Archilochus, Fr. 112."

λευτόν, *offending* (animal)? [IV] Tegea, Hoffmann, GD. I, p. 23, no. 29₃ εἰ δ'ἂν λευτὸν (ΛΕVΤΟΝ) μὴ ἰνφορβίη. As Danielsson, Epigraphica, p. 37, shows, the word may be a present participle in the nominative agreeing with the subject, i. e., the hieromnemon, or it may be an adjective in the accusative denoting the animal, object of ἰνφορβίω, or an adverb which, as Danielsson remarks, seems less likely. Solmsen, KZ. 34, 447, puts aside Meister's translation, *losgelassenes*, and Hoffmann's *böses Tier*, the latter assuming a root which he connects with O. B. ḷi̯utŭ, Gk. λύσσα. Solmsen then discusses Danielsson's suggestion that the word may be a present participle from a root connected with German *liederlich, lotter*, Ags. *lýpre, elend, schlecht*, Russ. *lytát, sich herumtreiben*, Serv. *lutati*, and translates finally by *dolo malo*. But Solmsen translates ἰνφορβίω by *Weidegebühr eintreiben*. Cf. ἰνφορβίω. Considering both words, I take λευτόν, with some hesitation, as a neuter noun in the accusative denoting the offending animal.

λίθιος = λίθινος. [III] Thess. 345₂₁.₄₄ ἐν στάλλας λιθίας. 1332₃₂ [ἐν σταλλαν λι]θίαν. Lobeck, Phryn., p. 124, cites ὀρθρινός· ὄρθριος. Cf. also Lebadaean ἀγριελάϊνος, CIGS. I, 3073₁₈₈: Attic ἀγριέλαιος.

λιποτελέω, *leave unpaid taxes.* [V] Locris 1478_{15} = CIGS. III, 334 hόσστις κα λιποτελέηι (ΛΙΓΟΤΕΛΕΕΙ).

λισσός, *petition, request.* [III] Drerus, Cauer 121, C_{29} αἰ δὲ λισσὸς εἴη ἀγγραψάντων ἐς Δελφίνιον – –. From λίσσομαι. Cf. Hesych. λισσούς· δεομένους.

λιτροπώλης, *seller of λίτρον* (= νίτρον). [IV] CIA. III, Add. $834c_{21}$.

λῶαν, *discus* (?). [I] Lac. M. 57 = LeB.-F. 162a νεικάαντερ κασσηρατόριν μῶαν καὶ λῶαν. M. 59 is incomplete, but probably contains the same expression. Baunack's reading and interpretation, Rh. M. 38, 295, are probably correct. He assumes a dialectic variation of λαῦαν (cf. ὠτῶ for αὐτῶ in the same inscription) from λαϝ-αν = λᾶαν, comparing Lac. Λαναγήτας and Arg. Λανδίκα. In the Homeric poems λᾶς is frequently used for a stone hurled by the warrior (cf. Il. III, 80, IV, 521, and elsewhere), and in the Od. VIII, 192, it is used of the δίσκος. It seems quite probable that this inscription records a triple victory.

λωτίς, *undergarment, tunic* (?). [380] Delph. Amphyctionic decree, Cauer 204_{26} = CIA. II, 545 λωτίς. ἁ λωτίς ἀμφ...... (with space for about forty letters). Ahrens misread this word as δῶτις. Kretschmer, KZ. 30, 578, thinks it a derivative from λη-, translating *Beschluss* = βούλησις. But Danielsson, IF. IV, 164ff., argues that this meaning would involve a restoration which would be too long for the space. He suggests λω- as seen in λῶμα, λώπη, λῶπος, etc. It would be similar in form to other nouns denoting articles of dress, as ἀπληγίς, διπληγίς, διπλοίς, etc.

μάλινος, *made of fiber from μαλιναθάλλη*. Boeot. 714_6 = CIGS. I, 2421 χιτῶνα μάλινον κοριδίω παρπόρφυρον. Cf. Dittenberger, who quotes Theophr., Hist. plant. IV, 8, 12, ἐν δὲ τοῖς ἀμμώδεσι χωρίοις, ἅ ἐστιν οὐ πόρρω τοῦ ποταμοῦ, φύεται κατὰ γῆς ὅ καλεῖται μαλιναθάλλη. Doubtless the fiber of this plant was used for making cloth. Theophrastus, however, describes it only as an excellent food for grazing animals.

μανάσιος, Elean measure. [V] Elis 1168_5 = Ol. 18 = Roberts 300 φάρην κριθᾶν μανασίως (ΜΑΝΑϟΙΟϟ) δύο καὶ ϝίκατι. Cf. Hesych. μνασίον· μέτρον τι διμέδιμνον.; Epiph. de mens. et pond.

II, 178 μνάσις τοίνυν παρὰ Κυπρίοις μετρεῖται καὶ παρ' ἄλλοις ἔνθεσιν. For the first vowel compare Σαλαμώνα (= Σαλμώνη) of the same inscription; further Meyer, p. 162.

μαστράα, *revision, audit* (of accounts). [VI] Elis 1152₆ = Ol. 2 = Roberts 292. αἰ ζὲ μῆνποι ζίφυιον ἀποτινέτω ἐν μαστράαι. Cf. Hesych. μαστρίαι· αἱ τῶν ἀρχόντων εὔθυναι. See Dittenberger, l. c., who says the word is for *μαστρεία, a for ε as in κατιαραῦσειε, λατραί[ω]μεν 1147₇. He thinks the loss of ι between vowels should occasion no trouble in Elean, since there are so many anomalous writings in this dialect. μαστρεία would be a regular formation from μαστρός.

μασχαλιαίᾱ, a sort of *corner block*. [V] CIA. I, 322₉₈ μασχαλιαία μῆκος τετράπους, πλάτος τρίπους, πάχος τριῶν ἡμιποδίων.

μέρεια = μερίς. [IV] Tab. Heracl. I₁₈·₂₂·₂₈ (com.) ἐν ταύτᾳ τᾷ μερείᾳ. Cf. Hesych. μέρεια· φυλῆς μέρος ἐκ δέκα τρι(ακ)άδων συνεστός. The word is used in the same sentence with μερίς and apparently with no specialization of meaning.

μερισμός, *division, portion.* [I] Ephesus, Ditt. Syll. 344₁₈ τοὺς δὲ γενομένους — μερισμοὺς. l. 20 τοὺς ὅρους τῶμ μερισμῶν, l. 23.

μέσποδι, *until.* [214] Thess. 345₁₃ μέσποδί κε οὖν καὶ ἕτερος ἐπινοείσουμεν ἄξιος τοῖ - -. See Meyer, p. 40; J. Schmidt, Plur., p. 245. Notwithstanding Schmidt's arguments, it seems fairly certain that we have in this word, as in πεδά, a variation of the stem found in πούς. For the use of this and similar words see the section on synonyms.

μεστ', μεττ', *until.* [V] Gort. Law-code IX₄₈ τῶ μείονος μεττ' ἐς τὸ δεκαστάτηρον δ[ύ]ο ; Arcad. 1222₃₀ μεστ' ἂν ἀφῆ[τοι] τὰ ἔργα τὰ πλέονα. Cf. preceding. See Brugmann I, p. 742 ; J. Schmidt, Plur., p. 351.

μεύς = μήν, μείς, μής. [VI] Elis 1151₁₅ = Ol. 16 = Roberts 298. This is a new analogical formation μεύς : μηνός = Ζεύς : Ζηνός. See Solmsen, KZ. 29, 62; Schulze, Berl. Phil. Woch. 1890, 1404; Meyer, pp. 37, 408.

μηδαμεῖ = μηδαμοῦ. [V] Delph. BCH. 1895, 1 ff., C₃₅. Cf. τηνεῖ C₄₇, ἁμεῖ D₄₈.

μικκιχίδδομαι = μικίζομαι. [I] Lac. M. 58 βουαγὸρ μικκιχιδδομένων. Cf. Bachmann, Anecd. 2, p. 355 παρὰ Λακεδαιμονίοις ἐν τῷ πρώτῳ ἐνιαυτῷ ὁ παῖς ῥωβίδας καλεῖται, τῷ δευτέρῳ προμικιζόμενος, τῷ τρίτῳ μικιζόμενος – –.

μωλέω, *contest, bring suit.* [VII] Gort. Comp. 1–2 ὅ κα πάθηι μωλέν (ΜΟΛΕΝ), 146 V, 151 (Law-code) I₁₄ αἰ δέ κα μωλῆι (ΜΟΛΕΙ) ὁ μὲν ἐλεύθε[ρ]ον ὁ δ[ὲ δ]ῶλον, ll. 17, 49, V₄₄ (com.). Cf. ἀντιμωλέω, ἀπομωλέω, ἀντίμωλος, ἀμωλεῖ, ἐπιμωλέω. Hesych. μ[ω]λεῖ· μάχεται. καὶ ἀντιμωλία δίκη, εἰς ἣν οἱ ἀντίδικοι παραγίνονται; μωλήσεται· μαχήσεται. See Baunack, Insc. v. Gort., p. 63; Comparetti, l. c., p. 140. The latter says that the word is certainly to be transcribed with -ω-, notwithstanding the form ἑτερομόλιος which is found in Suidas, Zonaras, etc. It is then to be directly connected with the Homeric μῶλος. This explanation of the word is generally accepted, but compare Bücheler u. Zitelmann, Das Recht v. Gort., p. 14, where it is taken from the root μολ-, *losgehen auf etwas.*

νᾱεύω, *seek refuge in a temple.* [V] Gort. Law-code I₃₉·₄₂ αἰ δέ κα ναεύηι ὁ δῶλος – –. Comp. 152 IV₈ τὸν δὲ ϝοικέα τὸν ἐπιδιόμενον μὴ ἀπόδοθθαι μήτε ναεύοντα – –. Cf. Hesych. ναύω· λίσσομαι. ἱκετεύω. See also ἀπονάϝω and ναόω.

νᾱόω, *bring into a temple.* Cret. Mus. It. III, p. 637₁₆ ναωσάντων δ᾽ ὁ κόσμος κατ᾽ ἕκαστον ἐ(νι)αυτὸν [τὰν ἀγέ]λαν – –. l. 24 αἰ δὲ μὴ ναώσαιεν τὰν ἀγέλαν ἀποτ[ει]σ[άντων] ὁ κόσμος.

ναῦσθλον, *passage-money*, ναῦλον. Troiz. 3362₁₃ ἐ]φ[ό]διον καὶ ναῦσθλον Φιλίσκωι. Cf. Hesych. ναῦσθλον· ναῦλον. See Töpffer, Mitth. 1891, 417.

ναῦσσον, *tax on sea-traffic.* [II] Cos 3632₁ ὁ τὰν ὠνὰν ἐωνημένος ναύσσου ἔξω, etc. l. 2 θυόντωι δὲ καὶ τοὶ ἐωνημένοι ὠνὰν ναύσσου ἄρτων, κάπων κατ(ὰ) [ταὐ]τό; Ion. 108b καὶ τοῖσιν Αἰσήπου παισὶν . . . . καὶ πρυτανεῖον δέδοται παρὲξ ΝΑΥ : ΠΤΟ. This last word was first explained by J. Töpffer, Mitth. 1891, 418. He discusses the Coan word and infers from this Cyzicus inscription that the traffic by sea was regulated by the state, which exacted a prescribed tax. Wackernagel, Rh. M. 48, 299, pronounces this "höchst scharfsinnig" and further discusses the result of this identification, p. 300; the -σσ- of the loan ναῦσσον is to be compared with the -σσ- of Ἁλικαρνασσός Πανύασσις, not with -σσ- in πρήσσω. It is not then a derivative from ναῦς, but a Carian loanword meaning *tribute, tax*. So also Meyer, p. 369, note, and Keil, Hermes 29, 270.

ναυτιλεῖον, *place for sailors.* [189/167] Cos 3632$_{11}$ ἐπὶ ναυτιλέοι. This word is taken by Bechtel, 1. c., as dative of ναυτιλεῖον with loss of ι as in Ἀλεξανδρεᾶν. For this meaning of the suffix -εῖον he compares ἀρχεῖον, διδασκαλεῖον.

νεϝώστατος, *last.* Cypr. 59$_2$ τὰν ἐ]παγομενᾶν τῶ πε(μ)φαμέρων νεϝοστάτας. There is no doubt as to the meaning of this word, but its formation is open to question. Meister, GD. II, pp. 147, 245, would see a compound of νεϝο- and στατός, comparing νεοκατάστατος, νεόσσυτος. Deecke-Siegismund, Curt. Stud. VII, p. 237, and Ahrens, Philol. 35, 77, take it as a superlative of νέος. This would be an irregular formation, but it might be easily due to analogy with stems in -ες and -ις. Hoffmann, GD. I, p. 275, suggests the reading taken above, and derives from νεϝωτ-. He compares νέωτα, νεώσσω, and for the form in -τατος from an adverb— κατώτατος, ὀπίστατος. This would dispose of the phonetic difficulty in Ahrens' suggestion, and seems to be preferable to the asumption of a compound.

ξενοδίκᾱς, *judge of cases in which strangers are concerned* [V] Locris 1479$_{10}$ = CIGS. III, 333 αἴ κ' ἀνδιχάζωντι τοὶ ξενοδίκαι – –; Phocis 1539a$_{38}$ μὴ ἔστω δὲ ἐπάναγ[κ]ες λειτουργεῖν τοὺς Μεδεωνίους ἐν Στίρι τὰς ἀρχάς, ὅσοι γεγένηνται ἐν Μεδεῶνι ἄρχοντες, ξενοδίκαι, πακτῆρες, etc. Cf. Roberts, p. 357.

ξοάνιον, *small image.* Anaphe 3430$_{12}$ [ὁ]πεῖ ὁ βωμὸς τοῦ Κτησίου καὶ τὸ ξοάνιον.

ξυλοπώλης, *wood-seller.* [III(?)] CIA. II, Add. 834c$_{17·35}$. Cf. Hesych. συρμιστήρ· ξυλοπώλης.

ὀδελονόμος, *official of Troizene.* [III] Troiz. 3364b$_{42}$ ὀδελον[ό]μοι Κλεωνίδας Κλει[σ]θέναος, etc.

οἴη, *village.* [IV] Ion., Bechtel 183$_{44}$ = BCH. 1879, 244 ff. πόλιν καὶ τὴν οἴην, 201$_{27}$ (no context). Cf. Hesych. οἰαταν· κωμητῶν, οἷαι γὰρ αἱ κῶμαι; Herodian I, 302$_9$ Οἴα, ἡ κώμη; also Attic

Οα, Ὦα, the name of a deme of the tribe of Pandionis; Ὤη (Οἰῆθεν), a deme of Oineus. See Smyth, Ionic Dialects, p. 21, note. The Chian inscription in which this word occurs, Bechtel 183, is Hellenistic, with traces of the local dialect. Cf. ἐνηλάσιον, ἀίδασμος, etc.

ὁλοκαύτησις, *holocaust.* [III] Epid. K. 244$_{1,12,15}$ εἰς τὴν ὁλοκαύτησιν. Cf. Hesych. ὁλοκαύτωμα· ὅλον πυρὶ καθαγιζόμενον. This inscription, with the exception of three words, is written in the Attic dialect.

ὁμάλιξις = ὁμαλισμός. [IV] Arg. BCH. 1893, 116$_{15}$ τῶι στρώματι καὶ ὁμαλίξιος τοῦ χ[ωρίου].

ὁμοστεγέω, *live under the same roof.* Cnid. 3540 ἐμοὶ δὲ ἦ<η>όσια καὶ ἐλεύθερα ὁμοστεγησάσῃ. This occurs in an imprecation against a slanderer. From ὁμόστεγος.

ὁμωμότᾱς, *one who takes the oath with another.* [VII/VI] Crete, Comp. 12–13$_{3}$ (without context) οἱ ὀμωμόται (OMOMOTAI); 203$_{13}$ (Lyttus.) O]MΘMOTAϟ (without context). See Insc. Jurid. Gr., p. 434.

ὄναιος, *profitable.* Thess. (found at Dodona) 1559 Κλεούτα(ς) asks the oracle αἴ ἐστι αὐτοῖ προβατεύοντι (ὄ)ναιον καί ὠφέλιμον. Cf. Hesych. ὄναιον· ἄρειον. From ὀνίνημι.

ὀνάλᾱ = ἀνάλωμα. [III] Thess. 345$_{22,45}$ καὶ τὰν ὀνάλαν κίσκε γινύειτει ἐν τάνε δόμεν. ὀνάλουμα occurs in 361A$_{13}$, B$_{25}$. ὄ(ν)αλον, 1332$_{20}$ = Hoffmann, GD. II, p. 15, no. 7$_{20}$, is doubtful, as the text is incomplete. From ἀναλίσκω.

ὀνημάξιον, *donkey carriage.* Cos PH. 36a$_{4}$ ἀνέθηκε [δὲ] καὶ τοὺς ξενῶνας τοὺς ἐν τῷ κάπῳ καὶ τὰ ὀνημάξια – –.

ὄπι, generalizing particle. [IV] Cypr. 60$_{29}$ (Edal.) ὄπι σίς κε τὰς ϝρήτας τάσδε λύσῃ, etc. Cf. Brugmann, Gr. Gr., p. 54, note, who takes -π- for -τ- by analogy. Meister, GD. II, p. 154, reads with Curtius (Stud. VII, p. 256) ὄφι σίς κε, *wo* (*in welchem Punkte*) *immer einer.* He compares ὅθι, Lat. *u-bi;* Hoffmann, GD. I, p. 73, takes as ὄπυι, setting up the equation ὄπι : ὄπυι = πληθί : πληθυῖ. The word seems to be rather generalizing in use than temporal.

ὄπυι, *where.* [V] Gort. Law-code IV$_{15}$ ὄπυι ἐπελεύσῃι—. See Meyer, pp. 202, 395; Brugmann I, pp. 185, 595.

ὄπυς, *where.* Rhodes 1568₂ (found at Dodona). ὄπυς κα δοκῆι σύμφορον ἔμειν. For full treatment of these forms see J. Schmidt, KZ. 32, 394 ff. Cf. Boisacq, DD., pp. 76, 77.

ὀπυστύς, *wedlock.* [VII/VI] Gort. Comp. 18 αἰ μή ϙ' ὀπυστυῖ (without context). Comparetti thinks this is a derivative from ὀπυίω, formed in the same way as ἀμφαντυῖ, from ἀμφαίνω. He would, however, consider the latter an adverb, although it is rather to be taken as a substantive. For the σ cf. ὠπυσμένος. See Solmsen, KZ. 29, 113; Kühner-Blass II, p. 503.

ὀρκυνεῖον, *place for keeping or curing tunnies* (ὄρκυνοι). Ion. Bechtel 240₄₄ καὶ τὴν θάλασσαν ὅπου τὸ ὀρκυνεῖον. See Ditt. Syll. 6, n. 12; Newton, Essays, p. 428.

ὀρκωμότᾱς, *juror, judge.* [V] Locris 1479 B₁₇ = CIGS. III, 333 δαμιωργὼς hελέσται τὼς hορκωμότας (HOPKOMOTAΣ) ἀριστίνδαν, τὰν πεντορκίαν ὀμόσαντας. Cf. Poll. I, 39 ὀρκωμοτέω - - ὀρκωμότας.

ὀρφανοδικαστᾱ́ς, *dicast who has oversight of orphans.* [V] Gort. Law-code XII₂₃ ταῖς πατρωιώκοις, αἴ κα μὴ ἴωντι ὀρφανοδικασταί, ἃς κ' ἄνωροι ἴωντι χρῆθαι κατὰ τὰ ἐγραμμ(έ)να.

ὀσπρεύω, *plant with beans.* [300] CIA. II, 600₂₃ σ[π]ερεῖ δὲ τῆς γῆς σίτῳ τ[ή]ν ἡμίσειαν, τῆς δὲ ἀργοῦ ὀσπρεύσει ὁπό[ση]ν ἂν βούληται. ὄσπριον occurs on a Coan inscription 3632₁₅.

οὐροφύλαξ, *official having to do with boundaries.* [V] Ion. Bechtel, 174a₁₇ πρηξάντων δ' οὐροφύλακες · ἢν δὲ μὴ πρήξοισιν, αὐτοὶ ὀφειλόντων, πρηξάντων δ' οἱ πεντεκαίδεκα τοὺς οὐροφύλακας.

παί, *generalizing particle.* [IV] Cypr. (Edal.) 60₁₂ ἰδέ παι; Corcyra 3206₁₂₇ ἢ καταχρήσαιτο ἄλλαι παι - -.

παιᾱνίας, *name of official.* [I] Lac. M. 55b₅₄. From παιάν.

πάιλλος, *infant boy.* Boeot. CIGS. I, 699, 709, 2900, 3118, 3515. Cf. SGDI. 643, 698. This word occurs alone, and Meister writes it as a proper name, but Dittenberger, l. c., 690, thinks πάιλλος and κορίλλα are rather to be taken as diminutives. They occur only on grave inscriptions and may be, as Dittenberger suggests, used of children who died before the time of naming.

πᾱματοφαγέω, *confiscate.* [V] Locris 1478₄₁ = CIGS. III, 334 ἄτιμον εἶμεν καὶ χρήματα παματοφαγεῖσται.

πᾱμωχέω, *possess*. [IV] Tab. Heracl. I$_{14}$ τὸν Κωνέας ho Δίωνος ἐπαμώχη, I$_{168}$ τὰ Φιντίας ho Κρατίνω παμωχεῖ. Cf. Hesych. παμωχιῶν· κεκτημένος ; παμῶχος· ὁ κύριος.

πανάζωστοι, *whole body of* ἄζωστοι. [III] Drerus, Cauer 121$_{10}$ τάδε ὠμόσαν ἀγελάοι πανάζωστοι. For full discussion of this term see Danielsson, Epigraphica, pp. 1 ff. He concludes that it is a word similar in form and meaning to παναχαιοί, πανέλληνες and means ἀγελάοι (= ἀζωστοί) πάντες. He then takes up the meaning of ἀζωστοί. It does not signify unarmed, but rather having the equipment which belongs to the oldest ephebes who have not yet come to the full rights of manhood. It is uncertain whether the form is original ἄ-ζωστος or for *ἄνζωστος = ἀνάζωστος. Cf. Danielsson, l. c., p. 12, note. See ἀγελάος.

παντοβαρής, *very grievous, oppressive*. [II] Acarn. CIGS. III, 489 ὁ παντοβαρής λάβε μ' "Αιδης (metrical inscription).

πανώνιος, *with all salable products*. [IV] Cypr. 60$_{10}$ δυϝάνοι νυ – – τὸν χῶρον – – κὰς τὰ τρέχνιϙα τὰ ἐπιόντα πάντα ἔχεν πανώνιον – – ἀτελην. l. 22 πανωνίος (acc. pl.). See Hoffmann, GD. I, pp. 71, 155, who would explain as compound of παν + ὄνιος, deriving the latter from ὀνίνημι and translating by *nützlich*. Cf. Meister, GD. II, p. 225. Solmsen, KZ. 32, 288, gives a full discussion with derivation and explanation as above.

παραμαξεύω, *drive aside from*. [IV] Arcad. (Teg.), Hoffmann I, p. 23, no. 29$_{23}$ εἰ κ'ἂν παραμαξεύη θύσθην τᾶς κελε[ύθ]ω τᾶς κακειμέναυ κατ' Ἀλέαν, etc. Cf. Danielsson, Epigraphica, p. 56.

πάραξ, *sacrificial cake*. [I] Thera Cauer 148 F$_3$ καὶ ἄρτον καὶ πάρακα καὶ ὀψάρια – –. Hesych. βάραξ· φύραμα στρογγύλον ἀφ' οὗ αἱ μάζαι γίνονται ; βήραξ· μάζα μεγάλη ; βήρηκες· μᾶζαι ὀρθαί. οἱ δὲ ἀπλῶς μάζας, ἄλλοι μάζας ἄνωθεν κέρατα ἐχούσας. Confusion between surd and sonant is not so common in labials as in dentals, but compare πιστάκια : βιστάκια Eust. Hom. 1210$_{42}$ and the Phocian βρυτανευόντων for πρυτανευόντων, BCH. 1887, 324. See Ahrens II, p. 584 ; Meyer, p. 273.

παραπιτνάω, *let fall around*. [346/5] Ion. 220$_{20}$ ἥντιν[α] τῆι θεῶι παραπιτνῶσι.

παραπροστάτας, *assistant presiding officer*. [211] Agrig. Cauer 199₃ = IG. Sic. et It. 952₃ ἐπὶ ἱεροθύτα Νυμφοδώρου τοῦ Φίλωνος, παραπροστά(τα) τᾶς βουλᾶς. Cauer reads παραπροστα-(τούσας).

παρεντυγχάνω, *happen to be near*. [II] Delph. 1716 κύριος ἔστω ὁ παρεντυχών.

παρετάζω = ἐξετάζω. [IV] Arcad., Hoffmann, GD. I, p. 23, no. 29₂₀ εἰ μὴ παρhεταξαμένος τὸς πεντήκοντα ἢ τὸς τριακοσίος., 1222₂₈ ὅτινι ἄμ μὴ οἱ ἁλιαστα[ὶ] παρετάξωνσι ὁμοθυμαδὸν πάντες, etc. Cf. Hesych. παρήτασεν· ἐξήτασεν. See Danielsson, Epigr., p. 53.

παρκάλισις, *removal of crating*. [IV] Epid. K. 242 παρκαλίσιος τῶν λίθων ἐπὶ λιμένι. See διακάλισις.

πασσυδιάζω, *assemble, convene*. [2 B. C./14 A. D.] Aeol. 311₅ πασσυδιάσαντος. Cf. Hesych. πανσυδίη. ὁμοῦ πάντες.

πάστᾱς, *owner*. [VI] Gort. Law-code II₃₂ τοῦ δὲ δώλου τῶι πάσται ἀντὶ μαιτύρων δυῶν. II₄₃, III₅₄, IV₂·₅·₂₀·₂₂. Comp. 152 I₁₆, 184₃, 171₁₀(?). From πᾰ- in πᾶμα, etc. For suffix compare θύστας· ὁ ἱερεὺς παρὰ Κρησί. Hesych. See Baunack, Ins. v. Gort., p. 75.

πατριαστί, *according to paternal descent*. [230] Cos. 3705₃₂ = PH. 367 εἰ δὲ μή, ἀπογραφέσθων αὐτοί, ἐπεί κα παραγένωνται, ἐν τριμήνωι τὸ ὄνομα πατριαστὶ ποτὶ τὸς ναποίας. From πατριάζω. For similar adverbs, ὀνομαστί, etc., see Blass-Kühner II, p. 303.

παύστωρ = παυστήρ. [II] Epid. 3340, IV₅₀ (Isyllus) τὸν νόσων παύστορα. This word is used of Aesculapius.

πεδίσκᾱ, *anklet*. [II] Boeot. CIGS. I, 2420₂₇ χειριπέδας κὴ πεδίσκας ἀργουρίας. Dim. of πέδη. This word occurs in a list of ornaments in the temple.

πειθόω = πείθω. [III] Boeot. 488₅₈·₁₁₆ ἐπίθωσαν, ἐπίθωσε. It is uncertain whether these forms are to be taken as representing πειθόω or πιθόω, but the former seems somewhat more probable.

πενθημίγυος, *land containing five semijugera*. [IV] Tab. Heracl. II₂₀·₃₀ ἀλλὰ πενθημίγυον μόνον κατελείπετο ἐκ τῶν δυῶν τριγύων.

πεντᾱμαριτεύω, *perform five days' sacrifice*. [V] Delph. BCH. 1895, 1 ff., D_{16} καίκα πενταμαριτεύων τύχηι. This clause occurs in a passage discussed under ἄλεκχος. The word is similar in form to μεσιτεύω, πολιτεύω, etc., hence *πενταμαρίτᾱs is to be assumed, which, as Keil says, Hermes 31, 512, would imply *hold office lasting five days*, rather than *perform a sacrifice on the fifth day*. Homolle, l. c., p. 25, offers both suggestions. The -αρ- is to be taken with Keil as dialectic and not due to derivation from ἆμαρ.

πεντορκίᾱ, *oath of the five gods*. [V] Locris 1479_{17} = CIGS. III, 333 τὰν πεντορκίαν ὀμόσαντες. The above is the interpretation given by Kirchhoff.

περιβολιβόω, *surround with lead*. [III] Rhodes, IG. Ins. 694_{10} = Ditt. Syll. 305 καὶ στᾶσαι (τὰν στάλαν) ἐν τῶι ἱερῶι τᾶς 'Αθάνας καὶ περιβολιβῶσαι ὡς ἔχηι ὡς ἰσχυρότατα καὶ κάλλιστα. See βόλιμος.

περιχύτρισμα, *space dug down around a tree*. [344/3] CIA. II, 1055_{44} καὶ μύκητας καταλιπεῖν μὴ ἔλαττον ἢ (π)αλα(σ)τιαίους ἐν τοῖς περιχυτρίσμασιν. Cf. χύτρα, χυτρῖνος.

περιστεμματόω, *wreathe around*. [I] And.$_{36}$ ἐν ᾧ ἂν τόπῳ περιστεμματώσωντι οἱ ἱεροί—.

περτ᾽ = πρός. Pam. 1260 δαμιοργίσωσα περτέδωκ᾽ εἰς ἐρεμνὶ καὶ πυλῶνα ἀργύρυ μνᾶς φίκατι; 1261 (same use). Cf. Gort. πορτί, Ep. προτί. One cannot help the conviction that these words are to be taken together, notwithstanding the fact that Brugmann, in his latest edition, I, p. 436, still considers them different formations   Meister, GD. I, p. 44, cites an Aeol. πρές from a late grammarian. It would seem that ablaut change and mixture between two of the forms gave rise to the four forms cited. Brugmann also still connects directly with the Umbrian form. For this comparison see Buck, Vocalismus, p. 71. Cf. also Meyer, p. 63.

πετρών, *rocky, stony place*. [III] Rhodes, Cauer $179b_{29\cdot 30}$ ἀπὸ δὲ τούτου ἀναβαίνουσι ποτὶ τὸν πετρῶνα ἄλλον ὅρον ἐπεκολάψαμεν εἰς τὸν πετρῶνα· ἀπὸ δὲ τούτου ἐν τῷ πετρῶνι – –.

πήποκα = πώποτε. [V] Lac. M. 27_5 νικάhας ταυτâ hâτ᾽ ο[ὐ]δὴς πήποκα (ΓΕΠΟΚΑ) τῶν νῦν. See Meyer, p. 484; Ahrens, DD. II, p. 363.

πίσσασις, *sealing with pitch*. [IV] Epid. 3325 B = K. 241[157]·-[238·245·255·278] πισσάσιος τοῦ ἐργαστηρίου and πισσάσιος θυρᾶν τοῦ ἐργαστηρίου. This word is the equivalent of Attic πίττωσις. See Aus Epid., p. 77.

πλάγος, *side*. [IV] Tab. Heracl. I[66·74] τὼς μὲν ἐς τὸ hιαρὸν πλάγος τῶ ἀντόμω ἐπιγεγραμμένως, etc.

πλανεῖος, *vagabond*. [II] Mant. BCH. 1896, 119 περὶ τ[ᾶς ἐξ]ώσεως τῶν πλανείων. Cf. note, p. 121. The meaning is somewhat doubtful, but the phrase would seem to refer to the expulsion of vagabonds.

πλῆμα (?), *water reservoir*. [I] And.[106] μήτε [τὸ] πλῆμα (ΗΛΕΜΑ) μήτε τοὺς ὀχετοὺς --. This is the reading given by Kumanudis and by Curtius, though the stone shows H. Cf. Sauppe, Ausgewählte Schriften, p. 282, n. 104; Hesych. πλῆμα· πλήρωμα.

πλύνιον, *pit holding water used in washing*. Acrae 3246[35] θέμ(α) ποτὶ πλυνίοις. Another rare diminutive, φρήτιον = φρεάτιον, occurs in this inscription.

πόθικες (pl.) = προσήκοντες. [V] Lac. M. 21b τοὶ (ἄσ)σιστα πόθικες ἀνελόσθω. See Roberts, p. 360; Meister, Ber. d. sächs. G. d. W. 1896, 273. The latter suggests a noun πόθιξ : ποθίκω = προίξ : προίκω, although he expresses some doubt as to the genuineness of the form.

ποθόδωμα = πρόσοδος. [III] Boeot. 488[160] πόρον δ' ε[ἶ]μεν ἐν οὔτο ἀπὸ τῶν τᾶς [π]όλιος ποθοδωμάτων πάντ[ων]; Epirus 1339[5] ποθόδωμα γραψαμένου Λυσανία τοῦ Νικολάου Καριώπου περὶ προξενίας Γαίω, etc.

ποῖ = πρός. [V] Locris 1479[14] = CIGS. III, 333 ποῖ τὸν ϝάστον; Arg. (Epid.) 3339[3·23·56·67·62], Troiz. 3362[9·21·27], Hermione 3385[19]. It is found in compounds in 3339[17]; Boeot. 553[13], and in the Delph. Ποιτρόπιος, name of a month. In origin it is the same as Lett. *pî*, Lith. *apē̃*. Cf. Bezzenberger, BB. VII, 94.

πολιᾱτεύω = πολιτεύω. [V] Gort. Law-code IV[33] πολιατεύηι (ΠΟΛΙΑΤΕVΕΙ).

πόλιστος = πλεῖστος. [IV] Tab. Heracl. I[130]. This word was first explained satisfactorily by Homolle, BCH. 1891, 627.

πορτί = πρός. [V] Gort. Law-code V_{44}, VI_{54}, XI_{30}, $IX_{30 \cdot 50}$, Comp. 153 II_2, and in compound 191_8. See περτ'. Cf. Meyer, p. 245.

πός = πρός. [IV] Cypr. 60 $A_{19 \cdot 21}$; Arcad. 1222_{54}, also in compounds. See Bechtel, BB. X, 287; Kretschmer, KZ. 30, 569. This word is to be taken from πότ-ς, not from ποτί. Cf. Hoffmann, GD. I, pp. 200, 311.

ποτεξορκίζω, *take an additional oath.* [I] And.$_8$ τὰς δὲ ἱερὰς ὁρκιζέτω ὁ ἱερεὺς καὶ οἱ ἱεροὶ - - τὸν αὐτὸν ὅρκον καὶ ποτεξορκιζόντω· Πεποίημαι δὲ, etc.

ποτιδατέομαι, *assign.* [IV] Tab. Heracl. $II_{54 \cdot 60 \cdot 68}$ (com.) ποτεδασσάμεθα.

ποτικλάίγω, *hem in, border on.* [IV] Tab. Heracl. II_{69} τὰν τρίταν διαστολὰν ἀφ' ἑκατομπέδω τὰν ποτικλαίγωσαν - -. II_{107} ϝέκτα μερὶς τὸ ἔγγωνον τὸ πὰρ τὰς ἀμπέλως τὸ ποτίκλαιγον - -. This is a new formation from the Doric aorist. Cf. κλαίγω. See Meyer, p. 294, note.

πράκτιμος, *subject to exaction.* [150-140] Delph. 1686_{10} πράκτιμοι ἐόντων κατὰ τὸν νόμον τᾶς πόλιος. 1694, 1697, and others. For similar expressions see section on synonyms. πρακτός is used in the Theran inscription, Cauer 148.

πρεγγευτάς, πρειγευτάς, πρεισγευτάς = πρεσβευτής. Cret., LeB.-F. $75_{4 \cdot 16}$ πρεγγευταί; Cauer 127_8 πρειγευτᾶ; 127_{11} πρεισγευτᾶν, while in l. 23 πρεσβευταί is found. See Brugmann I, p. 755; also Meyer, p. 184.

πρείγιστος = πρεσβύτατος. [V] Gort. Law-code VII_{18} πρειγίστωι, $VII_{23 \cdot 27}$ πρειγίστω. Cf. Brugmann I, 510, 595; Meyer, p. 184, note.

πρείγων = πρεσβύτερος. [VI] Gort. Law-code XII_{34} ὀπυίεθαι δὲ δυωδεκαϝέτια ἢ πρείγονα.

πρηγιστεύω, *act as πρεσβύς.* [I] Cos 3742 = PH. 117. Bechtel, l. c., compares the relation of πρη- to πρει- with that of ἤ to εἰ, which would make πρη- identical with the same form in πρηών, Att. πρών, and πρει-, with old Lat. *pri.* Cf. πρηγιστής, BCH. 1888, 282.

πρισγύς = πρεσβύς. [IV] Boeot. 705_6 πρισγείες.
See Brugmann, Grundriss I, p. 595. These forms are largely due to analogical formations, and nothing certain is known about

the latter part of the word, though probably the same element is to be seen in ἐγγύς, μεσσηγύ(ς), possibly also in Lith. *žmogùs*, Skr. *vanargú*. Cf. Brugmann, Ber. sächs. G. d. W. 1889, 53 ; Meyer, p. 268.

προάνγρεσις = προαίρεσις. [III] Thess. 361 B₁₄ ἔδο]ξε τοῦ κοινοῦ τᾶς πόλιος [ἐπαινεῖσθαι] Λίοντα ἑττᾶ προανγρέ[σι]. See ἀγρέω.

προκαυτεύω, *burn first*. [IV] Cos 3637₁₂ = PH. 38 κα[ὶ] χο[ῖ]ρος προκαυτεύεται καὶ προκαρύσσεται καθάπερ τῶι Πολιῆι. This is, according to Paton, the sacrifice indicated in the expression καθαίρεται χοίρωι.

προπραξίᾱ, *precedence in right of execution*. [IV] Acarn. CIGS. III, 442 προνομίαν καὶ προπραξίαν αὐτοῖς καὶ γενεᾶι.

προσχάραιος, *as a thank-offering*. [IV] Rhodes, IG. Ins. 791 προσχάραιος θυσία.

προτενσῖτεύω, *be first on the list of σιτηθέντες*. [I] Lac. LeB.-F. 281 B. προτενσιτε[ύ]οντος Νικηφόρου.

προτεράσιος = πρότερος. [168] Delph. 1746₄ τὰν προτερασίαν ὠνὰν, etc., 2143₁₀ ἁ δὲ προτερασία ὠνά. See Baunack, l. c. This formation is similar to that of δοκιμασία : δοκιμάζω : δόκιμος ; hence we may assume a verb *προτεράζω beside προτερίζω.

προτερεῖος = προτεραῖος. [IV] Tab. Heracl. I₁₀₁ μηνὸς προτερείαι.

προχαρής, *as a thank-offering*. [I] Lac. M. 56a₁₂ ἄρτον προχαρέα. Cf. προσχάραιος.

πρωγγυεύω = προεγγυάω. [IV] Tab. Heracl. I₁₅₅ πεπρωγγυευκῆμεν. προεγγυάω is cited in the Thesaurus as a late verb. Cf. κατεγγυεύω.

πρωτοκοσμέω, *be chief κόσμος*. Crete (Lyttus), BCH. 1889, 61, no. 6₃ τὸν δὲ πρωτοκοσμοῦντα κατ' ἔτος − −.

πρωτόκοσμος, *chief κόσμος*. Crete (Lyttus), Mus. It. III, p. 668 π[ρωτο]κόσμου, p. 669 πρωτοκόσμου.

πτοίνᾱ = κτοίνα. Rhodes, BCH. 1886, 261 τὸ κοινὸν τᾶς πτοίνας. Kretschmer, KZ. 33, 272, would take this as a phonetic equivalent of κτοίνα. For discussion and references see ὀπτίλλος (Rare Words).

ῥάκινος, *ragged*. [IV] Ion., Bechtel 220₁₈ περίβλημα λίνου ῥάκινον, l. 25 καταπέτασμα τῆς τραπέζης ῥάκινον. The Thesaurus gives this word as a gloss in Panneus.

ῥογεύς, *dyer*. [I] Lac. M. 56₂₆. The word occurs in a list of temple officials. Cf. Hesych. ῥογεύς· βαφεύς. This form, as compared with ῥεγεύς, ῥηγεύς, shows the normal ablaut form. Cf. τοκεύς, φορεύς, φονεύς, φθορεύς, etc.

ῥογός, *place for storing grain*. [IV] Tab. Heracl. I₁₀₂ ἀπάξοντι (grain) ἐς τὸν δαμόσιον ῥογὸν καὶ παρμετρήσοντι τοῖς σιταγέρταις – –. Cf. Hesych. ῥογοί· ὅροι σιτικοί, σιτοβολῶνες; Pollux 9₄₅ ἐν δὲ Μενάνδρου Εὐνούχῳ καὶ σιτοβόλια· ταῦτα δὲ ῥογοὺς Σικελιῶται ὠνόμαζον. Kaibel, IG. Sic. et It. 645, defines by *horrea frumentaria*, and thinks the word is of Italic origin. Cf. Meister, Curt. Stud. IV, p. 442; Jordan, Hermes 15, 13; Meyer, p. 238. In BB. XIV, 41, Foy discusses this word at some length, giving modern citations to prove that the word is not originally Italic. He thinks it is to be taken in the Heraclean Tables to mean *kellerartiger Aufbewahrungsort*, which would accord with the modern use of the word.

σαρμεύω, *dig holes or trenches*. [IV] Tab. Heracl. I₁₃₆ οὐδὲ γαιῶνας θησεῖ πὰρ τὼς ὑπάρχοντας οὐδὲ σαρμευσεῖ. Cf. Hesych. σαρμός· σωρὸς γῆς καὶ κάλλυσμα. ἄλλοι ψάμμον. ἄλλοι χόρτον; σάρματα· καλλύσματα· καὶ κόπρια παρὰ Ῥίνθωνι – –. Cf. Meister, Curt. Stud. IV, p. 442.

σιταγέρτᾱς, *supervisor of public supplies of grain*. [IV] Tab. Heracl. I₁₀₂·₁₁₀·₁₇₇. See ἀγέρτᾱς.

σιτωνικόν = σιτωνία. [I] Aeg. 3417₈ [ὅλου τοῦ] σιτωνικοῦ κατ[αναλισκομ]ένου εἰσ[φέρων στατῆρας, etc.

σκιλλαῖον, dim. of σκίλλα. [II] Aeol., Hoffmann, GD. II, p. 66, no. 90₁₄ ἐν τῷ χωρίῳ τῷ ἐπάνω τὰ σκιλλάω[ν καὶ σκορό]δω φύτα.

σπάδιον = στάδιον. [V] Arg. 3267 τετράκι τε [σ]πάδιον νίκη, etc. Cf. Hesych. σπάδιον· τὸ στάδιον. The word is also found in Etym. M. and Greg. Cor., p. 364 (Schaefer). See Meyer, p. 332. The relation of the word to στάδιον is uncertain. It would seem that this word is related to Lat. *spatium*.

σπονδαύλης, *flute player at a* σπονδή. Rheg., IG. Sic. et It. 617, 618.

στέγασις = στέγασμα. [IV] Epid. 3325₂₈₇·₃₀₄ = K. 241 στεγάσσιος, l. 41. Cf. Baunack, Aus Epid., p. 90; Keil, Mitth. 1895, 88.

According to the latter this designates a temporary covering to protect the pillars from the weather. He draws this conclusion from the small price paid for the work as well as from the early mention of the στέγασις.

στορά, *layer of stone slabs* (?). [IV] Epid. 3325 $A_{11\cdot 33}$ = Epid. K. 241 Ἀντίμαχος Ἀργεῖος ἥλετο στοράν τῷ σακῷ ταμὲν καὶ ἀγαγὲν καὶ συνθέμεν. Cf. Baunack, Aus Epid., pp. 63, 70. He thinks the στορά consists of stone slabs used, 1) for pavement (l. 11) and 2) for roofing (l. 33). Kavvadias thinks the same word would not be used for both and that the στορά was rather a layer of stone placed on the ground to hold the limestone slabs which formed the temple pavement. No trace of stone used for roofing has been found.

συμπέδιος, *bordering on the* πεδίον.[1] [II] Aeol., Hoffmann, GD. II, p. 66, no. 90_6 ἐν τᾷ συμπεδίῳ, etc. Cf. Hoffmann, l. c., note.

συμπρηίσκω, *burn together.* [V] Delph. BCH. 1895, 1 ff. D_{48} καὶ συμπρηίσκεν ἁμεῖ τοὺς Λαβυάδας. This is an iterative formation, but not from συμπράσσειν, as Homolle would take it, but rather with Keil, Hermes 31, 510, from συμπίμπρημι. Cf. θνῄσκω, ἐνδυδισκόμενος, Delph. SGDI. 1899. The compound συμπίμπρημι is late and rare. It is cited in the Thesaurus from Theod. Prodr., p. 5.

συναποδέχομαι, *accept.* [II] Aetol. 1413_{18} συναποδεδέχθαι τοὺς Αἰτω[λοὺς ἄσυλον] εἶμεν αὐτὸ τὰ ἀπ' Αἰτωλῶν καὶ τῶν ἐν Αἰτωλίαι κατοικεόντων, etc.

συναρχοστατέω, *establish archon in common.* [II] Phocis $1539a_{15}$ καὶ συνεκλησιάζειν καὶ συναρχοστατεῖσθαι. Cf. Ditt. Syll. 294. Dittenberger notes the Delphian month of Ἀρχοστάσιος, but the verb *ἀρχοστατέω does not occur.

συνεσάδδω, *act as accomplice in taking.* [VI] Gort. Law-code III_{13} αἰ δέ κ' ἀλλότριος συνεσάδδηι, δέκα στ[ατ]ῆρανς καταστασεῖ, τὸ δὲ χρεῖος, διπλεῖ, ὅ τί κ' ὁ δικαστὰς ὀμόσει συνεσσάκσαι. Related to σάττω. See Baunack, Ins. v. Gort., p. 30. Comparetti's view of this verb, Leggi di Gort., p. 176, that it is a compound, συν-εκσ-άγεν, is less likely, though approved by Meyer, p. 370.

---

[1] Meister, Stud. Nicol. 1884, takes this word as a proper name.

συνιατρεύω, *aid in practicing medicine.* [156–151] Delph. 1899₁₂ συνιατρευέτω Δάμων μετ' αὐτοῦ ἔτη πέντε. This is a manumission decree. It would seem that the freed person had been trained as a physician. See ἐνδιδύσκω for the peculiar conditions of this decree.

συνυπόλαμψις, *support.* [I] Lac. LeB.-F. 242a₂₁ εἰσδεδεγμένοι τέ εἰσιν εἰς τὰν τᾶς πόλεως χάριν καὶ συνυπόλαμψιν. From συνυπολαμβάνω, *aid in supporting*, a late verb and but little used.

σωπονπίᾱ, *certainty of manumission.* [182] Delph. 2133₁₁ τὰν ἐπίστευσε Νίκαια αὐτοσαυτᾶς ὠνὰν ἐπὶ σωπονπίαι Εὐμνάστωι τῶι πατέρι αὐτᾶν. The circumstances of this decree are unusual. Eumnastus, to whom Nicaea trusted the freeing of the slave, died before fulfilling the obligation, and it came as an inheritance to his daughters. This phrase ἐπὶ σωπονπίαι replaces the usual ἐπ' ἐλευθερίαι. It is explained by Cauer, in note to 212, "ita, ut pecunia salva permittatur," but Baunack's explanation is more satisfactory. The word is an abstract to *σώπομπος (*having assured freedom*, as σώφρων, *having sound sense*), hence πομπή is used in this compound in the sense of *release, manumission*, Lat. *missio*.

τάκτης, *assessor of tribute*, member of board in charge of tribute to be paid by the several states of the Athenian Federation. [V] CIA. I, 266 ἔτ]αξαν οἱ τάκται. See Gilbert I, p. 422. The τάκται formed an elective body before whom the states assessed themselves. If their own assessment was not satisfactory, ἔταξαν οἱ τάκται. There is no doubt that in CIA. I, 37, these same magistrates are meant; possibly also in CIG. 1086₁₀ (Fourmont) TETKKH should be so read. Köhler, l. c., thinks these officials were ten in number, but Gilbert says eight, "two for each of the four tribute districts then existing." Cf. Böckh, Staatshaushaltung I, p. 90, and II, p. 39,* n. 243.

τερμαστήρ, *boundary commissioner.* [243/223] Meg. 3025₈₅ τερμαστῆρες τῶν αὐτῶν δικαστᾶν.

τερμονίζω = τερμάζω. [III] Meg. 3025₉.₁₁ τοὺς τερμον[ιξ]-οῦ[ν]τας—, οὗτοι δὲ ἐπελθόντες ἐπὶ τὰν χώραν ἐτερμόνιξαν κατὰ τάδε. Cf. τέρμων : τέρμα.

τερμονισμός, *defining of boundaries.* [III] Meg. 3025₈ ἀντιλεγόντων δὲ τῶν Κορινθί[ων τῶ]ι τερμονισμῶι.

τεταρτεύς, a measure. [IV] Cos 3638₁₂ καὶ σπυ[ρ]ῶν τρεῖς τεταρτῆς καὶ μέλιτος τέτορες κοτυλέαι. Cf. PH. 325. This word is similar to ἐκτεύς.

τετάρτη, a prescribed tax (technical). [I] Ion. Bechtel, 108b₅ καὶ τοῦ ταλάντου καὶ ἱππωνίης καὶ τῆς τετάρτης καὶ ἀνδραποδωνίης. See Gilbert II, p. 369.

τοφιών, *quarry of tuff-stone* (?). [IV] Tab. Heracl. I₁₃₇ οὐδὲ τοφιῶνας ἐν τᾷ ἱαρᾷ γᾷ ποιησεῖ οὐδὲ ἄλλον ἐασεῖ. See Meister, Curt. Stud. IV, p. 443.

τροφεά = τροφή. [50] Delph. 2254₆ ἐν τᾶι τροφεᾶι.

τύμος = τύμβος. [VI] Corcyra 3186 = CIGS. III, 870; 3190 = 869 ἐπὶ τύμῳ. See Dittenberger's comment. He thinks Brugmann's comparison with Latin *tumulus* is to be approved. He also quotes Loch, De titulis Graecis sepulcralibus, to the effect that in these inscriptions σᾶμα refers to the whole sepulcher, while τύμος is the mound.

τυρώδης, *shaped like a cheese.* Cos 3636₄₉ = PH. 36 ἐφ' ἑστίαν θύεται ἀλφίτων ἡμίεκτον, ἄρτο[ι δύ]ο ἐξ ἡμιέκτου,— ὁ ἄτερος τυ[ρ]ώδης, etc.

τυτυῖ, uncertain. [VII/VI] Cret. Comp. 12–13 καὶ ϝαρὴν τυτυῖ ἔτι δὲ ϙοῖρο[s]. Comparetti suggests that it is an adverb to τυτθός.

ὑ = ἐπί. [IV] Cypr. 74₃, 123₆ ὐ τύχα. In compounds ὐϝαῖς (below) ὐχήρων, ὐευξάμενος. Meister, GD. II, p. 302, takes as ὔν for ὄν = ἀνά; Hoffmann, GD. I, p. 312 (cf. note, p. 313), thinks it is to be taken as a short form to εὐ (found in three glosses) and would connect with Ags. *up;* Baunack, Stud. I, p. 16, connects with Sanskrit *ud.* Cf. Brugmann, Gr. Gr., p. 219. Kretschmer, KZ. 31, 415, thinks it is probably to be read ὐ(ν) τύχα as ὑν = σύν in the Hesychian gloss ὕγγεμος· συλλαβή. Σαλαμίνιοι. Solmsen, KZ. 34, 450, in an article on the Tegean temple inscription, after rejecting the assumption made by Keil, Gött. Nachr. 1895, 357, that the ϝ- of ϝοφλεκόσι is the same as the Cyprian ὑ, and speaking briefly of the other suggestions as to its derivation, favors that given by Baunack. He also says rightly that there is no need of assuming a change of meaning in the formula ὐ τύχα, since ἐπί could quite as well be used as ἐν.

ὑδατώλενος, *having arms like water* (?), *bright* (?). Acrae, IG. Sic. et It. 219₅. This word occurs in a fragment and refers to the water nymphs.

ὑδράνᾱ, *urn containing water for lustration.* [I] And.₃₇ χωραξάντων δὲ καὶ ὑδράνας. Cf. Hesych. ὑδρανός· ὁ ἁγνιστὴς τῶν Ἐλευσινίων.

ὑϝαῖς = ἐπὶ ἀεί. [IV] Cypr. (Edal.) 60₁₀·₂₂·₂₈. Cf. Meister, GD. II, pp. 227, 284; Hoffmann, GD. I, pp. 312, 313.

ὑλωρέω, *be* ὑλωρός. [V(?)] Thess. Mitth. 1896, 248, with the reading of Meister, Ber. d. sächs. G. d. W. 1896, 251, ἧς (= ἥν) hυλωρέοντος (HVΛOREONTOS) Φιλονίκω. The correct reading of this word was also discovered independently by Danielsson, Eranos I (1896), 136 ff. The ὑλωροί, according to Arist., Pol. 7 (6), 8, correspond to ἀγρονόμοι. See Gilbert II, p. 333.

ὑπερχρονέω = ὑπερχρονίζω. [I(?)] Lac., LeB.-F. 194b τῶν ὑπερχρονούντων (πραγμάτων).

ὑπέχθεμα, *supplementary statement* (in accounts). [I] And.₆₁ ὁ δὲ ταμίας ὅσον κα παραλάβει διάφορον λοιπὸν ἐκ τούτων, γραφέτω ἐν ὑπεχθέματι, etc. ἔκθεμα is a later word for πρόγραμμα. See Lobeck, Phryn., p. 249. ὑπέκθεμα therefore indicates an account which is appended. Cf. Dittenberger. For χ cf. the following word.

ὑπεχθέσιμος, *deposited for reëxportation.* Crete, Cauer 119₂₅.

ὑποδιασύρω, *jeer at.* [IV] Epid. 3339₂₄ Θεωρῶν δὲ τοὺς ἐν τῶι ἰαρῶι [π]ίνακας ἀπίστει τοῖς ἰάμασιν καὶ ὑποδιέσυρε τὰ ἐπιγράμματα.

ὑποδόκιον (coll.), *beams placed on top of the wall to sustain the rafters.* [IV] Epid. 3325₅₉ = K. 241 ἔγκαυσιν τοῦ ὑποδοκίου κα(ὶ) κ(υ)ματίου. 1. 233 ὑποδοκίου ἐργασίας. Kavvadias, l. c., translates as above and thinks that θρᾶνος of the Delos inscription is the same as ὑποδόκιον in this. He compares Hesych. θράνιον· τὸ ὑπὸ τοῖς φατνώμασι σανίδωμα, καὶ τὸ ὑπὸ τὴν δοκόν τι. Baunack, in Aus Epid., p. 73, translates "Untergebälk," and thinks the word denotes the same part of the construction as ποίστασις of l. 41, only that here it is named with reference to the στρωτῆρες which are to be placed upon it.

ὑποδομά, *foundation built underground.* Troiz. 3362₃₇ χοεύσαντι τὰ ὑπὲρ τᾶς ὑποδομᾶς. Cf. χοεύω.

ὑποθοιναρμόστρια, *vice-president of a feast* at Sparta (f.). [I] And.₃₂. Cf. θοιναρμόστρια.

ὑπόμαστρος, *answerable to the μαστρός.* [I] And.₅₁ καὶ ἔστωσαν ὑπόμαστροι. Cf. Hesych. μαστρίαι· αἱ τῶν ἀρχόντων εὐθῦναι. ὑπόμαστρος is therefore probably synonymous with ὑπεύθυνος. Cf. κατάμαστρος.

ὑποτιτθίδιος, dim. of ὑποτίτθος, ὑποτίτθιος. [156/151] Delph. 1954 σῶμα γυναικεῖον ἆι ὄνομα ᾽Αριστονίκα καὶ ταύτας παιδάριον ὑποτιτθίδιον ἆι ὄνομα ᾽Αρίστων – –.

ὑστερομεινιᾶ, *day following the full moon.* [III] Thess. 345₄₀ τᾶ ὑστερομεινία. This is the interpretation given by Bischoff, De fastis Graecorum antiquioribus, quoted in Prellwitz, De dial. Thess., p. 50.

φαρετρίτᾱς, *bowman.* Boeot. 573₂ τῶν φαρετριτάων. Cf. φάρετρα, φαρετρέων.

φαωτός, *dark, violet.* [V] Delph. BCH, 1ff., C₂₄ τὰν δὲ παχεῖ[α]ν χλαῖναν φαωτὰν εἶμεν. See BCH. 1895, 15, 54. From φαιός.

φοροφορέω, *serve as carrier.* [150/140] Delph. 1938₂₁ κυριευέτω δὲ καὶ τῶν ἔχει καὶ κατεσκεύωται φοροφορέων Σωτήριχος πάντων, καὶ οἱ βεβαιωτῆρες βέβαια παρεχόντω, Σωτηρίχωι παντα. E. Curtius, Gött. Nachr. 1864, 148, would read φορεαφορέων and thinks that Σωτήριχος was a *Sänfteträger.* Baunack, after quoting Curtius, makes two suggestions: 1) that it indicates the regular bringing in of the φόρος, and 2) that it is equivalent to φορτο-, φορμο-φορέων, and designates the *trade* which Σωτήριχος followed. This seems the simpler understanding of the word and, on the whole, the most satisfactory.

φραδᾱτήρ, *notary.* IG. Sic. et It. 211 γραμματεύς καὶ φραδατήρ Πύρριχος ᾽Αριστογείτου. From φραδάω.

φύγιμος, *giving refuge.* [I] And.₈₂ τοῖς δούλοις φύγιμον ἔστω τὸ ἱερόν.

χάραδος, τό, = χαράδρα. [IV] Tab. Heracl. I$_{61}$ ἐπὶ τᾶς ἀμαξιτῶ τᾶς διὰ τῶ χαράδεος ἀγώσας, etc.

χαριστεῖον, thank-offering. [Late.] Cnidus 3577 χαριστεῖα καὶ ἐκτίματρα ἀνέθηκε. 3528 Σαράπιδι - - χαριστεῖα. Thera, Dittenberger, Hermes 16, 162 τῷ θεῷ χαριστεῖον. See ἐκτίματρον.

χελληστυάρχᾱs = commander of a χιλιαστύς. [222–205] Aeol. 276$_6$, 277$_{3·4}$. For χέλλιοι see Meyer, pp. 37, 504; Brugmann I, pp. 264, 722, 751.

χελληστυαρχέω, act as χελληστυάρχας. [III] Aeol. 278$_2$ χελληστυαρ(χ)[ήσαντα].

χέλληστυs, body of one thousand men. [222–205] Aeol. 276$_{9·13·14·19·23·24}$; 277$_{6·11}$; 278$_1$; χιλιαστύς Ion. 147$_{20}$.

χειριπέδᾱ, bracelet. [II] Boeot. CIGS. I, 2420$_{26}$ χειριπέδας κὴ πεδίσκας [ἀρ]γουρίας, ὁλκὰ τρὶς δραχμή.

χοεύω = χώννυμι (?). Troiz. 3362$_{37}$ χοεύσαντι τὰ ὑπὲρ τᾶς ὑποδομᾶς. Cf. ὑποδομά, which seems to have been a construction below the surface. χοεύσαντι denotes the work of covering with earth.

χοροψάλτρια, chorus singer (f.). [II] Delph. BCH. 1894, 82 = LeB.-W. 257 χοροψάλτης is quoted in the Thesaurus.

χραύζομαι = χραύομαι. [IV] Cypr. (Edal.) 60$_{18}$ τὸ(ν) χραυζόμενον Ἀμηνίᾳ ἄλϝω. Cf. χραυόμενον 60$_9$.

χρεοφύλαξ, official in charge of the accounts of debtors. [III] Cos. 3706, VI$_{36}$ καθ' ὑθεσίαν δὲ τὰν ἐπὶ χρεοφυλάκων. Cf. χρεοφυλακέω and χρεοφϋλάκιον, which occur frequently in late inscriptions found in Asia Minor. See L. & S.

χρημάτιξις = χρημάτισις. [Late.] Crete, Mus. It. III, p. 696 ἀπ]ολαγάξιος κα[ὶ τ]ᾶς χρηματίξιος, etc.

χύλωμα, a kind of liquor (?). [IV] CIA. II, Add. 834b, II$_{64}$ χυλώματος χόες Γ.

χωράζω = χωρίζω. [I] And.$_{37}$ χωραζάντω.

ψιλινοποιός, maker of ψίλινοι (στέφανοι). [I] Lac. M. 56$_{23}$ ψίλινος is a rare word. Cf. Ath. 678b οὕτω (θυρεατικοι) καλοῦνται στέφανοί τινες παρὰ Λακεδαιμονίοις - - ψιλίνους αὐτοὺς φάσκων νῦν ὀνομάζεσθαι, ὄντας ἐκ φοινίκων.

RARE WORDS AND RARE MEANINGS.

ἀγελαῖος, *belonging to an ἀγέλα.* [III] Crete (Drerus), Cauer 121a$_{10}$ = Mus. It. III, pp. 657 ff. τάδε ὤμοσαν ἀγελάοι. See Danielsson, Epigr., pp. 1 ff.; Gilbert II, pp. 223 f.; Ins. Jurid. Gr., p. 412; Gardner and Jevons, Manual Gr. Antiq., p. 436. Cf. πανάζωστος.

ἀγέλη, class of Cretan ephebes (technical). [III] Crete (Drerus), Cauer 121c$_{10}$ = Mus. It. III, 657 ff. τὰν ἀγελᾶν (written by Haussouillier τὰν ἀγέλαν), Malla, Mus. It. III, p. 637, ll. 17, 24, τὰν ἀγέλαν, CIG. 2554$_{35}$ τὰς ἀγέλας. See preceding with references. Cf. also Haussouillier, Rev. d. Philol. 1894, 167.

ἀγή, *breaking, cutting.* used of wood. [IV] Ion. (Chios) 183$_{15}$ = BCH. 1879, 244 ff. ἀποδί[δ]οντος ἐμοῦ Κλυτίδαις ἔτεος ἑ[κάστου] τριάκοντα τάλαντα ξύλων ἐν [τῶι . . . .]τωι ἄλσει κείμενα, ὅταν ἡ ἀγή ἦ[ι]. In Aesch., Pers. 425 ἀγαῖσι κωπῶν, and in Eur., Suppl. 693 πρὸς ἁρμάτων τ' ἀγαῖσι the word has the concrete meaning *fragments.*

ἀγρέω = αἱρέω. [IV] Aeol. 214$_{33}$ ἀγρέθεντες, 215$_{49}$ ἀγρ[έ]θεντες, 214$_{15}$ κατάγρεντον, 311$_{6}$ προαγρημμένω ; Thess. 345$_{14}$ ἐφανγρένθειν ; Pamphylian 1267$_{15}$ hαγλέσθω. Cf. ἐφάνγρεσις (New Words) and Aeol. 215$_{31}$ . . ρέσιος which may, in view of the verb form in this inscription, be read [ἀγ]ρέσιος. This verb is found in various poetical writers, but only in the present system. Cf. Kühner-Blass II, p. 347. The Thessalian forms point to ἀνγρέω. The Pamphylian hαγλέσθω shows the dialectic variation between ρ and λ seen also in Cretan αἰλέω : αἱρέω, but the Cretan λ is directly traceable to the aorist εἶλον, which cannot be affirmed of the Pamphylian word. Compare, however, στλεγίς : στεργίς ; κρίβανος : κλίβανος, and others. See Meyer, p. 234 ; Kühner-Blass I, pp. 73, 145. For use of αἱρέω, ἀγρέω, λαμβάνω, λάζομαι in the inscriptions see section on Synonyms.

ἀδηλόω, *conceal*. [IV] Tab. Heracl. I$_{57}$ ὡς μὴ καταλυμακωθῆς ἀδηλωθείη καθὼς τοὶ ἔμπροσθα ὅροι. The verb occurs in Philo., Jud. 1, 539. It is explained by Suidas as ἀγνώριστον ποιέω.

ἀδίαυλος, *having no returning road*. [III] Boeot. CIGS. I$_{2535}$ ἀδίαυλ[ον ἔφθας ἐξανύ]ων ἀτραπόν εἰς ’Αίδ[α].; Cyz. Kaibel, Epig. Gr. 244$_9$ Φερσεφόνας δ᾽ἀδίαυλον ὑπὸ στυγερὸν δόμον ἦλθον παυσιπόνῳ λάθας λουσαμένα πόματι. Both inscriptions are metrical. The word is found in literary Greek only in a citation in Bekker, Anecd. I, p. 343, ἀδίαυλος τόπος : ὅθεν μὴ ἔστιν ἐπανελθεῖν. οὕτως Εὐριπίδης, θεοὶ χθόνιοι ζοφερὰν ἀδίαυλον ἔχοντες ἕδραν φθειρομένων ’Αχεροντίαν λίμνην. So far as our occurrences go, it is used only of the realms of Hades.

ἄδος, *decree*. [V] Ion. 238$_{19}$ ἀπ᾽ οὗ τό ἄδος ἐγένετο. Cf. Hesych. ἄδημα· ἄδος· ψήφισμα, δόγμα, Eustath. 1721$_{60}$ f., where, starting from ἄδος ὁ κόρος, he cites from Hipponax in l. 64 ἄδηκε βουλή, ἤγουν ἤρεσκε τὸ βούλευμα. ἄδος, *decree*, derives its meaning from the technical use of ἀνδάνω. See below.

ἀιδής, *blind*. [IV] Epid. 3339$_{125}$ παῖς ἀιδής. οὗ[τος] ὕπαρ ὑπὸ κυνὸς τῶν κατὰ τὸ ἱαρὸν θ[εραπ]ευόμενος τοὺς ὀπτίλλους ὑ[γιὴ]ς ἀπῆλθε. The word occurs in Bacchylides, Fr. 46, δυσμενέων δ᾽ ἀιδής. It is used in a passive sense in Schol. Hes. 477 τοῦ δὲ τάφον καὶ σῆμ᾽ ἀιδές ποίησεν ῎Αναυρος.

αἱμασιά, *wall*. Anaphe 3430$_{10}$ ἐν τῶι τόπωι, ἐν τᾶι αἱμασιᾶ, ὁπεῖ ἁ ἐλαία ἁ ποτὶ τὸ[ν] Εὐδώρειον οἶκον, etc.

αἴρω, ἀρμένος (in phrase ἀρμένα καὶ ἀτελής). Phocis 1529$_{11}$ καὶ ἁ συνγραφὰ ἀτε[λ]ὴς καὶ ἀρμένα ἔστω, 1545 ἄκυρος καὶ ἀρ<ε>μένα ἔστω. 1546$_{13}$ (same); Delph. 1746, 2143, et al.; Aetol. 1425$_7$. This meaning of the perf. pass. part. is a further development of the poetic use of the word found in Aesch., Eum. 880; Eur., El. 942, etc.

αἰσυμνάω, *rule, govern*. [IV] Ion. 156b$_8$ αἰσυμνῶ(ν); Meg. 3054 αἰσιμνῶντες, 3068 αἰ]σιμνῶν[τες]; 3052$_{12}$ ὅς δέ κα εἴπηι ἢ προαισιμνάσηι [ἢ ἐν βουλᾶι] ἢ ἐν δάμωι ἢ ἄλλει καὶ χ᾽ὁπειοῦν, etc., 3087, II$_{57}$ προαισυμνῶντος Μηνίος. See the following.

αἰσυμνήτης, *ruler*, official title in Megara. [IV] Ion. 156b$_5$ ε[ὐθ]ύνωι ἢ αἰσυ[μ]νήτηι; Meg. 3016 συναρχίαι προεβουλεύσαντο

ποτί τε τοὺς αἰσιμνάτα[ς τὰν] βουλὰν καὶ τὸν δᾶμον. 3045_5 [χρή]-
ματα δαμε[ύειν τοὺς] αἰσιμνά[τ]ας, etc., 3068 (fragment) ϚΙΜΝΩΝ.
The verb is found in literary Greek only in Euripides, Med. 19
γήμας Κρέοντος παῖδ', ὃς αἰσυμνᾷ χθονός. The Megarean αἰσυμνᾶ-
ται correspond to the πρυτάνεις or προστάται. See Gilbert II,
p. 317.

ἄκεσις, *mending, repairing.* [IV] Epid. 3325 $B_{276·297}$ = K. 241
θυρᾶν ἀκέσιος ; Delph. BCH. 1896, 198 ff.$_{62}$ τοῦ μαχανώματος ἀκέσιος. This word is used to denote *healing, cure,* in Herod. 4, 90,
109 ; Plut., Lyc. 12, Hippocrat. (com.), and in an inscription, CIA.
III, 900 ; to denote *a plaster,* Galen, p. 666. ἀκέομαι means *mend,
repair,* and is used of a building in Boeot. CIGS. I, 3074. We
have also a new compound ἐφακέομαι, used of repairing bridges,
Delph. Cauer 204_{37}. Bourguet, l. c., p. 219, notes that another
medical word ἴασις is found in the phrase ζυγάστρου ἴασιος in an
unedited Delphian inscription. Cf. also ἐξαῖρεν ὑγιῆ τὸγ κώθωνα
γεγενημένον Epid. 3339_{87}.

ἀκρόθις = ἀκροθίνιον. [V] Delph. BCH. 1895, 1 ff. D_{47} τὠπόλ-
λωνι τὰν ἀκρόθινα καὶ συμπρηίσκεν ἁμεῖ τοὺς Λαβυάδας· Cf. ἀκρόθινα πολέμου Pind., Ol. 2, 7. ἀκροθίνιον is generally used in the
plural. Homolle, l. c., p. 61, comments : "Le dessus du tas, les
prémices et particulièrement la dîme des fruits des récoltes, offerte
aux dieux."

ἁλίᾱ, *assembly,* 1) of a clan (Delphi), 2) of the people,
ἐκκλησία. [V] Delph. BCH. 1895, 1 ff. A_{21} ἔδοξε ἐν τᾶι ἁλίαι, A_{41}
καταγορείτω ἐν τᾶι ἁλίαι, D_{26} [αἰ δ' ἁ]λίαν ποιόντων ἄρχων (gen. pl.) ;
Tab. Heracl. I_{11} ἐν κατακλήτωι ἁλίαι, I_{118} ἀναγγελίοντι ἐν ἁλία,
II_{10} ; Acarn. 3180 γραμματε[ύον]τος ἁλίας ; Corcyra 3199 ποιεῖ ἁ
ἁλία, 3201–3 ἔδοξε τᾶι ἁλίαι, 3206_{47} ἐμ βουλᾶι ἢ ἁλία(ι), l. 72 βουλὰ
καὶ ἁλία ; Agrigentum, Cauer 199_{10} ἔδοξε τᾶι ἁλίαι καθὰ καὶ τᾶι
συνκλήτωι ; Gela, Cauer 198_7 τᾶι ἁλίαι καὶ τᾶι βουλᾶι, l. 20 στεφα-
νῶσαι ἐν τᾶι ἁλίαι ; Rheg., IG. Sic. et It. 612 ἔδοξε τᾶι ἁλία[ι]
καθάπερ τᾶι ἐσκλήτωι καὶ τᾶι βουλᾶι. Gilbert, II, p. 236, n. 5,
thinks the word was also used in Epidamnus. See also p. 309,
n. 1. This word is used by Herodotus, I, 25, V, 29, 79, VII, 34,
of gatherings of the Persians, Milesians, Thebans, and Spartans

respectively. It occurs in this general sense in a letter of Periander, Diog. Laert. I, p. 99, and it is used technically in a ψήφισμα Βυζαντίων quoted in Dem. de Cor. 90. In the Delphian inscription it evidently denotes the formal meeting of the whole clan. The heavy fine to be inflicted for absence is noticeable. The literary tradition shows the aspirate for this word, but there is no inscriptional evidence for it. On the contrary, the word is now found in two inscriptions which consistently show the aspirate and is not aspirated in either. Thumb, Spir. Asp., p. 11, cites this correctly among the words in which the unaspirated form is the more original. Cf. ἀλιάσσιος, Argos, Blass, Jbb. Philol. 143, p. 159.

This word should not be separated from Attic ἡλιαία, ἡλιαστής, though Herodotus retains ᾱ. It is probably not an Ionic word. There is no occurrence in an Ionic inscription, while ἐκκλησίης is found in an inscription from Miletus, Bechtel 248$_3$. See Smyth, § 158, for retention of ᾱ by Herodotus. Cf. also ἀλιαίαι Argolis 3320, ἀλιασταί Arcad. 1222$_{24}$, ἀλίασις and ἀλίασμα (above). E. Meyer, Philologus 48, 187, suggests that, since ἀλιαία is certainly Argive, it may have been borrowed by the Athenians and falsely Ionicized. The lengthening which Meister, Curt. Stud. IV, p. 402, assumes for the Attic form seems improbable.

ἀμαξήα, *carriage road.* Troiz. BCH. 1893, 116$_{20}$ (new fragment of SGDI. 3362) ἐννέα ποὶ τῶι ναῶι ἀμαξήας ἐκ Κιθ[αιρῶνος]. Cf. Suid. ἁμαξεία. ὁ τῶν ἁμαξῶν φόρτος.

ἄμπαλος, *auction.* [III] Aetol. 1415$_{15}$ κατ' ἄνπαλον μισθούντω καθὼς καὶ τὸ πρότερον. ἄμπαλος occurs in Pind., Ol. 7, 110, in the sense of *allotment.* From ἀναπάλλω. Cf. ἀνάπαλσις.

ἀμφαίνομαι, *adopt.* [VII–VI] Gort. Comp. 19$_3$ ἀμφαντός ; Law-code X$_{34}$, XI$_{18}$ ἀμφαίνεθαι ; X$_{37\cdot43}$, XI$_{3\cdot5\cdot9\cdot11}$ ἀμφανάμενος ; X$_{50}$, XI$_{22}$ ἀμφαντός. Cf. ἄνφανσις, ἀμφαντύς. See Comp., p. 228, Ins. Jurid. Gr., p. 481. In the Gortynian Law-code the mode of adoption and the result with respect to the rights and obligations of both parties are carefully defined. Though differing in some details from the Attic law, the Gortynian also requires public action and is accompanied by the sacrifice usual on the admission of a new member to the phratry. Cf. Bücheler and Zitelmann, Das Recht v. Gort., pp. 160 ff.

ἀμφίσταμαι, *investigate*. [IV] Tab. Heracl. I₁₂₅ τὼς δὲ πολιανόμως τὼς ἐπὶ τῶ ϝέτεος ποθελομένως μετ' αὐτὸς αὐτῶν ἀπὸ τῶ δάμω μὴ μεῖον ἢ δέκα ἄνδρας ἀμφίστασθαι ἤ κα πεφυτεύκωντι πάντα κὰτ τὰν συνθήκαν - -. Cf. Hesych. ἀμφίστασθαι· ἐξετάζειν; ἀμπιστάτηρ· ἐξεταστής.

ἀνδάνω = δοκέω (technical use). [V] Locris 1478₃₈ = CIGS. III, 334₃₈ ὅσστις κα τὰ ϝεϝαδηϙότα (ϜΕϜΑΔΕϘΟΤΑ) διαφθείρῃ - - ἄτιμον εἶμεν καὶ χρήματα παματοφαγεῖσται; Crete, Comp. 148, τάδ' ἔϝαδε τοῖς Γορτυνίοις ψαφίδονσι. The same use is found in Herodotus, also in Eustathius 1721₆₀ f. See ἄδος, *decree* (above).

ἀνέγκλητος, *without a blemish* (of stones). [II] Boeot. 3073₁₆₄ ἐν ταῖς ἰδίαις χώραις βεβηκότας ὅλους (λίθους) ἀσχάστους ἀνε[γκλῆ]-τους. This word in its ordinary use occurs very frequently in the manumission decrees.

ἀνοικοδομή, *rebuilding*. Rhodes, IG. Ins. 9₅ = Cauer 186 εἰς τὰν ἀνοικοδομὰν τοῦ τοίχου καὶ τῶν μναμείων τῶν πεσόντων ἐν τῶι σεισμῶι. The noun is rare, occurring only in Byzantine literature, while ἀνοικοδομέω is used by Herodotus, Thucydides, Xenophon, etc.

ἀνώγεον, *upper story*. Dodona 1581 [ἦ]κα (λ)ώιο(ν) Θέμι ἔ(σ)[ται . . . .] τὸ ἀνώγεον τ[ὸ ἔδωκε 'Αριστοφ[άντωι, ἀπ(ο)-δ[ομεν - -]. Hoffmann, l. c., note, derives from ἀνά and -ωγέον (= -ωγέιον), to ἀνάγω. It is found with the spelling ἀνώγαιον in Xen., Anab. V, 4, 29, and in the New Testament.

ἀξιάζω = ἀξιόω. Aeol. 318₃₃ ὅστις παραγενόμενός πρὸς Λαμψακάνοις [τό τ]ε ψάφισμα ἀποδώσει καὶ ἀξιάσει. This verb is quoted in the Thesaurus from Nicetas Annal. 10, p. 322 D.

ἀξίως, *cheaply*. Anaphe 3430₆ [ὑ]πὲρ τᾶς ἐφόδου, ἇς ἐποιήσατο Τιμ[ό]θεος Σωσικλεῦς, κατ[ὰ δὲ ὑοθεσίαν Ἰσοπόλιος, ἀξίως αὐτῶι δοθῆμεν ἐν τῶι ἱερῶι τοῦ Ἀπόλλωνος τοῦ Ἀσγελάτα τόπον, ὥστ[ε ναὸ]ν Ἀφροδίτας οἰκοδομῆσαι, etc. Cf. note which cites an Olbian inscription, Latyschew 11₂₃ τὸ δὲ χρυσίον πωλεῖν καὶ ὠνεῖσθ[αι τὸ]ν μὲν στατῆρα τὸν Κυζικηνὸν [. . . . .]του ἡμιστατήρου καὶ μήτε ἀξιώτερο[ν μή]τε τιμιώτερον – –. For occasional examples of the same meaning in Attic, see L. & S.

ἄοζος, *servant in the temple*. Corcyra 3212 μάγιρος, – – ὑπηρέτας, – – ἄοζος, – – οἰνοχόος. Cf. Aesch., Ag. 231 φράσεν δ' ἀόζοις πατὴρ μετ' εὐχὰν δίκαν; Bekk., p. 413₃₁ ἄοζος, ὑπηρέτης, διάκονος.

ἀποβάλλω, *expose* (a child). [V] Gort. Law-code IV₉ αἰ ἀποβάλοι παιδίον – –. In use this verb corresponds to Attic ἀποτίθημι, ἐκτίθημι.

ἀποδινέω, *thresh out grain*. [IV] Tab. Heracl. I₁₀₂ κ[αὶ] αἴ κ' ἔμπροσθα ἀποδίνωντι ἀπάξοντι ἐς τὸν δαμόσιον ῥογὸν, etc. Cf. Hdt. 2, 14 (end) ἀποδινήσας δὲ τῇσι ὑσὶ τὸν σῖτον οὕτω κομίζεται.

ἀπόλογος, *auditor*. [III] Ion. (Thasos) Bechtel 72₁₅ δικασάσθων δὲ ἀπόλογοι· ἂν δὲ μὴ δικάσωνται αὐτοὶ ὀφειλόντων, δικασάσθων δὲ ἀπόλογοι οἱ μετὰ τούτους αἱρεθέν[τες]., Becht. 71₁₀ δικάζεσθαι δὲ τοὺς ἀπολόγους ἢ αὐτοὺς ὀφείλε(ι)ν. These officials correspond to the Athenian λογισταί. For their various special duties, also for the titles used in the different dialects, see Gilbert II, p. 339.

ἀπολύτρωσις, *ransom*. Cos 3629₇ μηδὲ ποιε[ύντω – – – – τ]ᾶς ἀπολυτρώσιος. Cf. l. 3 θυέτω καὶ τῶν ἐλευθε[ρουμένων]. From ἀπολυτρόω, but the noun is cited only from Plutarch, the New Testament, and writers of the Christian era. Cf. λυτρόω.

ἀποπυρίς, *sacrifice consisting of small fish*. Cos 3634b₅ ποιεῖν δὲ καὶ τὰν ἀποπυρίδα [κ]ατὰ τὰ πάτρια· l. 24 θύεν δὲ ἐκκαιδεκάται [μ]ηνὸς Πεταγειτνύου κα[ὶ] τὸν ξενισμὸν ποιεῖν τῷ[ι Ἡ]ρακλεῖ τὰν δ'ἀποπυρίδα ἑπτακαιδεκάται· See PH. 29, and note p. 75, which in substance is as follows: ἀποπυρίς means anything plucked off the coals and eaten at once (Hesych. ἀποπυρίζων· ἀπὸ πυρὸς ἐσθίων). Epicharm. in Athen., p. 277 F ἀφύας ἀποπυρίζομες and Tel., Stob. 97, 31 τῶν μαινίδων ἀποπυρὶν ποιήσας. Here it probably means a sacrifice to the dead, consisting of fish. Paton cites as a parallel the three fish to be offered to the heroes according to the will of Epicteta VI₁₂. This word occurs also in a story from Hegesandrus, Ath. 334 E, and from Clearchus, Ath. 344 C. In these two places it means only *small fish*.

ἀπορροή, *brook, small stream.* [IV] Tab. Heracl. I$_{17·22·27·32·56·87}$· ἀπορροαί is found in Eur., Hel. 1587 αἵματος δ' ἀπορροαί. The word is frequently used by the philosophers to denote *emanations, effluences.* Cf. especially Empedocles.

ἀράω, *damage, injure.* [IV] Tab. Heracl. I$_{133}$ οὐδὲ τὰς ὁδὼς τὰς ἀποδεδειγμένας ἀράσοντι οὐδὲ συνέρξοντι οὐδὲ κωλύσοντι πορεύεσθαι.

ἀριθμός, *verse.* [II] Delph. BCH. 1894, 80 προφερόμενοι ἀριθμούς τῶν ἀρχαίων ποιητᾶν. Cf. Dion. H. c. 54 φέρε γὰρ ἐπιχειρείτω τις προφέρεσθαι τούσδε ἀριθμοὺς Ὄλυνθον μὲν καὶ Μεθώνην καὶ Ἀπολλωνίαν – –. See also Larfeld, Ber. ü. d. Epigr. 1896, p. 208; Couve, l. c., p. 81.

ἄρρηκτος, *unbroken, untilled.* [IV] Tab. Heracl. I$_{19·24}$ (com.). Homer uses ἄρρηκτος of νεφέλη, δέσμος, τεῖχος, and it is used by Aeschylus of σᾶκος and πέδαι, but it is used of land in the Heraclean Tables only, where it forms one in the series; σκίρω, ἀρρήκτω, δρυμῷ.

ἄρταμος, *slayer of the victim,* official. [VI] Calabria, IG. Sic. et It. 643 ϙυνίσϙος με ἀνέθηκε ὤρταμος ϝέργων δεκάταν. This is the famous "axe-inscription." ἄρταμος, *butcher, cook,* occurs in Xenophon, while in Sophocles the word means *murderer.* Here it could be taken with Roberts, p. 304, and others, as *butcher,* but Dittenberger, Hermes 13, 391, offers the suggestion adopted in the definition given, which seems more satisfactory. Though the word does not occur in any list of temple officials, it is nevertheless quite probable that a certain person was appointed for this duty.

ἀρτύω, *arrange by will, leave as a legacy.* [IV] Tab. Heracl. I$_{106}$ καὶ αἴ τινί κα ἄλλωι παρδῶντι τὰν γᾶν, hάν κα αὐτοὶ μεμισθώσωνται, ἢ ἀρτύσωντι ἢ ἀποδῶνται τὰν ἐπικαρπίαν ἂν αὐτὰ τὰ παρhέξονται πρωγγύως hοι παρλαβόντες ἢ hοῖς κ' ἀρτύσει ἢ hοι πριαμένοι τὰν ἐπικαρπίαν – –. Cf. Hesych. ἀρτῦναι· διαθεῖναι; Ἄρτυμα· διαθήκη; ἀρτυθῆναι· παρασκευασθῆναι. See Ins. Jurid. Gr., p. 203, where, with stress on the first two glosses, the word is translated as above. Kaibel, IG. Sic. et It. I, 645, comparing the last gloss, thinks the meaning rather *pledge, mortgage.* But the former meaning does no violence to any gloss and certainly suits the context admirably. Legatees would probably be required to furnish new security, while in case of a mortgage the land would remain in the possession of the original owner, who would still be liable for any infraction of the contract, so that the necessity for new security would hardly exist. The verb is very general in meaning, hence either specialization is quite possible.

ἀτάω, 1) *fine,* 2) *defeat* (in a law-suit). [V] Gort. Law-code IV$_{29}$ αἰ δέ τις ἀταθείη, ἀποδάτταθθαι τῶι ἀταμένωι, ἆι ἔγρατται. X$_{21}$ (cited below). Comp. 152 V$_{14}$ αὐτὸν ἀτῆθαι, 155$_7$ (same). The second meaning is seen only in X$_{21}$ ἀτάμενον, which seems to plainly correspond to the νενικάμενος of XI$_{32}$. See Comp., p. 183; Ins. Jurid. Gr., p. 436; Roberts, p. 334.

ἄτη, 1) *damage, harm,* 2) *fine.* [IV] Gort Law-code VI$_{23\cdot 43}$, IX$_{14}$ κ'αἴ τι κ' ἄλλ' ἄτας ἦι, τὸ ἀπλόον; 2) X$_{20}$ f. αἰ δὲ τις ὀφήλων ἄργυρον ἢ ἀταμένας ἢ μωλιομένας δίκας δοίη, αἰ μὴ εἴη τὰ λοιπὰ ἄξια τᾶς ἄτας μηδὲν ἐς χρέος ἦμεν τὰν δόσιν. XI$_{31}$ f. αἰ κ' ἀποθάνηι ἄργυρον ὀφήλων ἢ νενικαμένος, αἰ μέν κα ληίωντι οἷς κ' ἐπιβάλληι ἀναιλῆθαι τὰ χρήματα, τὰν ἄταν ὑπερκατιστάμεν καὶ τὸ ἀργύριον οἷς κ' ὀφήληι, ἐχόντων τὰ χρήματα. l. 41 ἄλλαν δὲ μηδεμίαν ἄταν ἦμεν – –. Cf. Comp. 152 VII, 173$_6$. Cf. ἀτάω and ἄπατος (New Words).

ἀφεστήρ, *presiding officer* of the Cnidian βουλή. Cnid. 3505$_{17}$ ἐλέσθαι δὲ [κα]ὶ ἄνδρα, ὅστις ἀποδεξάμενος παρὰ τοῦ ἐν ἀρχᾶ ἀφεστῆρος τὰν ἐπιμέλειαν τᾶς εἰκόνος, etc. Cf. Plut., Quaest. gr. 4, p. 360 τίνες ἐν Κνίδῳ οἱ ἀμνήμονες καὶ τίς ὁ ἀφεστήρ. – – – ὁ δὲ τὰς γνώμας ἐρωτῶν ἀφεστήρ. See Gilbert II, p. 171.

ἀφέταιρος, *not a member of the* ἑταιρεία. [V] Gort. Law-code II$_5$ αἰ δέ κ' ἀφεταίρω δέκα, αἰ δέ κ' ὁ δῶλος – – διπλεῖ καταστασεῖ, αἰ δέ κ' ἐλεύθερος – –. II$_{25}$ (same), II$_{41}$ τῶ δ'ἀφεταίρω τρίτον αὐτόν, τῶ δὲ ϝοικέος – –. See Ins. Jurid. Gr., p. 418. The word is also found in a passage from Theop. Hist. 332, cited by Poll. 3, 58 ἀπολῖται καὶ ἀφέταιροι καὶ ἀπαθηναῖοι. The Cretan form of ἑταιρεία is ἑταιρηία, as shown by Comp. 153 II$_{12}$ τὰν ἑταιρηιᾶν (ETAIPHIAN).

ἄφωνος, *intestate.* [IV] Tab. Heracl. I$_{152}$ αἰ δέ τίς κα τῶν καρπιζομένων ἄτεκνος, ἄφωνος ἀποθάνει, τᾶς πόλιος πᾶσαν τὰν ἐπικάρπιαν ἦμεν.

βουνός, *hill.* [III] Rhodes, Cauer 179b$_{31}$ ὡς παραφέρει παρὰ τὸν βουνόν; Corcyra 3204 τὸν βουνὸν ἄνω καθὼς - -. Cf. Anthol. Pal. 11, 406. Phrynichus, Rutherford, p. 56, says the word is common among the Syracusan poets. βοῦνις occurs in Aesch., Supp. 117. Cf. βουνίτης, etc.

βύβλιος, βύβλινος, *having βύβλος plants.* [IV] Tab. Heracl. I$_{58}$ πὰρ τὰν βυβλίαν καὶ τὰν διώρυγα. I$_{92}$ πὰρ τὰν βυβλίναν μασχάλαν καὶ πὰρ τὰν διώγυρα. See μασχάλη.

γίγλυμος, *pivot on which the door turns, hinge.* [IV] Epid. 3325$_{74}$ = K. 241 Δαμοφάνης εἵλετο δακτυλίους τοῖς γιγιλύμ[οις ἐς τ]ὸ μέγα θύρ[ω]μα - -. Cf. Hesych. γίγγλυμος· ὁ στρεφόμενος γόμφος ἐπὶ τῶν θυρῶν. Cf. Kavv., 1. c., and Baunack, Aus Epid., p. 79.

γναφικός, *pertaining to a fuller.* [II] Delph. 1904$_6$ μανθάνων τὰν τεχνὰν τὰν γναφικὰν - -, also 11. 7, 9. κναφικός is a late word found in Diosc. 4, 163, and in Suidas. For γν- : κν- see Meyer, p. 335.

γόνος, *descendants* (collective). [VI] Elis 1153$_3$ = Ol. 11 = Roberts 294 Χαλάδριον ἦμεν αὐτὸν καὶ γόνον. See Roberts, p. 366.

γύης, *measure of land.* [IV] Tab. Heracl. II$_{13·14·15}$ γυᾶν, γύαι. Cf. τρίγυα πενθημίγυον, τρίγυον, τριημίγυον. Cf. Ins. Jurid. Gr., p. 227.

δεξίωσις, *reception of members* or *entertainment of guests.* Cos. 3634b$_{30}$ ἐπιμελέσθων δὲ τοὶ ἐπιμήνιοι ὦγ κα δέηι ποτὶ τὰν δεξ[ίωσιν]. See PH. 36, where it is noted that the two meanings given above are possible.

διαλείπω, *die.* [179] Delph. 1920$_9$ ἐπεὶ δέ κα διαλίπη Ἀρίσστα, 2082$_5$ ἐπεὶ δέ κα δι[α]λίπηι Σωτίων, etc. The use of this word intransitively is one of the many peculiarities of diction to be found in these decrees.

δόμος, *layer of brick or stone.* Ion. 159$_4$ καὶ τοῦ [προ]σεχέος αὐτῶι τείχους δόμοι ἕξ. Cf. Herod. I$_{179}$ διὰ τριήκοντα δόμων πλίνθου. It is used also in the Septuagint, Eccl. 6, 25.

δουλαγωγία, *enslaving.* Phocis 1545$_{12}$ εἰ δέ τις ἐπιλανβάνοιτο αὐτῶν ἢ καταδουλίζοιτο, ἅ τε γενηθῖσα δουλαγωγία αὐτῶν ἄκυρος καὶ ἀρ<ε>μένα ἔστω. This occurrence is earlier than any literary use of the word.

ἔγκαυσις, *encaustic painting.* [IV] CIA. IV, 834b, col. II$_{26}$ καὶ ἔνκαυσις Λεύκωνι ; Epid. 3325$_{24}$ τᾶς περιστάσιος, l. 31 τοῦ σάκου, l. 51 ἀκάνθων, etc. ἐγκ- Epid. K. 242$_{38\cdot 65}$. CIG. 2297 (Delian) τῶν θυρῶν. It is used as a medical term, Diosc. 5, 21 ; Plut. 2, 127 B.
εἰλέω, *exclude, hinder.* [380] Delph. Amphyctionic decree, Cauer 204$_{20}$ αἰ δέ κα μὴ ἀποτίνῃ ὁ - - - - - εἰλέσ[θω τ]οῦ ἰαροῦ. Cf. Tab. Heracl. I$_{152}$ αἰ δέ χ' hυπὸ πολέμω ἐγϝηληθίωντι, hώστε μὴ ἐξῆμεν τὼς μεμισθωμένως καρπεύεσθαι - - ; Elis 1150$_4$ κὠπόταροι μηνπεδέοιαν, ἀπὸ τῶ βωμῶ ἀποϝηλέοιαν κα τοὶ πρόξενοι καὶ τοὶ μάντιε(ς), 1154$_7$ ἀποϝηλέοι κ'ἀπὸ μάντειας. This development in meaning is not so strange for the compounds as for the simple verb. Cf. κατειλέω.

ἔκθεμα, *proclamation.* [III] Cos 3706$_{61}$ = PH. 367$_{61}$ ἐμ πόλει ἐκχθέματα κατὰ τὰν ἀγοράν. Cf. ὑπέχθεμα, Andania. Lob., Phryn., p. 249, explains πρόγραμμα as Attic, ἔκθεμα as Hellenistic. See Keil, Mitth. 1895, p. 37. For the writing see Meyer, p. 287.

ἐκκάθαρσις, *cleaning, polishing.* [IV] Epid. 3325$_{283}$ = K. 241 θυρᾶν ἐκαθάρσιος, l. 20 [τῶ ναῶ (?)] ἐκαθάρσιος. Cf. l. 109 καὶ τῶ ναῶ ἐπικαθάρσιος.

ἐκλεαίνω, *cancel.* [III] Boeot. 488$_{73}$ ἐσλιανάτω Νικαρέτα τὰς οὑπεραμερ(ί)ας ἃς ἔχι καττᾶς πόλιος. Cf. διαλιαίνω. See Ins. Jurid. Gr., p. 302, n. 4.

ἐκτός, *besides* (adv.). [170–169] Delph. 1742 μάρτυροι· τοὶ ἱαρεῖς - - καὶ ἐκτὸς ᾿Αλέξων, Μνασίθεος ; Rhodes 789$_8$ (time of Hadrian) πρῶτον μὲν καὶ τὸ μέ[γ]ιστον· χεῖρας καὶ [γ]νώμην καθαροὺς - - καὶ τὰ ἐκτός, ἀπὸ φακῆς ἡμερῶν γ', etc. ἐκτός (prep.), *besides,* occurs in Plato, Gorg. 474 D ἐκτὸς τούτων.

ἐλατήρ, *broad, flat cake.* Cos 3637$_8$ καὶ θύ[εται] ἐπὶ τᾶι ἱστίαι ἐν τῶι ναῶι τὰ ἔνδορα καὶ ἐλατὴρ ἐξ ἡμιέκτου [σπ]υρῶν· τούτων οὐκ ἐκφορὰ ἐκ τοῦ ναοῦ. Etym. M., p. 325, 46 μᾶζα ἐλάτης καὶ ἐλατήρ. Cf. Aristoph., Knights 1183 ἡ Γοργολόφα σ'ἐκέλευε τουτουὶ φαγεῖν ἐλατῆρος, ἵνα τὰς ναῦς ἐλαύνωμεν καλῶς.

ἔνδικος, *liable.* [V] Gort. Law-code III$_{24}$ and elsewhere, Comp. 152, I$_{12}$, III$_3$, always in the phrase ἔνδικον ἦμεν, equivalent to Attic ὑπόδικος. For similar words, ἔντιτος, ἔνοχος, etc., see section on Synonyms.

ἐνδιδύσκω, *clothe*. [156–151] Delph. 1899₁₃ εἰ δὲ χρείαν ἔχοι Διονύσιος, συνιατρευέτω Δάμων μετ' αὐτοῦ ἔτη πέντε λαμβάνων τὰ ἐν τὰν τροφὰν πάντα καὶ ἐνδυδισκόμενος καὶ στρώματα λαμβάνων. There is little question that the form should be ἐνδιδυσκόμενος, as corrected by Baunack, who cites τιτύσκομαι as a similar formation. ἐνδιδύσκω occurs in the New Testament, meaning *to have put on*.

ἔνδυμα, *garment*. [II] Delph. 1716₂ καὶ τὰ ἐνδύματα πάντα, 2141₂₃ τὰ δὲ γυναικῆα ἐνδύματα καὶ ἱμάτια φ[υλασ]σέστων —; Cnid. 3537 τὰ ὑπ' ἐμοῦ ϝαταλιφθέντα ἱμάτια, καὶ ἔνδυμα καὶ ἀνάκω[λ]ον. This word is used by Plutarch and other writers of the Christian era.

ἐνεστηκώς, *plaintiff*. [453] Halicarnassus, Bechtel 238₂₈ τὸν δὲ ὅρκον εἶ[ν]αι παρεόντος [τοῦ ἐ]νεστηκότος. From ἐνίστημι.

ἐπαρή, *curse*. [IV] Ion. 156, B₃₀ οἵτινες τιμουχέοντες τὴν ἐπαρὴν μὴ ποιήσεαν, l. 36 ἐν τῆπαρῆι ἔχεσθαι, 174 C₁₁ ἐπὴν τὰς νομ[α]-ίας ἐπαρὰς ποιῆται., 248 A₁₂ καὶ πρόσθετα ποιήσαντες Μαυσσώλλωι ἐπαρὰς ἐποιήσαντο, B₁₂, C₁₅. Aeol. 281 A₂₆ ποήσασθαι δὲ καὶ ἐπάραν ἐν τᾶ ἐκλησία α[ὔτ]ικα, B₃₄ (same). This is a rare poetic word. It occurs but once in the Iliad, IX, 456 θεοὶ δ' ἐτέλειον ἐπαράς. Cf. also Ath., p. 466a ἐπαρὰς (ἐπ' ἀρὰς) ἀργαλέας ἠρᾶτο.

ἐπελαύνω, *take action, enforce*. [II] Arcad. 1222₂₃ εἰ δὲ μή, ὀφλέτω ἕκαστος πεντήκοντα δαρχμάς, ἐπελασάσθων δὲ οἱ ἁλιασταί. Cf. ἐπελάω, Tab. Heracl. I₁₂₇ (New Words).

ἐπελεύσομαι, used in the active (fut. and aor.) in the sense of *bring, carry*. [V] Gort. Law-code V₁₅ ἐπελευσεῖ, III₅₂ ἐπέλευσαν, III₄₅·₅₃, IV₇, Comp. 152, I₉, II₁₅, VII₃. Cf. Hesych. ἐλευσίω· οἴσω. Cf. Baunack, Ins. v. Gort., p. 40; Comparetti, pp. 260 f. In inscription 152 this verb is used in direct contrast with ἐπιδίομαι.

ἐπήκοος, *witness*. [V] Lac. M. 29 ἐπάκοε Μενεχαρίδας, 'Ανδρομέδης. M. 28 ἐπακόω, M. 30 ἐπακό. Cf. Hesych. ἐπάκοοι· οἱ μάρτυρες; ἐπήκοοι· κριταί, καὶ οἱ μάρτυρες, καὶ οἱ δικάζοντες. The words are certainly to be taken as nouns in the dual, with Boisacq, DD., p. 124; Müllensiefen, De tit. Lac. dial., p. 96, and others. Blass, Misc. Epigr. 130, thought the first form could be verbal, = ἐπήκουε.

ἐπιβάλλων, ὁ, *the one to whom it is due, the next in succession*. [V] Gort. Law-code III₂₈ τά τε ϝὰ αὐτᾶς τοῖς ἐπιβάλλουσι ἀποδόμεν.,

III$_{33}$, V$_{25\cdot49}$, VII$_{28}$ (com.). ὁ ἐπιβάλλων is used in this inscription to denote οὗτος ᾧ ἐπιβάλλει τι. The verb occurs in its ordinary sense in V$_{23}$, VI$_{29}$, IX$_{23}$, XI$_{33}$. Cf. ἐπαβολά. See Ins. Jurid. Gr., pp. 462, 470; Baunack, Ins. v. Gort., p. 147; Roberts, pp. 331 f.

ἐπικάθαρσις, *cleaning*. [IV] Epid. 3325$_{109}$ = K. 241. See ἐκκάθαρσις.

ἐπικαταβάλλω = ἐπιβάλλω, *inflict penalty*. [IV] Tab. Heracl. I$_{134}$ hότι δέ κα τούτων τι ποίωντι πὰρ τὰν συνθήκαν τοὶ πολιανόμοι τοὶ ἀεὶ τῶ ϝέτεος ἐπικαταβα[λ]ίοντι καὶ ζαμιώσοντι.

ἐπικαταλλαγή, *difference in exchange*. [IV] Epid. K. 242$_{41}$ Τύχωνι ἐπικαταλλαγὰ ἐπὶ τὸ καταλλαχθὲν ἀργύριον ἐς 'Αθάνας. Cf. Theophr., Char. 30 τοῦ χαλκοῦ τὴν ἐπικαταλλαγὴν προσαπαιτεῖν. See Keil, Mitth. 1895, 66, who thinks that καταλλαγή also has this meaning in this inscription.

ἐπίουρος, *nail*. [IV] Epid. 3325 A$_{63}$ Δαμοφάνη[ς] εἵλετο ἄλους καὶ χοινίκας καὶ δακτυλίο[υς] καὶ ἐπιούρους ποὶ τὰ διὰ στύλων θυρώματα. l. 73 Δαμ[οφ]άνης εἵλετο τῶι μεγάλωι θ[υρώματι] χοινίκας καὶ πλίνθους καὶ ἐπιούρ[ους]. Hesych. ἐπίουροι· ἐπίσκοποι καὶ ἦλοι ξύλινοι. See Aus Epid., p. 79.

ἐπίποκος, *having wool on, unshorn*. Cos 3731$_6$ = PH. 401 ['Εκ]άται ἐμ πόλει [οἶν] ἐπίποκον τελέ[αν]. Cf. Mitth. 16, 414, n. 1. Töpffer notes that this custom of sacrificing a sheep unshorn is analogous with Jewish custom, but is not found elsewhere in Greece. In Athens it was directly forbidden. Cf. Ath. I, 9; IX, 375. See also Paton, l. c., where it is said that the word in the form ἔποκον is still used by the shepherds of Cos. ἐπίποκος occurs in Kings IV, 3, 4.

ἐπισπένδω, *promise solemnly*. [V] Gort. Law-code IV$_{52}$ ὄτειᾳ δὲ πρόθθ' ἔδωκε ἢ ἐπέσπευσε, ταῦτ' ἔχεν, ἄλλα δὲ μὴ ἀπολαν[χά]νεν. V$_3$, VI$_{11\cdot13\cdot19\cdot21}$, X$_{28}$. This word is evidently used on account of the libation which accompanied the formal act of transferring property in Gortyn. Cf. Lat. *spondeō*.

ἐπίτεξ, ἐπίτοξ, *pregnant*. [VII/VI] Cret. Comp. 10$_3$ ὄι]ς ἐπίτεκ[ς]. And.$_{34}$ καὶ θυσάντω τᾷ μὲν Δάματρι σῦν ἐπίτοκα. See Schulze, Quaest. Ep., p. 180, note 2: "*τριχάϝεικες : accus. ϝοῖκα (in ϝοίκαδε) = ἐπίτεξ : accus. ἐπίτοκα."

ἐρίζω, *contest at law.* [IV] Tab. Heracl. II₂₆ καὶ τοὶ μὲν ἐρίξαντες ἀπέσταν, τοῖς δὲ ἐδικαξάμεθα δίκας τριακοσταίας. ἐρίζω is not used elsewhere of legal contests.

ἔροτις, *feast.* [IV] Arg. LeB.-F. II, 122 = Kaibel, Epigr. Gr. 846 Ἥραι ὃν εἰς ἔροτιν πέμπο[ν ἄε]θλα νέοις. Cf. Hesych. ἔροτιν· ἑορτήν. Κύπριοι. This word occurs in Eur., Electra 625 Νύμφαις ἐπόρσυν' ἔροτιν, ὡς ἔδοξέ μοι. Cf. Meyer, p. 165.

ἔρρω = φεύγω. [VI] Elis 1153₅ = Ol. 11 = Roberts 294 αἰ δέ τις συλαίη, ϝέ(ρ)ρην (FEPEN) αὐτὸν πο(τ)τὸν Δία, αἰ μὴ δάμοι δοκέοι. 1152₂ = Ol. 2 = Roberts 292 αἰ ζέ τις κατιαραύσειε, ϝάρρην (FAPPEN) ὢρ ϝαλείω. This explanation is not without difficulties. See ll. cc. and especially Dittenberger, Ol., p. 30.

ἑστιᾱτόριον, *hall for feasting.* [III] Rhodes, IG. Ins. 677₁₆ = Cauer 177 [θ]έμειν δὲ τὰς στάλας μίαμ μὲν ἐπὶ τᾶς ἐσόδου τᾶς ἐκ πόλιος ποτιπορευομένοις, μίαν δὲ ὑπὲρ τὸ ἱστιατόριον. The form ἑστιατόριον is found only in Theopomp., Hist. 33, and Dion. H. 2, 23. Philostr. 605 has ἑστιατήριον; Herod. IV, 35 ἱστιητορίου. For the initial vowel of this form and examples see Meyer, p. 109 (who takes it from a √ves); Kretschmer, KZ. 31 (who thinks the derivation from √ves uncertain on account of the aspirate in Attic); Boisacq, DD., p. 69. Brugmann, I, p. 836, explains the ι-vowel as due to assimilation.

ζύγαστρον, *box containing the archives.* [IV] Delph. BCH. 1896, 201₄₉ γραμματισταῖ στατῆρες πέντε· κάρυκι δραχμαὶ τρεῖς· ζυγάστρου ὀβολοὶ πέντε, ἡμιωβέλιον· πινακίων ὀβολός. There are numerous glosses on this word. Etym. M. ζύγαστρον· παρὰ Δελφοῖς ζύγαστρον καλεῖται τὸ γραμματοφυλάκιον. In Soph., Trach. 692, it is used for κιβώτιον. Cf. Hesych. ζύγαστρος· κιβωτός, (σ)ορὸς ξυλίνη.

In II₃₉ of this Delphian inscription four ναοποιοί ἐπὶ τοῖς ζυγάστροις ἐφεστάκεον. Cf. p. 218, where it is stated that the word is common on the unedited fragments.

ἤθησις, *polishing, cleaning.* [IV] Epid. K. 242₁₂₄ ἠθήσιος ἔλαβε Λααρχίδας τῶν λίθων τῶν εἰς τὸς σακὸν τὰς θυμέλας. Cf. Aristot., Probl. 870b₁₇ ἠθίσει for ἠθήσει = καθάρσει. Kavv., l. c., takes the word from ἠθέω. Keil, Mitth. 1895, 426, notes that with this derivation we should expect ἄθησις. He suggests that it may be a technical building-word which keeps its Ionic-Attic form. It may have been ἤθησις, as the Sigean ἠθμός. But Meyer, Alb. Stud. III, p. 42, derives *σάω from σιᾱ- in Lith. sijoti for *siōti. Beside this there is an I. E. √sei-, sift, O. B. sito, sêjati. This root is further connected with √sē, throw, sow, from which ἠθέω may be taken. The loss of aspiration is probably due to dissimilation.

ἡλίασις. [V] Arg. Mon. Ant. I (1891), 593 ff. ἐ(τ)τᾶς ἁλιάσσιος (ΕΤΑϚ ΑΛΙΑϚϚΙΟϚ). Cf. Brugmann I, p. 662; Danielsson, Zur argiv. Bronzeinschrift, Eranos I, 31 f. Otherwise Robert, l. c., who would connect with λιάζειν. The inscription as a whole has not yet been satisfactorily explained.[1]

ἡμίνα, half. [V] Gort. Law-code II₄₉, III₃₆, and elsewhere, Malla, Mus. It. III, p. 637. In Epicharmus, p. 124, this means half the ἐκτεύς; so also in other poets. But in Crete it seems to be always an equivalent of ἥμισυς. But cf. ἡμιτύεκτος.

θέμα, deposit, fund. [V] Delph. BCH. 1895, 1 ff. Β₅₀ μηδὲ κοινανείτω τῶν κοινῶν χρημάτων μηδὲ τῶν θεμάτων. Here the word plainly means funds. In Plut. 2, 116 A, B, and Sept. Tob. 4, 9, it means pledges, deposits. That it was a word of general meaning is shown by the gloss of Hesychius, θέμα· ἕξις. τόπος. στάσις. μνῆμα.

ἱεροργός, sacrificial priest. Crete, Mus. It. III, p. 697 οἱ κόρμοι οἱ σὺν Ἀρατογόνω(ι) τῶ Ἀρτέμωνος κὼ ἱεροργὸς ἐπεμέληθει τῶ ταύ[ρ]ω κ[αὶ] τᾶς ἐρίφω. ἱεροεργός occurs in Callim. Fr. 450, -ουργός in Ammon., p. 92.

ἱεροσκόπος, inspector of victims, diviner. Rheg. IG. Sic. et It. 617. This official is named in Dion. H. 2, 22, and Orph. H. 1, 23.

ἵζω = ἱδρύω. [V] Corcyra, Brugmann, IF. III, 87 M]ῦς με hίσατο. Epid. K. 138 τὸν δ' ὑμῖν Βρασίδας ξυνήιον ἵσατο βωμὸν. Brugmann compares ἵσσατο in an Argive inscription discussed by Baunack, Philologus 48, 396. These are the only occurrences of

---

[1] In addition to the above, compare also Reinach, Rev. d. Ét. Gr. IV, 171 ff.; Peppmüller, Woch. f. klass. Phil. 1891, N. 31; Meister, I. F. Anz. 200. The last gives a review of previous translations.

the middle aorist of ἵζω, though εἴσατο, from *ἕζω, is used in the same sense in literature as well as in the Carian inscription quoted by Brugmann. See also for the Corcyrean inscription Six, Mitth. 1894, 341. For various words used for *dedicate* see section on Synonyms.

ἵστωρ, *witness.* [III] Boeot. 429_7, 430_6, 482_{13}, 488 (com.), 811_{25} ϝίστωρ and ϝίστορες, always written with ϝ. Cf. Hom., Il. Σ 501 ἐπὶ ἵστορι πεῖραρ ἑλέσθαι, and Ψ 486 ἵστορα δ' Ἀτρείδην Ἀγαμέμνονα θείομεν ἄμφω. It is used also for *witness* in the oath of the ephebes, Poll. 8, 106. Cf. Hesych. ἵστωρ· συνετός, σοφός, ἔμπειρος. μάρτυρ. συνθηκοφύλαξ.

καθαρτής, *cleanser, purifier* (official). [I] Lac. M. 56_{24}.

καλάσῖρις. [I] And.$_{17}$ αἱ δὲ παῖδες καλάσηριν ἢ σινδονίταν καὶ εἱμάτιον μὴ πλείονας ἄξια μνᾶς, αἱ δὲ δοῦλαι καλάσηριν ἢ σινδονίταν καὶ εἱμάτιον μὴ πλείονος ἄξια δραχμᾶν πεντήκοντα – –. l. 19 καλάσηριν ἢ ὑπόδυμα, l. 20 καλάσηριν καὶ εἱμάτιον. Cf. Herod. II, 81 ; Poll. VII, 71 ; Aristoph., Fr. 330b (Blaydes).

καρτερός, *valid.* [V] Halicarnassus, Bechtel 238_{22} ὅτ[ι] ἂν οἱ μνήμο[νες ε]ἰδέωσιν, τοῦτο καρτερὸν εἶναι. See Br. Mus. IV, 886 ; Roberts 145 and p. 342. In l. 29 the adjective occurs in the meaning *possessed of,* which is sometimes found in literature καρτεροὺς δ' εἶναι γ[ῆς κ]αὶ οἰκίων, οἵτινες τότ' εἶχον. See also Gort. Law-code IV$_{24}$, VI$_{33}$, and others. The comparative is used in a technical sense, describing *those whose testimony is entitled to the greater weight,* in the Gort. Law-code I$_{15}$ αἱ δέ κα μωλῇ ὁ μὲν ἐλεύθε[ρ]ον, ὁ δ[ὲ δ]ῶλον, καρτόνανς ἦμεν, [ὅττο]ι κ' ἐλεύθερον ἀποφωνίωντι.

καταδατέομαι, *reapportion.* [IV] Tab. Heracl. II$_{28}$ ταύταν τὰν γᾶν κατεδασσάμεθα. See δατέομαι, Poetical Words.

κατάκειμαι, *be personally pledged for debt.* [V] Gort. Law-code I$_{55}$ τὸ]ν δὲ νενικαμένο[ν] κα[ὶ τὸν κα]τακείμενον ἄγοντι ἄπατον ἦμεν, X$_{26}$ ἄνθρω[π]ον μὴ ὠνῆθα[ι] κατακείμενον πρίν κ' ἀ(λλ)ύ(σ)ηται ὁ καταθένς, – –. Comp. 152 (Lesser Code) V$_{13}$, VI$_{3·10·16}$. This word is used of the free man as well as of the slave.

κατάλογος, Epidaurean official named by the senate. [IV] Epid. K. $242_{2·9·13}$, etc., 273, 275. See Keil, Mitth. 1895, 27 f., who discusses the various duties of the κατάλογος. In inscription 273 he seems to have been γραμματεύς of the βουλή. The name occurs in close relation with sums of money, so that one would conclude that some sort of financial officer is meant. But in 242 he makes no payments, receives no money, and does not keep the records. Keil suggests that the κατάλογος may have been named as a supervising official on behalf of the state. The form καταλογεύς would be expected, but compare ἀπόλογος and Keil's note, l. c., p. 26.

κατατίθημι, *take a personal pledge from another for debt.* [V] Gort. Law-code X$_{26}$. See κατάκειμαι for use and citation. This passage is somewhat obscure, but these words hardly admit of any other translation. See Ins. Jurid. Gr., pp. 450, 481, 487.

κατειλέω, κατείλω, *assemble.* [V] Gort. Law-code X$_{35}$, XI$_{13}$ καταϝηλμένων (KATAFEΛMENON) τῶμ πολιατᾶν. This is the transcription of Baunack, Ins. v. Gort., p. 38, who takes it as originally reduplicated ϝεϝελ-. So Blass-Kühner II, p. 412. Brugmann II, 1213, prefers -ϝελμένων.

κλᾶρος, *division of land* to which the κλαρῶται (= ἀφαμιῶται = ϝοικεῖς) are attached. [V] Gort. Law-code V$_{26}$ αἰ δὲ μὴ εἶεν ἐπιβάλλοντες, τᾶς ϝοικίας οἵτινές κ' ἴωντι ὁ κλᾶρος τούτους ἔχεν τὰ χρήματα. Cf. Hesych. κλαρῶται· εἵλωτες, δοῦλοι. See Ins. Jurid. Gr., p. 423, and citation from Ath., p. 263e καλοῦσι δὲ οἱ Κρῆτες τοὺς μὲν κατὰ πόλιν οἰκέτας χρυσωνήτους· ἀφαμιώτας δὲ τοὺς κατ' ἀγρόν, ἐγχωρίους μὲν ὄντας, δουλωθέντας δὲ κατὰ πόλεμον· διὰ τὸ κληρωθῆναι δὲ κλαρώτας.

κόμιστρον, *provision, gift.* [V] Gort. Law-code III$_{37}$ κόμιστρα αἴ κα λῆι δόμεν ἀνὴρ ἢ γυνά, ἢ ϝῆμα ἢ δυώδεκα στατῆρανς ἢ δυώδεκα στατήρων χρῆος, πλῖον δὲ μή. The general meaning of this word is clear, but there has been much discussion as to the occasion of giving the κόμιστρα in Gortyn. It is taken by the editors of Ins. Jurid. Gr., pp. 363 f., as also by Baunack, Ins. v. Gort., p. 126, as a gift made at the time of the divorce. Comparetti, Leggi di Gort., p. 180, connects it with what precedes, and thinks it denotes a gift for funeral expenses. Bücheler and Zitelmann discuss the word, Das Recht v. Gortyn, p. 128, but do not come to any definite conclusion as to its specific meaning. As Comparetti remarks, the literary use of the word does not limit its meaning beyond the general idea of *carrying*. Cf. Aesch., Ag. 965 : Eur , Herc. Fur. 1387, and Poll. VI, 186 τῷ φέροντι, κόμιστρα, which occurs in a list of names of gifts peculiar to certain classes of people. One would incline to think with the French editors and Baunack that this is given to the one who leaves the house after the divorce. It may be that the meaning *provide for* is the prominent idea rather than *bring, carry*.

ληίω, λείω, *wish, will*. [V] Gort. Comp. 150_{12}, 151, Law-code (common); El. $1151_3 =$ Ol. 16 (inscriptions which do not have H); Gort. Comp. 152 (3 occurrences), 153 II_8 (inscriptions which have $Ⱨ = η$ and use it in this word); Oaxus, Comp. 183_5, $184_{8\cdot 12}$, and Cnossus, Mus. It. II, 678 (inscriptions which have Ⱨ, but do not use it in this word). Cf. Hesych. λεῶμι· θέλοιμι ἄν. The inscriptional evidence would seem to be conclusive and to show that both forms of the stem exist. Cf. Bechtel, Nachr. d. Gött Ges. d. Wiss. 1888, 400, and Solmsen's discussion, KZ. 32, 515. Solmsen, p. 517, would take the form used in the Law-code from the long vowel stem, but thinks, p. 515, nqte, it is impossible to decide for the Elean λΕοίταν. Meyer, p. 581, would take both from the short form of the root. Cf. Brugmann II, 1087, 1160; Meister, Berl. Philol. Wochenschrift 1885, 1450; Dittenberger Ol., p. 43, and the literature cited. For the use of verbs denoting *will, wish*, see section on Synonyms.

λιμήν = ἀγορά. [214] Thess. 345_{42} τὸς ταγὸς ἐνγρά[ψαν]τας ἐν λεύκωμα ἐσθέμεν αὐτὸς ἐν τὸν λιμένα - -. See Prellwitz, De dial. Thess., p. 50, who cites Hesych. ἀγορά· ὄνομα τόπου ἢ λιμένος, Θετταλοὶ δὲ καὶ τὸν λιμένα ἀγορὰν καλοῦσι; also Dio Chrys. orat. 11, I, p. 315 ; Strabo XVI, 683.

λυτρόω, *pay expenses*. Delph., Cauer 207_5 καθὼς ἦν λελυτρωμένοι ὑπ' αὐτῶν. Cf. Ditt. Syll. 207, note. This word generally means *release on ransom, redeem*, cf. Plat., Theaet. 165 E, Polyb., Dem., etc.; but here it plainly means *having expenses paid*.

μαστρός, 1) member of a special Rhodian council, 2) prosecutor of those misusing the sacred funds at Delphi. Rhodes, IG.

LEXICOGRAPHICAL STUDY OF GREEK INSCRIPTIONS 99

Ins. 694₁₃ ἐγ δὲ ταυτᾶν τᾶν κτοινᾶν ἀποδεικνύειν τοὺς κτοινάτας μαστρόν ἐν τῶι ἱερῶι τῶι ἁγιωτάτων ἐν τᾶι κτοίναι · κατὰ τὸν νόμον τῶν Ῥοδίων, Ialysus 677, Lindus 761, 762, 828, 829a, 837, 839, 861, Camirus 696; Delphi, Ditt. Syll. 233₂₀ εἰ δέ τις τούτων τι ποιῆσαι ἢ ἄρχων ἢ ἰδιώτας κατάμαστρος ἔστω ἱερῶν χρημάτων φωρᾶς καὶ οἱ μαστροὶ καταγραφόντω κατ' αὐτοῦ κατὰ τὸ ψαφισθὲν – –. Cf. Hesych. μάστροι· παρὰ Ῥοδίοις βουλευτ(αί). Arist., Fr. 526, quoted by Harpocration, ὡς οἱ ζητηταὶ καὶ οἱ ἐν Πελλήνῃ μαστροί, ὡς Ἀριστοτέλης ἐν τῇ Πελληνίων πολιτείᾳ. Cf. And.₅₁ ὑπόμαστροι = ὑπεύθυνοι. See Gilbert II, pp. 37 (Delph.), 181 (Rhodes). In Rhodes the μαστροί stood at the head of the assembly, they had a γραμματεύς (828), and were chosen from the ἐπιστάται of the assemblies. Cf. 694₁₃, cited above. They seem also to have formed an auditing board for the accounts of the magistrates, and to have controlled the administration of the property belonging to the temple. See Br. Mus. II, 351.

μασχάλη, *grotto*. [IV] Tab. Heracl. I₉₂ ἐπὶ δὲ τῶ πὰρ τὰ Φιντία ἑπτὰ σὺν τῷ πὰρ τὰν βυβλίναν μασχάλαν καὶ πὰρ τὰν διώρυγα. Cf. IG. Sic. et It. 645 and note. Kaibel compares Strabo VI, 268 ἡ μὲν Μεσσήνη τῆς Πελωριάδος ἐν κόλπῳ κεῖται καμπομένης ἐπὶ πολὺ πρὸς ἕω καὶ μασχάλην τινὰ ποιούσης.

μέρος, τό, = ὁ κλῆρός. [V] Locris 1479 B₁₉ = CIGS. III, 333 αἴ κα μὴ διδοῖ τοῖ ἐνκαλειμένοι τὰν δίκαν, ἄτιμον εἶμεν καὶ χρήματα παματοφαγεῖσται, τὸ μέρος μετὰ ϝοικιατᾶν. See Gilbert II, p. 40, note 1, who translates "sein bestimmter Theil." Cf. also Meister, Ber. d. sächs. G. d. W. 1896, p. 325, who discusses at some length ; Dittenberger, l. c., fully indorses this explanation.

μετάβολος, *merchant, trader.* [II] Cos 3632₂₀ θυόντω δὲ κα[τὰ τ]αὐτὰ καὶ (τ)οὶ μετάβολοι τοὶ ἐν τοῖς ἰχθύσιν Ποτειδᾶνι καὶ Κῶ οἶν – –. This is a rare use found in Isai. 23, 2, 3. Cf. Lob., Phryn., p. 315, for this word and others in -ος where -εύς would be expected.

μυχός, *storehouse for grain.* [IV] Tab. Heracl. I₁₃₉·₁₄₁·₁₄₄ οἰκοδομήσηται – – μυχόν. τὸν δὲ μυχὸν πέντε καὶ δέκα ποδῶν παντᾶι. – – πὰρ δὲ τὸν μυχὸν τρῖς μνᾶς ἀργυρίω. In Ath. X, p. 414 C, mention is made of a general storehouse μυχοὶ πόλεως.

νεωλκός, *one who hauls up the ship.* [II] Cos 3632₂₃ θυόντωι δὲ κατὰ ταὐτὰ καὶ τοὶ νεωλκοί. Cf. Pollux VII, 190 νεωλκοί· τὰ δὲ τῶν νεωλκῶν ξύλα, οἷς ὑποβληθεῖσιν ἐφέλκονται αἱ νῆες, φάλαγγες καὶ φαλάγγια. νεωλκία is found in CIA. II, 467₃₇. See Töpffer, Mitth. 1891, 431. The only occurrence of this noun in literature which I have found is that cited by L. & S., Aristot. Phys. 7, 4, εἰς γὰρ ἂν κινοίη τὸ πλοῖον, εἴπερ ἥ τε τῶν νεωλκῶν τέμνεται ἰσχὺς εἰς τὸν ἀριθμὸν καὶ τὸ μῆκος ὃ πάντες ἐκίνησαν. The verb νεωλκέω is quite common.

νεωποιέω, νᾱοποιέω, *serve as νεωποιός.* [IV] Delph. BCH. 1896, 198 ff., I₆₉ Νικομάχου δὲ τοῦ Μενεκράτεος ναοποιέοντος; inscriptions of Asia Minor, CIG. 2930, 2956, etc. Cf. Poll. I, 11. In literature it is used only by Greg. Naz., Orat. 37, p. 610, et al.

νεωποίης, νεωποιός, νᾱποίᾱς, νᾱπόᾱς, νᾱοποιός, magistrate who superintends the building of a temple. [IV] Delph. BCH. 1896, 198 ff., I, πὰρ τὰν πόλιν τῶν Δελφῶν λοιπὰ χ[ρ]ήματα τοῖς ναοποιοῖς (com.); Cos 3705₃₃·₄₆·₉₁·₉₈ = PH. 367 τοὶ ναποίαι τοῖς Ἡρακλείοις, 3707₅₁ = PH. 369₅, 3705₁₀₆, PH. 373 *ναπόαι*; Ion. 147₁₅ τοὺς νεωποίας, Ins. of Asia Minor, CIG. 2656, 2785, 2824, etc. Cf. Arist., Rhet. I, 1374b οἷον ὃ Μελανώπου Καλλίστρατος κατηγόρει, ὅτι παρελογίσατο τρία ἡμιωβέλια ἱερὰ τοὺς ναοποιούς.

ὀβελίᾱ, ὀβελίᾱς, *baked or toasted on a spit,* bread or cake. [II] Cos 3632₄ τοὶ ἀγοράξαντες τὰν ὠνὰν τᾶς ὀβελίας. Cf. Poll. VI, 75 ὀβελίαι δὲ ἄρτοι, οὓς εἰς Διονύσου ἔφερον οἱ ὀβελιαφόροι; Ath. 111 B ὁ δὲ ὀβελίας ἄρτος κέκληται, ἤτοι ὅτι ὀβολοῦ πιπράσκεται -- ἢ ὅτι ἐν ὀβελίσκοις ὠπτᾶτο. Ἀριστοφάνης Γεωργοῖς Εἴ τ' ἄρτον ὀπτῶν τυγχάνει τις ὀβελίαν. Töpffer, Mitth. 1891, 419, gives the above explanation. He further suggests the possibility that ὀβελία may denote a *tax of an obol,* and the whole phrase may designate those selling the right of collecting this tax.

οἰκεύς, *serf.* [V] Gort. Comp. 18₃, Law-code II₈ (com. in columns II, III, and IV). A full discussion of the status of the ϝοικεύς is to be found in Ins. Jurid. Gr., pp. 424 ff.

ϝοιζῆα, Crete, Comp. 77-78, 145, and **ϝοιζήαζε,** 17, would seem to be the same word and derivative, but as yet there is no satisfactory explanation of the phonetic difficulty. See Comparetti, p. 54, who thinks of a phonetic change by which κ came to be pronounced as a palatal. Cf. Baunack, Berl. Phil. Wochenschrift, 1887, 57. There is no context.

ὀπτίλλος, *eye.* [IV] Epid. 3339$_{92}$. Cf. ἀτερόπτιλος 1. 72. See Schmidt, Plur., pp. 380, 401, 407; Collitz, BB. 18, 206 ff.; and especially the comprehensive discussion of the various Greek words for *eye,* Brugmann, Ber. d. sächs. G. d. W. 1897, 32 ff. ὀπ-τίλλος is from the root ὀπ- seen also in ὄπ-ωπα, but ὄκταλλος is to be taken with Collitz from the same stem as Skr. *akṣi,* *akṣan,* Av. *aši,* and hence to be entirely separated from ὀπτίλλος. These words with Rhodian πτοίνα, κτοίνα have led to various attempts to establish a derivation which might account for a double development in Greek, and give under different conditions πτ- and κτ- from the same root. But so far the evidence is not sufficient. Cf., however, in addition to the above, Kretschmer, KZ. 33, 272.

The suffix -τίλλος is rare; ναυτίλος, ναυτίλλομαι furnish the only good parallel. ὀπτίλος is found in Stob. 50, 15, and Plut., Lyc. 11, ὀπτίλλος, Plut., Arcad. 54, 15.

ὄρεγμα, measure of land. [IV] Tab. Heracl. II$_{33\cdot34}$, et al., καὶ ἐγένοντο σχοίνοι ἑκατὸν τριάκοντα ὀκτώ, ὀρέγματα ὀκτώ.

πατροῦχος. [V] Gort. Law-code VIII$_{1,21}$ (com.) ἁ πατρωιῶχος (ΓΑΤΡΟΙΟΚΟΣ), *the heiress* = Att. ἐπίκληρος. πατροῦχος with παρθένος expressed occurs in Herod. 6, 57 πατρούχου τε παρθένου. πέρι – –. The legislation concerning the "heiress" forms an important part of columns VII, VIII, and IX of the Law-code. For discussion of these laws see Ins. Jurid. Gr., pp. 475 ff., and the various editors of the inscription.

πεῖρα, *mercantile venture.* [V] Gort. Law-code IX$_{43}$ αἴ τίς κα πήραι συναλ[λάκ]σηι, ἢ ἐς πῆρ[α]ν ἐπιθέντι μὴ ἀποδιδῶι. Hesych. ἐπὶ πείρᾳ· ἐπὶ διαπείρᾳ ἢ ἐπὶ λῃστείᾳ καὶ πειρατικῇ βλαβῇ. This passage is much effaced, but the reading is reasonably certain. The meaning is hardly that of *piratical undertaking,* as Comparetti says, Le leggi, p. 225, but rather according to Ins. Jurid. Gr., p. 385, simply *traffic, business.*

περιέχω, *stipulate.* [50] Delph. 2208₁₀ εἰ δὲ μὴ παραμένοι καθὼς ἁ ὠνὰ περιέχει. This extension of the meaning of περιέχω is, so far as I know, unique. It is, however, a quite natural development.

περίστασις = περίστυλον (?). [IV] Epid. 3325 = K. 241₆·₁₃·₂₄, K. 242₄₉·₆₀·₁₆₃. This word occurs also in the inscription of Lebadaea. Fabricïus defines it as that part of the stylobate "quae inter locum, quo columnae constituuntur, et cellae parietem interest." Kavvadias interprets, however, as above. Cf. also Baunack, Aus Epid., p. 64.

πέτευρον, *raised tablet.* [IV] Ion. (Oropus), Bechtel 18₄₂ τὸ ὄνομα τοῦ ἐγκαθεύδοντος, ὅταν ἐμβάλλει τὸ ἀργύριον, γράφεσθαι τὸν νεωκόρον καὶ αὐτοῦ καὶ τῆς πόλεος καὶ ἐκτιθεῖν ἐν τοῖ ἱεροῖ γράφοντα ἐν πετεύροι σκοπεῖν τοῖ βουλομένοι. Cf. Hesych. πέτευρον· σανίς, ἐφ' ἧς αἱ ὄρνεις κοιμῶνται· καὶ πᾶν τὸ ἐμφερὲς τούτῳ· καὶ ὄργανόν ποιον, καὶ πᾶν τὸ μακρὸν καὶ ὑπόπλατυ. ἔστι δὲ λεπτόν, ὅταν ἐν μετεώρῳ κείμενον. Cf. Photius, p. 426, 11. It is used to denote a perch for fowls in Aristoph., Fr. 667, Theocr. 13, 13. Its general meaning, however, is simply *raised, in the air,* and in formation it corresponds to Att. μετέωρον. The first part of the compound is πετα-, a compromise between πεδά and μετά, such as is seen also in Πεταγείτνιος = Att. Μεταγείτνιος, the second part being the stem of αὔρα, *air,* seen also in the Attic form. *πεταυρον becomes Ion. *πετηυρον, πέτευρον. For further discussion see Kretschmer, KZ. 31, 448.

πληθύς, *majority.* [V] Locris 1479₁₈ = CIGS. III, 333 πληθὺν δὲ νικῆν. Cf. πλήθαι 1478₃₉ = CIGS. III, 334. See Meister, Ber. sächs. G. d. W. 1896, 323.

ποίστασις, building term. [IV] Epid. K. 241₄₁ λατομίαν τῶι στρώματι καὶ τᾶι ποιστάσει. Kavvadias asks if ποίστασις, πρόστασις may denote the *ramp* for mounting to the stylobate. Baunack thinks this word is synonymous with ὑποδόκιον.

πολιᾱνόμος, official title. [IV] Tab. Heracl. I₉₅ ha πόλις καὶ τοὶ πολιανόμοι, I₁₀₅ τοῖς πολιανόμοις τοῖς ἀεὶ ἐπὶ τῶν ϝετέων - -, I₁₁₇·₁₃₄·₁₇₈. This officer seems to be the same as the ἀστυνόμος of other cities. The word is used in later Greek to translate the Roman *aedile.*

προάρχω, *be first archon*. [III] Orchomenus 488₁₁₄ τὸν ταμίαν τὸν προάρχοντα τὰν τρίταν πετράμεινον. This word does not occur in a technical sense until late. Dio Cass. 47, 21 ; 57, 14, et al.

προδικέω = προδικάζω. Aen. 1432b₅ ἔκριναν οἱ δικασταὶ καθὼς οἱ προδικέοντες – –. This verb occurs in Plutarch, Mor. 2, 787 B, 973 A, where it means *be patron* or *advocate*. Cf. Hesych. προδικεῖν· ἐπιτροπεύειν.

προπωλέω, *negotiate a sale*. Aetol. 1425₆ καὶ ὁ προα[π]οδότης μὴ προπωλ(ε)ίτω. Cf. Plato, Laws 954 A ἐγγυητὴς μὲν δὴ καὶ ὁ προπωλῶν ὁτιοῦν τοῦ μὴ ἐνδίκως πωλοῦντος ἢ καὶ μηδαμῶς ἀξιόχρεω· ὑπόδικος δ' ἔστω καὶ ὁ προπωλῶν, καθάπερ ὁ ἀποδόμενος.

προσελαύνω, *proceed against*. [V] Arg., Meister IF. I, 200 = Blass, N. J. f. Phil. 143, 559 = Danielsson, Eranus I, 28 ff. ha δὲ βωλὰ ποτελάτω hαντιτυχόνσα. For similar aorist forms compare Cos 3636₁₁·₈, etc., ἐλάντω and ἐπελάντω. See Bechtel, SGDI. III, p. 360. This meaning of the verb is rare. Cf. ἐλάω, ἐλαύνω, ἐπελαύνω. See Danielsson, l. c., p. 36, note 5.

πρόχοος, a measure. [V] Gort. Law-code X₃₉ καὶ πρόχοον ϝοίνω, Comp. 150₇. This word is commonly used in the Il., Od., Hesiod., Soph., etc., to denote a *jar* or *pitcher*, and especially a *vase* or *ewer* for pouring water. Cf. Hultsch, Metrol., p. 324, πρόχοος, ξέστης, μέτρον.

πρωτομύστης, *one newly initiated*. [I] And.₇₀ ὑπὲρ τοὺς πρωτομύστας. This word does not occur in literature until 500 A. D., Achill., Tat. 3, 22. Cf. Sauppe, Ausgewählte Schr., p. 271.

πυαλίς, *basin* (of a stream). Troiz. 3362₄₃ ἐ]κ τοῦ δαπέδου κάτωθε ᾠκοδομήθη καὶ τᾶς πυαλίδος – –.

ῥήγνυμι, *break, cultivate*. [IV] Tab. Heracl. I₁₈ (com.) καὶ ἐγένοντο μετριώμεναι ἐν ταύται τᾶι μερέλαι ἐρρηγείας μὲν διακάτιαι μία σχοῖνοι – –. This form is not used elsewhere to denote cultivated land. Cf. ἄρρηκτος of the same inscription.

ῥῑπίς, *missile* (?). [VI] Elis 1165 = Ol. 718 = Roberts 293 ῥιπίρ ἐγὼ Ξενϝάρε[ορ]. Cf. Hesych. ῥιπίρ· ῥιπίς, τὸ πλέγμα, ἢ ἐκ σχοίνων πέτασος · Ἀττικοὶ δὲ ῥιπίδα, ᾧ τὸ πῦρ καίουσι· καὶ τραπέζας οὕτω λέγουσι, and ῥιπίς· τοῦ σκέλους τὸ ἀκροκώλιον. See Meister, Berl. Phil. Wochenschrift, 1886, 323, who thinks this word does not mean *bellows*, as Röhl translates it, following the literary tradition. He takes it as a word applied to the stone itself and translates as above. This inscription would then be similar to that of the Bybon stone, Ol. 717. Dittenberger sees some objection in the character of the stone. In form the word would be a derivative similar to κοπίς from κόπτω, τυπίς from τύπτω, etc.

σελίς, technical building word. [IV] Epid. K. 242$_{163}$ ff. ἐξιδώκαμες τὰς θυμέλας τὸ στρῶμα ποιῆ[σ]αι τὸ ἐν τᾶι περιστάσι σελίδας πεντήκοντα δύο, τὰν σελίδα, etc. See Keil, Mitth. 1895, 106 (note). The technical use of this word seems to be confined to the inscriptions, where it has three distinct uses : 1) in the inscriptions from Ephesus, Brit. Mus. 481, 339, 310, it indicates the sections of the κερκίδες made by the διαζώματα ; 2) in our inscription it indicates the divisions of the floor of the θόλος ; 3) in CIA. I, 234, it is used to designate divisions of the ceiling of the Erectheum. Cf. Fabricius, Hermes XVII, 586$_1$.

σημεῖον, *stripe*. [I] And.$_{16}$ μηδὲ τὰ σαμεῖα ἐν τοῖς εἱματίοις πλατύτερα ἡμιδακτυλίου – –. Cf. Hesych. σάμεα· τὰ ἐν ταῖς ὤαις τῶν ἱματίων παράσημα. Λάκωνες.

σιτεύω, *supply with provisions*. Rhodes, Br. Mus. IV, 827 ἡμέρας] ἐξ σιτεύσαντα τὰς κοίνας τραπέζας. Similar benefactions are recorded in inscriptions from Miletus, LeB.-F. III, 227, and Amorgus, BCH. VIII, 450.

σκῖρος, *barren land*. [IV] Tab. Heracl. I$_{19\cdot23}$, etc. σκίρω δὲ καὶ ἀρρήκτω καὶ δρύμω ϝεξακάτιαι τετρώκοντα ϝ[εξ] σχοῖνοι ἡμί[σχοινον]. See C. Robert, Hermes 20, 349.

σκῦρος, *clippings of stone*. [IV] Epid. 3325 A$_{28}$ = K. 241 Εὐτερπίδας Κορίνθιος ἥλετο τὸν σκῦρον ἐς τὸ ἐργαστή[ριον ταμ]ὲν καὶ ἀγ[αγ]ὲν καὶ συνθέμεν. This word is found in the schol. to Pindar, Pyth. 5, 93 σκῦρον γὰρ λέγουσι τὴν λατύπην τὴν ἀπὸ τῆς κατεργασίας τῶν λίθων ἀποπίπτουσαν and Eustath. to Dionys. Per. 520 σκῦρος γὰρ ἡ λατύπη, – – ἤγουν τὰ ἐκπαλλόμενα λιθίδια ἐν τοῖς λαξεύμασι. Cf. Hesych. σκῦρος – – ἡ λατύπη. Kavvadias thinks the small stones used in the construction of the ἐργαστήριον are intended here. Baunack, Aus Epid., p. 76, agrees with this, but thinks the use of the word in Epidaurus is extended so that it applies to the larger stone also.

σπεῖρα, 1) an article of dress; 2) *large rounded molding.* And.$_{24}$ ἢ σπῖραν λευκὰ μὴ ἔχοντα μήτε σκιὰν μήτε πορφύραν; CIA. IV, 1054$_9$ A$_4$ κίονας καὶ τὰς σπείρας. For the first compare Hesych. σπεῖρον· τὸ καλὸν ἱμάτιον καὶ τὸ ῥακῶδες. Both these uses are easy developments from the general meaning of the word.

στοιβή, *foundation, substructure* (technical building term). [IV] Epid. 3325$_3$ στοιβὰν ἥλετο Μνασικλῆ[ς]. K. 242$_{19}$ πὰρ Εὐνίκου ἐπιτιμὰν τᾶς στοιβᾶς ἐπιξοᾶς ἀπήνικε - -. Troiz. BCH. 1893, 116$_{25}$. Kavvadias reports this word also from an unedited inscription found in the Hieron, [τῶν] εἰς τὰν στοιβὰν πώρων ἀγωγᾶς τὰν πράταν. From στείβω as στοιβή, which denotes a *shrubby plant, cushion, pad.* It is used here technically. Cf. Baunack, Aus Epid., p. 62, who translates as above. Keil, Mitth. 1895, 434, criticises this as too broad. He would rather think of distinct parts of the foundation. He compares the double meaning of εὐθυντήρια, for which see Fabricius, Hermes 17, 568.

στρατός, *subdivision of tribe or clan.* [V] Gort. Law-code V$_5$ Αἰθαλεὺς (σ)τάρτος ἐκόσμιον οἱ σὺν Κύλλωι; Lyttus, BCH. 1889, 61 τῆς δώσεως τοῖς στάρτοις κατὰ τὰ πάτρια ... Cf. Hesych. Στάρτοι αἱ τάξεις τοῦ πλήθους. The word is, of course, στρατός, but with specialized meaning. It denotes a division containing those members of the tribe who are entitled to be κοσμοί. Cf. Ins. Jurid. Gr., pp. 414 f. Comparetti thinks this was a military division, since the κοσμοί in time of war became στρατηγοί. Cf. Hesych. κόσμος· στρατηγός, also Arist., Polit. II, 70, 3.

συνείκω, *be of advantage.* Aeg. 3418 Μὴ ἄνοιγε· οὐ γὰρ μὴ συνείκῃ τοι ἄλλον τινὰ κατθέντι ἐς ταύταν τὰν σόρον· αἱ δὲ μή, αὔταυτον αἰτιασῆ. Cf. Hesych. συνείκει· συμφέρει. Bechtel suggests that this form may be an aorist subjunctive belonging to the εἶκα cited in Cramer, Anecd. Ox. 1, 287$_4$, the third singular of which, εἶκε, is found in Hom. Σ 520.

συνευαρεστέω, *consent, approve.* [II] Thera, Cauer 148 A$_5$ συνευαρεστούσας καὶ τᾶς θυγατρὸς Ἐπιτελείας τᾶς Φοίνικος.; Phocis 1555d$_7$ συνευαρεστέοντος καὶ τοῦ υἱοῦ αὐτῶν - -; Delphi 2146 ὁμολογέω καὶ συνευαρεστέω τὰ προγεγραμμένα, 2168, 2200, 2201, 2342. This is a late word. Diod., Excerpt. Vat., p. 131 οὔπω συνευαρεστουμένων ἡμῶν τῇ γραφῇ. In the inscriptions it is always used in the active.

συνεύνη, *wife.* Astyp. 3485 *Ὦ συνεύνα χρηστά, χαῖρε.* There is only one example of the feminine form of σύνευνος, and that is somewhat doubtful, Anth. Pal. V, 195, a fragment of Meleager. σύνευνος, *wife,* occurs in Pind., O. 1,143; Aesch., Ag.1116; Soph., Eur., etc. It is rarely used as a masculine.

ταγεύω, *act as ταγός.* [V] Delph. BCH. 1895, 1 ff. A ταγε[υ]σέω δι[καίως κ]ατὰ τοὺν νόμους; Thess. 345₂₄ ταγευόντουν Ἀριστονόοι, Εὐνομείοι, etc.; 1332₃₇, 1329 Ia₃, 326₅, 345₁, 361 B₃, 327 A₃.

ταγή. [IV] Thess. Mitth. 1896, 110 κὲν ταγᾶ(ι) κὲν ἀταγίαι. This phrase was understood by Chatzisoyidis as equivalent to ἐν τάξει καὶ ἐν ἀταξίᾳ. Meister, Ber. d. sächs. G. d. W. 1896, 254, explains more satisfactorily. He cites Xen., Hell. 6, 1, to show that at times there was no ταγός in Thessaly, and understands the whole phrase to mean "at a time when there is a ταγός and at a time when there is not." Danielsson also, Eranus I, 141 f., explains the phrase in this way, and for ἀταγία compares ἀκοσμία. ἀταγία does not occur elsewhere, and should have been cited in the list of New Words.

ταγός, *chief.* [IV] Thess. 345₃.₄, et al., 361 B₂₂; Mitth. 1896, 110; Delph. BCH. 1895, 1 ff. Cf. Homolle, pp. 26, 40 ff. This Delphian inscription is the only instance of the technical use of this word to denote any official not Thessalian. Xenophon, Hellenica 6, 1; 6, 4, etc., uses it of the Thessalian official. The word occurs in the general sense, *leader,* in the tragedians. See Gilbert II, p. 15.

τέθμιον, *agreement, contract* or *bond.* [III] Orchomenus 488₁₆₅·₁₆₉·₁₇₂·₁₇₅ = CIGS. I, 3172 = Ins. Jurid. Gr., p. 276 τἀππάματα μούριη ὀγδοείκοντα πέντε δίου[ο] ὀβολίω κὴ τῶ τεθμίω ρίστωρ Ἀριστόνικος Πραξιτέλιος. Meister, Dareste, and Latyschew place a period after τεθμίω and translate it variously, but connect with what precedes. This is on account of the κή, since Foucart, BCH. III, 460, punctuated after ὀβολίω. But by separating entirely from what follows, a more serious difficulty is caused by the use of the genitive. Cf. Ins. Jurid. Gr., p. 294, n. 2, where it is suggested that the case of τεθμίω may be connected with that of the preceding numerals. The reading adopted above is given by Dittenberger.

τελαμών, 1) *support* of stone used under the stele, 2) *stele*. [500] Argive, AJA. 1896, 43 ά στάλα καὶ ho τελαμὼ (ΤΕΛΑΜΟ); Meg. 3078$_{11}$ τὸν δὲ ταμ[ί]αν ἀναγράψαντα τὸ ψάφισμα τοῦτο εἰς τελαμῶνα λευκοῦ λίθου ἀναθέμεν εἰς τὸ ἱερὸν τοῦ Ἀπόλλωνος. With the second citation compare Latyschew II, 29, 351, 353, 438, 439, 452, 456, 459, where the τελαμών corresponds to the Attic στήλη. Richardson, l. c., p. 47, compares CIG. 2056d [ἀναγράψαι εἰς σ]τήλην λευκοῦ λίθου [καὶ] ἀνα[θεῖναι αὐτὴν ἐπὶ τελα]μῶνος. and later in the same inscription ἀνάθεσιν τοῦ τελαμῶνος. This explains the στάλα καὶ ὁ τελαμώ of the Argive inscription.

τέρχνος, τρέχνος, *shrubs, trees.* [IV] Cypr. (Edal.) 60$_9$ τὸ(ν) χῶρον τὸν ἰ(ν) τῶι ἔλει - - κὰς τὰ τέρχνιμα τὰ ἐπιό(ν)τα, ll. 18, 22 (same). Cf. Hesych. τέρχνεα φυτὰ νέα. ἢ ἐντάφια and τρέχνος· στέλεχος, κλάδος, φυτόν, βλάστημα.

τέτρωρον, *group of four boundary-stones.* [IV] Tab. Heracl. I$_{90}$ ἀριθμὸς ὅρων - - hοκτὼ σὺν τῷ τετρώρωι (ΤΕΤΡΩΙΡΩΙ), I$_{159}$ διὰ τῶν τετρώρων. L. & S. define by *land inclosed by four boundary-stones*. But that is impossible for the first citation, while the definition given suits both places. The general meaning of τέτρωρος, of which τέτρωρον is the neuter, is *of four* —. It is used with a noun and absolutely. Cf. Eur., Alc. 483 τέτρωρον ἅρμα; Eur., Hipp. 1229 τέτρωρος ὄχος; Ael. N. A. 1, 36 τέτρωρον, *a team of four;* also Soph., Tr. 507 τετραόρου φάσμα ταύρου.

τίτᾱς, *guardian, protector.* [V] Crete, Comp. 148$_{5.7}$ αἰ δὲ [μὴ συλ]οῖεν, ἑκατὸν στατήρανς ϝέκαστον τοὺς τίτανς [κατιστάμεν καὶ τὰν δ]ιπλήιαν τῶν χρημάτων ἐστεισάντανς ἀποδόμ[εν]. αἰ δὲ οἰ τίται μὴ ϝέρκσιεν ἆι ἐγράται, τὰν διπλήιαν - - ἀποδόμεν - -. 150$_{20}$ τ[οὺς τίτανς, 55-57$_{20}$ τῶν τιτᾶν. τίτας is used for τιμωρός Aesch., Cho. 67. Cf. Hesych. τίται· εὔποροι ἢ κατήγοροι τῶν ἀρχόντων; ἀτίτην· ἄπορον. Cf. ἐντιτός. Evidently in the manumission decrees the τίται correspond to the βεβαιωτῆρες of the Delphian inscription.

τρέω, be banished. [V] Arg. Fröhner, Rev. Arch. 1891 = Meister, IF. I, Anz., p. 200 ὲ τᾶς ἀλιάσσιος τρήτω καὶ δαμενέσσθω ἐνς 'Αθαναίαν. This special use of τρέω, so common with φεύγω, is, so far as I know, not elsewhere found. Cf. also Danielsson, Eranus I, p. 36.

ὑπώμαιον, shoulder blade. Cos 3636_{53} [ν]ώτου δίκρεας, ὑπώμαια, αἱματίου ὀβελὸς τρικώλιος - -. Cf. PH., p. 87.

φθοίς, cake. [IV] Cos 3636_{31} ἔπειτα ἄγοντι τὸ[μ βο]ῦν καὶ τὸγ καυτὸν καὶ [φ]θοῖας ἑπτὰ καὶ μέλι καὶ στέμμα. Cf. Hesych. φθόις· πλακοῦς· καὶ τὰ πρὸς λεπτὸν ἀληλεσμένα - -. Aristoph., Plut. 677 φθόις.

φιλόζωος, fond of one's life. [II] Rhodes, IG. Ins. 842 ἅ τε φιλόζωος ψυχὰ τ—. See Löwy, Ins. gr. Bildhauer 186.

φρήτιον = φρεάτιον. Acrae 3246_{18} ποτὶ φρητίοις. Cf. πλύνιον.

ὠβά, small division of a tribe. Sparta. [I] ὠβά M. 47_{10}, ὅπως ἀ[εὶ] ἁ ὠβὰ μναμονευοῦσα τῶν γεγότων φι[λ]ανθρώπων εἰς αὐτὰν ἀποδιδοῦσα φαίνηται τὰς καταξίους τιμάς. CIG. 1272_5, 1273_7, 1471_4. Cf. Müllensiefen, De tit. Lac. dial., p. 49, who thinks the word certainly from ὄϝις. See also Brugmann, Curt. Stud. IV, p. 145. The word is found in Plut., Lycurg. 6.

ὤρᾱ, shoulder blade. [V] Ion. $100_{2\cdot6}$ ἦν ἐν θ[ύη]ται, λά[ψεται γλῶσ]σαν, ὀσφύν, δασέαν, ὤρην. This was first correctly explained by Bechtel. The word has nothing to do with οὐρά, but is Lat. sura = ὠμοπλάτη. Cf. schol. to Od. XII, 89 ἀώρους. 'Αρίσταρχος ἀκώλους· τοὺς γὰρ "Ιωνας λέγειν φασὶ τὴν κωλῆν ὤρην καὶ ὠραίαν.

ὠνέω = πωλέω. [V] Gort. Law-code V_{47} ὠνὲν (ONEN) τὰ χρήματα, κ' ὅς κα πλεῖστον διδῶι ἀποδομένοι, τὰν τιμὰν δια[λ]αχόντων τὰ ἐπαβολὰν ϝέκαστος. Cf. Hesych. ὠνεῖν· πωλεῖν. The middle form in the usual sense of ὠνέομαι occurs in VI_4, X_{25}.

POETICAL WORDS IN PROSE INSCRIPTIONS.

ἀγορά = ἐκκλησία. Delph., Cauer 208 ἐν] ἀ[γ]οραῖ τελείωι σὺμ ψάφο(ι)ς ταῖς ἐν[νόμοις], WF. 11 ἔδοξε ταῖ πόλει τῶν Δελφῶν ἐν ἀγοράι τελείαι. Cf. 14, 16, 475. Thess. Mitth. 1884, p. 128 τῶ[ν] Θ[ε]σσαλῶν, ἀγορὰ μηνὶ....δευτέ[ραι], etc. Cf. Swoboda, p. 307. Kleemann, Voc. Hom., p. 4, adds an inscription from Halicarnassus, Sauppe, Gött. G. d. W. 1863, 305, ἐν τῆι ἱερ[ῆι] ἀγορῆι, and Gort. XI, 12 ἀποϝειπάθθω κατ' ἀγοράν. But ἀγορά in the Gortynian may be used in the ordinary sense, though Bücheler and Zitelmann, Das Recht v. Gort., p. 164, take it as *assembly*.

ἀγρέω = αἱρέω. See Rare Words.

ἀγχίμολος. Crete, Comp. 19 ὅστις μέζατ[ος] ἴοι|....τῶι ἀνπαντῶι μ' ἦμεν ἀνκέμο[λον. Cf. Comp., p. 34. The reading is doubtful. Comparetti cites Homeric ἀγχέμαχος for the second vowel. He thinks the word in this place probably has the special meaning of ἀγχιστεύς.

αἰδής. See Rare Words.

αἶσα, *portion.* Cypr. 73 τῶ Διὸς τῶ ϝοίνω αἶσα - -; Lac. LeB.-F. 352h₃₃ πέμπειν δὲ αὐτᾶι καὶ αἶσαν. This is a late honorary decree in the Doric κοινή. See Schulze, Berl. Phil. Wochenschrift 1890, 1471. Cf. Ath. VIII, 365d τὴν συμβολὴν τὴν εἰς τὰ συμπόσια ὑπὸ τῶν πινόντων εἰσφερομένην 'Αργεῖοι χῶν καλοῦσι· τὴν δὲ μερίδα αἶσαν. This is a quotation from Hegesander. In actual literary use the word occurs with this meaning only in poetry. Smyth cites Pind., Pyth. IX, 61, Simonides, and Empedocles.

ἀμεύομαι = ἀμείβομαι. Crete, Comp. 12–13 μὴ ἀμεϝύσασθαι, 201₃ (ἀ)μεύσονται. For the writing with ϝ compare the various spellings αὐτ-, ἀϝτ-, ἀϝυτ-. See Meyer, p. 193 (end). Cf. Hesych. ἀμεύσασθαι· ἀμείβεσθαι, διελθεῖν, περαιώσασθαι. Etym. M. explains ἀμεύω by πορεύομαι. The word occurs in Pindar,

Pyth. I, 45, and is cited by L. & S. as used by the Aeolic poets. It does not occur in the present. Cf. Baunack, Stud., pp. 268ff.; Blass-Kühner II, p. 366. See also ἀμοιϝή (New Words).

ἄμπαλος. See Rare Words.

ἀμφιμάχομαι. Crete (Drerus), Cauer 121 D_{25} ἕνεκα τᾶς χώρας τᾶς ἄμας, τᾶς ἀμφιμαχόμεθα. There are several poetical words in the latter part of this inscription, λισσός, ὀνομαίνω, δατέομαι.

ἄναξ. Cypr. 18 ὁ ϝάναξ Στασίας, 59_2 τό(ν)δε κατέστασε ὁ ϝάναξ—. Cf. Καρστιϝάναξ 68_1. Smyth, AJP. VIII, 468, notes that ϝάναξ occurs with βασιλεύς perhaps only in Cyprian. The word is used by Herodotus, also by Isocrates, 203 D, speaking of Evagoras, "the champion of Hellenism" in Cyprus. Cf. CIA. I, 489. For -αναξ, -ϝάναξ in compounds see Schulze, Quaest. Ep., p. 453.

ἄνασσα. Cypr. 38_4 τῶ ἱερέος τᾶ ϝανάσ(σ)ας, 39_2 τᾶς ϝανάσ-(σ)ας, 40_1 ὁ ἱερεὺς τᾶς ϝανάσ(σ)ας. Without digamma 33_1 ὁ ἱερὴς τᾶς ἀνάσ(σ)ας.

ἀνδάνω. See Rare Words.

ἄνδιχα. Cf. ἀνδιχάζω (New Words).

ἄνω, *accomplish, finish.* Aeol., Hoffmann, GD. II, 156_{18} μῆννος Τέρφεος ἐνάτα ἀνομένω; Cos. PH. 39_8 τρίται ἀνομένου. The occurrence in Cyprian, quoted by Smyth, AJP. VIII, 470, is very uncertain. The inscription is cited by Hoffmann, GD. I, 182. For a similar use of the participle compare Hdt. 7, 20 ἔτος ἀνόμενον and Ap. Rhod. 2, 494 ἦμαρ ἀνόμενον.

ἄνωγον. Cypr. 60_2 βασιλεὺς Στασίκυπρος κὰς ἁ πτόλις Ἡδαλιέϝες ἄνωγον Ὀνάσιλον, etc. This word is used by Herodotus in two speeches, III, 81, and VII, 104.

ἄοζος. See Rare Words.

ἀρά = εὐχή, εὐχωλή. Cypr. 97 ἀρὰ Ἀνάω, Hoff., GD. I, 83 = Meister 25i ἀρὰ Διί, and probably also Hoff. 147 ὀνέθηκε Ὀνασίτιμος τῶιθεῶι τῶι Ἀπόλ(λ)ωνι ι̯αρᾶ ἰ(ν) τέμενος, ἰ(ν) τύχαι. The interpretation of ι̯αρα as ἱαρά (SGDI. 72) is not likely in view of the common ἱερ- ι̯ερ-. Meister, GD. II, pp. 159f., considers the reading uncertain. Hoffmann takes the word as a dative and compares the use of εὐχωλᾶ in 27.

ἀράω. See Rare Words.
ἀριστεύς. Miletus, CIG. 2881_{12}. Cf. Kleemann, Voc. Hom., p. 9.
ἄρουρα. Cypr. 60_{20} κὰς τὸ(ν) κᾶπον τὸν ἰ(ν) Σίμ(μ)ιδος ἀρούραι; Ion. 156_{16} ἐν ἀρού(ρ)ηι περὶ (π)ό[λιν].
ἀρχός, *chief.* Locris 1148_{41} = CIGS. III, 334 τὠνκαλειμένωι τὰν δίκαν δόμεν τὸν ἀρχόν; Delph., BCH. 1895, 1 ff. D_{26} a[ἰ δ' ἀ]λίαν ποιόντων ἄρχω[ν ἀ]πείη; Boeot. 382 ['Επ]ιτίμω ἀρχῶ (com.). LeB.-Wad. III, 2798, Cyprus(?), ὁ ἀρχὸς τῶν κιννυραδῶν.
ἀσκηθής. Arcad. (Teg.), Hoff., GD. I, p. 25, no. $29_{5\cdot6}$ τὸν ἱεροθύταν νέμεν ἰν 'Αλέαι ὅτι ἂν ἀσκηθὲς ᾖ τὰ δ' ἀνασκηθέα ἰνφορβίεν. Epidaurus 3340_{109} ἀσ[κ]ηθὴς ἐξῆλθε. See Danielsson, Epigr., p. 43. ἀνασκηθέα belongs under New Words. Danielsson thinks this word is to be taken as a compound with ἀνά rather than as ἀνασκηθής, with double negative prefix. But in the absence of a *σκηθής it is doubtful whether the ἀ was felt as the negative prefix, so that a later ἀν-ασκηθής would offer no difficulty.
ἀτή, ἀτάομαι. See Rare Words.
ἀτιτάλλω. Cf. Gort. ἀτιτάλτας (New Words).
αὐτάρ. Cypr. 2_2 αὐτάρ μι κατέ[θηκε] 'Ονασίθεμις, 3_2 (same), 15_2 αὐτάρ με κατέθηκε --.; CIA. IV, p. 477 ἀϝυτάρ occurs in a metrical inscription. Cf. Kretschmer, Vas. Ins., p. 37.
βουνός. See Rare Words.
γαλαθηνός. Halicarnassus, CIG. 2656_{31} ἐπὶ δὲ γαλαθείνῳ ὀβολόν. See Kleemann, Voc. Hom., p. 11.
γέγωνα. Lacon., Cauer 30_{12} [κ]αὶ ἐπὶ τοῖς [γ]εγωναμένοις ...
γύης. See Rare Words.
δαίζω. Boeot. 1145_{12} δεδόχθη τοῖ δάμοι ὁπόττοι κα παργινύωνθη Σιφείων ἐν τὰς κοινὰς θυσίας ἃς δαίζοι[1] ἁ πό[λ]ις, ὑπαρχέμεν αὐτοῖς καθάπερ κὴ τοῖς πολίτης.
δατέομαι. Drerus, Cauer $121_{123\cdot134}$ δασσάσθωσαν. Cf. also ποτεδασσάμεθα, Tab. Heracl. $II_{60\cdot68}$ (com.); κατεδασσάμεθα II_{28}.

[1] For the form of this word see SGDI. I, p. 309. The inscription contains a renewal of friendly relations between Megarean Aegosthenae and Boeotian Sipha. It is sent from Megara, but written in the Boeotian dialect. There are some other forms besides this which are not Boeotian.

δέατο. Arcadian, Tegean building inscription, 1222_{10} εἴ κ' ἂν δέατοί σφεις πόλεμος ἦναι ὁ κωλύων ἢ ἐφθορκὼς τὰ ἔργα – –; 1. 18 ὅσαι ἂν δέατοί σφεις ζαμίαι, 1. 45. Mantinea, BCH. 1892, 570, 1. 23 εἰ δ' ἀλάξαι [δ]έατοι κατῶννυ.

δηλέομαι. See κα(δ)δαλέομαι (New Words).

δίδημι. Delph. 2156_{18}, 2216_{20}, 2171_{10}, 2324_{13} μαστειγοῦντες καὶ δίδεντες. This is a rather rare Epic verb. It occurs also in Xen., An. 5, 8, 24. Cf. Kühner-Blass II, p. 400.

δρίος. Acrae 3246 = IG. Sic. et It. 217 ἐν δρίει Κακκρικοῖς.

ἔδνα. Crete, Comp. 25 ὅς κα ἔκς ἔδνω[ν . . . This word is common in Homer and belongs also to the tragic poets, but finds its way into prose late. The above is its earliest prose use. Cf. Comparetti, p. 38.

ἐλατήρ. Cos 3637_8 καὶ θύ[εται] ἐπὶ τᾶι ἰστίαι ἐν τῶι ναῶι τὰ ἔνδορα καὶ ἐλατὴρ ἐξ ἡμιέκτου [σπ]υρῶν· ταύτων οὐκ ἐκφορὰ ἐκ τοῦ ναοῦ. Etym. M., p. 325, 46 μᾶζα ἐλάτης and ἐλατήρ, Aristoph., Knights 1183.

ἕλος. Cypr. 60 A_9 τὸν ἰ(ν) τῶι ἔλει, τὸ(ν) χραυόμενον Ὀ(γ)κα(ν)τος ἄλϝω—; Ion. 183_{36} τὸ ἕλος καὶ τὴν λίμνην τὰ ἐμ Πάρβαντι. In the latter inscription it is used in its usual significance, *pool, lake*. In Cyprian we have rather the Homeric meaning, *low-lying place, meadow*. It is to be taken with Solmsen, KZ. 32, p. 283, from *σελος, Lat. *solum*. See also Osthoff, BB. XX, p. 258.

ἐπᾱρά. See Rare Words. Cf. ἐπαρέομαι (New Words).

ἕρπω, *go*. Crete 156 I_3 μ]ὴ νυνατὸς ἦι ἔρπεν, Cauer 117, 119, etc.; Delph. 1780 καὶ ἐρπούσας οἷς κα θέλωντι; Epid. 3339_{86} ἦρπε ἐς τὸ ἱερόν. Cf. εἰσέρπω Astyp. 3472, παρέρπω And.$_{35}$. Cf. also Hesych. ἐς πόθ' ἔρπες· πόθεν ἥκεις Πάφιοι; common in epic poetry and the tragedians.

εὐχωλή. Cypr. 27 κατέστασε εὐχωλᾶ, 59 τᾶς εὐχωλᾶς ἐπέτυχε – –. This word occurs in Lucian, Syr. Dea 28, 29, but Smyth, AJP. VIII, 468, thinks it was probably a borrowing from Herodotus II, 63 εὐχωλιμαῖος.

ἦμαρ. Mantinea, BCH. 1893, 568 f.$_{22}$ ἄματα πάντα; Tegea, BCH. 1893, 12 νόμος ἱερὸς ἰν ἄματα πάντα. Cf. Keil, Gött. Nachricht. 1895, 363, and Danielsson, Eranus II, 27.

ἠπύω. Arcad. 1222_3 ἀπνέσ[θ]ω δὲ ὁ ἀδικήμενος τὸν ἀδικέντα ἰν ἀμέραις τρισὶ – –. This verb is common in poetic use of all periods. Cf. Schulze, Quaest. Ep., p. 338.

θεοπροπέω. Boeot. 864_5 θ]ιοπροπίοντος Οἰνοχίδαο Εὐμενίδαο.

ἰατήρ. Cypr. 60_3 ἰατῆραν. This word is used for *surgeon* in Homer. It has the more general meaning of *healer* in Theocritus, Soph., etc.

ἰδέ, and. Cypr. $60_{12\cdot 26}$. This is a Homeric word, occurring in tragedy only in Antigone 979. Cf. ἰ, Cypr. 60_{24}.

ἴνις, son. Cypr. 40_2 ὁ βασιλέος Τιμάρχω ἴνις. υἱός was formerly read in inscription 41. But cf. Deecke, BB. XI, 317, who reads now from left to right, so that there is no evidence for the occurrence of υἱός in Cyprian. ἴνις is used by Aesch. and Euripides. The latter has also the feminine ἡ ἴνις.

καρτερός. See Rare Words.

κασίγνητος. Cypr. 60 $A_{3\cdot 5\cdot 7\cdot 11\cdot 14}$; Ion. 23_2; Corcyra 3188, Aeol. 281 C_{19}.

κέ. With ἄν only in Arcadian $1222_{2\cdot 10\cdot 15\cdot 25}$. κέ occurs in Cypr. (Edal.) $60_{10\cdot 23\cdot 29}$. It is common in Aeolic and Thessalian. κά is universal in Doric. Cf. Boisacq, DD., p. 37.

κέλευθος. Tegea, Hoffmann, GD. I, p. 23, N. 29_{23} εἴ κ᾽ ἂν παραμαξεύῃ θύσθην τᾶς κελε[ύθ]ω τᾶς κακειμέναυ κατ᾽ ᾽Αλέαν—. Cf. Danielsson, Epigr., pp. 56 f.

κέλομαι = κελεύω. Delph. 1852_{14} ποιοῦσα ὅ κα κέληται Πάσιχον; Epid. $3339_{50\cdot 62}$, $3340_{112\cdot 126}$.

κέραμος. See Rare Words.

λᾶας = λίθος. Gort. Law-code IX_{36} ἀμφαίνεθαι δὲ κατ᾽ ἀγορὰν καταϝηλμένων τῶμ πολιατᾶν, ἀπὸ τῶ λάω (ΛΑΟ) ὦ ἀπογορεύοντι; XI_{12} αἰ δ[έ κα λῆι] ὁ ἀνφάμενος ἀποϝηιπάθθω κατ᾽ ἀγορὰν ἀπὸ τῶ λά[ω ὦ ἀπα]γορεύοντι καταϝηλμένων τῶν πολιατᾶν. "The stone" at Gortyn was evidently a public tribune, corresponding to the Athenian Bema.

λάζομαι = λαμβάνω. Meg. 3052a; Boeot. 3054_6; Aeol. 214_4 (? Hoffmann ἐπιλα]ζέσθω, Cauer μεταλα]ζέσθω). See section on Synonyms.

λίσσομαι. Cf. λίσσος (New Words).

νέομαι. Crete, Cauer 116$_{25}$ μήτε γυναῖκας τίκτεν κατὰ φύσιν, τῶι τε πολέμωι μή με σῶον νέεσθαι.

νύ. Cypr. (Edal.) 60 A$_{6 \cdot 16}$. Cf. Smyth, AJP. VIII, 471. The only instance of prose use of this word is in Aretaeus, p. 66. Smyth further notes that Aretaeus, like Lucian, tried to follow the Ionic of the fifth century. But since νύ is not to be found in either Herodotus or Hippocrates, it is to be accounted a pseudo-Ionism.

ξῦνός. Ion., Bechtel 156 A$_3$, b$_{25}$; Olb. Latyschew 48$_7$. Cf. Smyth, Ion. D, § 380. The word is cited as Arcadian in Bekker, Anecd. III, p. 1095 'Αρκάδων. ξυνόν· κοινόν.

οἶος = μόνος. Cypr. 60$_{14}$ κὰς 'Ονασίλωι οἴϝωι. Cf. Bekk., Anecd. III, p. 1095 'Αρκάδων - - οἶος μόνος.

ὀνομαίνω in ἐξονομαίνοντες. Drerus, Cauer 121$_{121}$ καὶ τὸ πλῆθος τοῦ ἀργυρίου ἐξονομαίνοντες.

οὔρεια = φρούρια. Drerus, Cauer 121$_{52}$ καὶ μήτε τὰμ πόλιν προδωσεῖν τὰν τῶν Δρηρίων μήτε οὔρεια τὰ τῶν Δρηρίων - -.

πίτνω, πιτνάω. See παραπιτνάω (New Words).

πολιήτης = πολίτης. Gort. Law-code X$_{35}$ καταϝηλμένων τῶν πολιατᾶν.

ῥέζω. Cypr. 156 ῥέζω, 71 ἔϝρεξα. Cf. Smyth, AJP. VIII, 470, who cites Plato, Laws 642 C ἔρρεξε as the only prose example outside of Cyprian. The word occurs in Rhodes in a compound, ἐπιρρέζω. See Rare Words.

σπέος. Cypr. 31 ἐξβα]σιν τῶ σπέως τῶ[δε ἔκε]ρ[σε].

συνεύνᾱ. See Rare Words.

χραύω. See Rare Words.

ὤρια. Phocis 1545$_8$ τὰ ὤρια. This is a poetical form which occurs in late prose.

ὤριμος = ὡραῖος. Gort. VIII$_{39}$ ἀ δὲ πατρωιῶκος ὠρίμα εἴη—.

www.ingramcontent.com/pod-product-compliance
Lightning Source LLC
Chambersburg PA
CBHW071140090426
42736CB00012B/2183